WHO WAS DRACULA?

WHO WAS DRACULA?

Bram Stoker's Trail of Blood

JIM STEINMEYER

JEREMY P. TARCHER/PENGUIN
a member of Penguin Group (USA) Inc.
New York

JEREMY P. TARCHER/PENGUIN
Published by the Penguin Group
Penguin Group (USA) Inc., 375 Hudson Street,
New York, New York 10014, USA

USA · Canada · UK · Ireland · Australia
New Zealand · India · South Africa · China

Penguin Books Ltd, Registered Offices: 80 Strand, London WC2R 0RL, England
For more information about the Penguin Group visit penguin.com

Most Tarcher/Penguin books are available at special quantity discounts for bulk
purchase for sales promotions, premiums, fund-raising, and educational needs. Special
books or book excerpts also can be created to fit specific needs. For details, write
Penguin Group (USA) Inc. Special Markets, 375 Hudson Street, New York, NY 10014.

Library of Congress Cataloging-in-Publication Data

Steinmeyer, Jim, date.
Who was Dracula? : Bram Stoker's trail of blood / Jim Steinmeyer.
p.   cm
Includes bibliographical references and index.
ISBN 978-0-14-242188-8
1. Stoker, Bram, 1847–1912. Dracula.   2. Dracula, Count (Fictitious character)
3. Vampires in literature.   4. Horror tales, English—History and criticism.   I. Title.
PR6037.T617D788   2013   2012047834
823'.8—dc23

Printed in the United States of America
1   3   5   7   9   10   8   6   4   2

Book design by Meighan Cavanaugh

While the author has made every effort to provide accurate telephone numbers and
Internet addresses at the time of publication, neither the publisher nor the author
assumes any responsibility for errors, or for changes that occur after publication.
Further, the publisher does not have any control over and does not assume
any responsibility for author or third-party websites or their content.

Remembering Orson Welles,

who first told me, "You know, it was Irving!"

He would have enjoyed the whole story.

If you want a happy ending, that depends, of course,
on where you stop your story.

—*Orson Welles*

CONTENTS

———

INTRODUCTION

Pity Bram Stoker.

He was one of the lucky authors who managed to create a character more mysterious and more interesting than he was. And he paid for it. He suffered careful dissection and analysis by generations of literary sleuths, biographers, and psychologists, attempting to find the man behind the vampire. Bram Stoker was a proper Irishman and a careful Victorian. For almost thirty years, his job was to keep his head at the Lyceum Theatre in London, and then to remain perfectly unobtrusive in service to Henry Irving, London's leading actor. Bram Stoker performed that job well.

Late in his career, he wrote a thick novel called *Dracula*, which garnered surprised reactions from his business acquaintances and mild praise from the critics. Stoker may have suspected that it was his best book. He had no way of calculating that it would become a phenomenon. As his great-grandnephew the novelist Dacre Stoker has written, "Bram would surely be surprised at the great number of works, books, movies, television shows, comics, et cetera, apparently inspired by . . . the vampire figure he created." In the middle of the twentieth century, the character seemed to have become a patron saint for every desperate filmmaker on a budget. But amazingly, Dracula's reputation has remained untarnished, continually inspiring some of entertainment's leading lights, like Orson Welles, Roman Polanski, and Francis Ford Coppola. Dracula is one of fiction's greatest, most recognizable, and most popular characters. He has glided through every type of medium with a seemingly supernatural power, commanding respect and always attracting audiences.

In the intervening years, Dracula proved too interesting, and Stoker apparently proved too dull, to perfectly satisfy critics, who re-created Dracula in their own image or dressed him in the fashions of their own age. Bram Stoker was burdened with suspicions and speculations—psychological motivations, physical ailments, and literary revenge—in an effort to properly explain his vampire. Annoyingly, Dracula has done his best to resist explanation. A psychological understanding of the novel seemed to elude even Bram Stoker.

Dracula was the very first adult novel I ever read—that is, a big, thick book from the adult section of the public library that didn't have any pictures in it. When I was eight years old, a classmate named Aiden gushed over the novel, recalling the frightening events in the castle and the dramatic execution of Dracula. "They cut off his head!" At that time, the classic horror movies made only occasional late-night appearances on television, and the novel was a revelation. I checked the book out of the library and slogged through it, almost four hundred pages of daunting gray text, glimpses of Victorian Whitby and London that became personal challenges for a fourth-grader. When I finally closed the back cover, Bram Stoker's abject horror was mixed with my own personal sanctimony. I tried to indulge in a conversation about the book with Aiden, but he just wrinkled his nose. "What? I didn't see that part," he said. "I just read the very beginning and the very end."

I later learned that most of us have been reading just "the very beginning and the very end." *Dracula* has survived for over a century, despite the shortcuts—or maybe because of the shortcuts. We know about the castle in Transylvania, we know about the stake through the heart, and we can all fill in the rest. Generally, we've depended upon the theater producers and motion picture screenwriters to reconfigure and redefine *Dracula* for us.

The West End, Broadway, and Hollywood quickly came to the rescue, and seem to have concurred that there were too many strange settings and incidents in the story—Dracula's castle where he makes dinner and does the dishes; his exit out the window and down the wall; the attack of the sensual vampire brides; Dracula's multiple houses in London; the vampire hunters sharing quarters in an insane asylum; the vampire's dapper daytime outfit, complete with a straw hat; and the part–Wild West, part–Gypsy caravan chase at the conclusion.

So they omitted them.

They also determined that there were too many characters and plot twists—a beautiful young vampire victim who becomes a vampire seductress in miniature, terrorizing children; Stoker's familial band of vampire hunters, which included a stuffy British lord and a good old Texas cowboy; a return to Transylvania to murder Dracula's three brides and purify his imminent bride.

They pushed them out of the story, focusing on a handful of characters.

For most of the twentieth century, the result had been a defanged vampire story, quite literally. In most of *Dracula*'s reincarnations, men in 1930s tuxedos stand around a sofa or morosely consult at a bedside, adjusting wreaths of garlic as the heroine dozes. The French doors offer the necessary threat. There's an occasional flapping bat. The vampire looks like a Latin lover in a long cape.

———

For Bram Stoker, his story was probably also about "the very beginning and the very end." We now know that he assembled the novel in a gradual, meticulous fashion, between the years 1890 and 1897, when it was published. In 1890, when he first began taking notes on his vampire story, Stoker worked at London's Lyceum Theatre; the theater was at the height of its popularity and Stoker was at the height of his powers. A glittering array of guests came to see Henry Irving's remarkable shows, and many stayed to be hosted by Irving and Stoker at elaborate dinners in the Beefsteak Room—the Lyceum's prestigious private dining club. There the mysterious journalist Henry Stanley purred of imperialism in Africa; the idealistic traveler Arminius Vambery described the strange, wonderful people of the Balkans; the adventurer and translator Richard Burton wove fanciful images from his visits to the Mideast. These were rich pickings for Bram Stoker, and his imagination was fired. The tales were wonderful; the storytellers were even more interesting. The theatricality of Irving and the guests at those dinners formed an important influence on Stoker's fiction, and various characteristics, bits of history and personal traits, worked their way directly into his vampire story. When he created Dracula in his Transylvanian lair—haughty, controlling, surrounded by lascivious lovers, and desperate for blood—it was a new twist on an old Gothic formula.

By the time *Dracula* was nearing completion in 1896, the fortune of the Lyceum had begun a slow decline. Bram Stoker's array of friends had been cursed with failure and surrounded by scandal. The story of the vampire in retreat—a frightening and powerful man now chased from London and hunted like an animal—seems to have fictionalized the desperate straits of many of Stoker's professional friends and dramatized the loss of their own mysterious, daunting influence over society.

———•◦•———

At some point as he assembled notes for his novel, Bram Stoker recorded a name that he found in a book on Eastern Europe, a fifteenth-century Wallachian voivode named Dracula. It was the right name at the right time—he wove it into his outline (he'd been using the name "Wampyr") and even gave *Dracula* pride of place as the title of his book (he'd been using *The Un-Dead*).

Vlad Tepes, also known as Dracula, has since become one of literature's greatest red herrings—a genuine mystery behind the horror. For decades it seemed logical that Bram Stoker had carefully researched this murderous voivode and concealed his source, a fantastic inside joke for fans of European history. The truth is even more surprising. Dracula's name was virtually picked out of a hat by Stoker: an incredible bit of luck and good fortune. It is now apparent that the real history of Vlad Tepes would have surprised Bram Stoker—he knew virtually nothing about him.

———•◦•———

A simple explanation is that Stoker's novel is so interesting because it was compiled at a fascinating time in his life, when he was surrounded by amazing people. It calls for very little speculation to see Stoker's inspirations, from the people and events that surrounded him in Victorian London, and the colorful characters that befriended him in America. I believe that the most important elements of *Dracula* were inspired by four people: poet Walt Whitman's bold carnality; author Oscar Wilde's corrupting immorality; actor Henry Irving's haunted characters; and murderer Jack the Ripper's mysterious horrors.

The real surprise is that Stoker knew these men—maybe even the mysterious Jack! They played important roles in his professional life. They weighed heavily on his personal life. For decades, scholars and critics have speculated whether these personalities had elbowed their way into the world's greatest vampire novel.

It would have been remarkable if they hadn't.

—Jim Steinmeyer
Los Angeles

"BLOOD OF MY BLOOD"

T o those who have never read the novel, who feel that they must know Bram Stoker's remarkable creation because they've seen the movie or heard most of the details—the wolves, the bats, the stake through the heart—*Dracula* is full of surprises.

In fact, it is not a great novel, and it has been criticized for its host of implausibilities, coincidences, and overwrought characters. At some point after the well-known adventure in Transylvania and the discovery of one of Dracula's disciples in a London cemetery, the novel slows to a torpid pace. There is a great deal of Victorian moralizing from sweet Mina Harker, the good woman, and Jonathan Harker, her stalwart new husband, as well as the manly men who stalk the vampire. The wise Dutch professor, Van Helsing, seems determined to fill the pages with lectures on his theories about the undead. The vampire hunters concern themselves with real estate sales, deliverymen, and typewritten copies of journals. The teasing and temptingly lewd touches of vampirism disappear. Dracula himself, who makes only sporadic appearances in the book, seems to go missing completely. A modern reader begins to wonder just how Bela Lugosi ever found a place in all of this, or why this odd, clunky detective story has earned such an enviable reputation.

And then, about three-quarters of the way through the book, there is an unexpected murder in the insane asylum. Renfield, the lunatic who has seemed obsessed with life and death, and devoted to his new mysterious "lord and master," Dracula, is found with a shattered skull. Before he collapses and dies, Renfield confesses that Dracula has been secretly visiting Mina in the night. It's something that, as readers, we have begun to suspect.

The band of vampire hunters race to Mina and Jonathan's room, pound on the door, and then push it open. They're too late.

Jonathan Harker, Mina's husband, is lying across the bed, breathing heavily as if in a stupor.

Mina kneels on the bed, her white nightdress smeared with blood. A "tall, thin man, clad in black," grips the back of her neck, pressing her face tightly against his bared chest, "forcing her face down on his bosom." Dracula has pierced a vein in his own chest and forced Mina to drink his blood, with "the terrible resemblance to a child forcing a kitten's nose into a saucer of milk to compel it to drink."

Mina later explains how the vampire came into the room, transfixed her husband, leaving him helpless, and snarled his threats to the men hunting him. "And you, their best beloved one, are now to me flesh of my flesh, blood of my blood, kin of my kin," Dracula said to Mina. "You have aided in thwarting me, and now you shall come to my call." He pulled open his shirt and pierced a vein with a long fingernail, pressing Mina's face close, so that she was forced to lap up his blood.

The scene forms the emotional climax of the book. A reader might anticipate the usual "bite on the neck" vampire attack, but this is something very different. The image of Mina forced to ingest the vampire's blood is completely unexpected and horrific. It stops the book cold. It stops the characters, who gaze upon the scene as Dracula's eyes turn to them "flamed red with devilish passion." They regain their senses and drive Dracula away with their crucifixes.

The stodgy Victorian novel seems to momentarily collapse under the weight of this bizarre terror and then struggles to right itself and overcome Dracula's suggestive assault. Bram Stoker constructed the scene to echo a marriage, a rape, and an unholy ritual that bristles with sexual energy. It is telling us a different story about vampires and hinting about a very different nature to their threat.

Mina is devastated by her weakness and her fate as one of the "unclean." The story is hot-wired with a jolt of violent energy. The plot shifts suddenly. The wise professor proclaims that it is no longer enough to drive Dracula away. Mina will survive only if she is cleansed through the vampire's destruction. The chase begins in earnest and propels us to the end of the book, where Dracula meets his fate in Transylvania.

For over a century since its publication in 1897, *Dracula* has tempted audiences with the hint of something more, something darker, something concealed. The Transylvanian folklore, the rules of the undead, provide a comfortable frame for the Victorian novel, but Dracula, the wily old vampire, seems to accomplish something different. He refuses to be pinned to the story and adds his own unexpected, animalistic plot twists. If Bram Stoker's work was never a great novel, it was always a great story—a swirl of nightmarish images that had been borrowed from real heroes, villains, heightened dramas, and theatrical tragedies. *Dracula*'s nightmares were first printed on the pages, and quickly imprinted into the world's subconscious.

One

THE DEMON, "IN A WAY YOU CANNOT DREAM OF"

T he Lyceum Theatre, London's most prestigious playhouse, had been turned into a laboratory.

In December 1885, the principal scientist and England's leading actor, Henry Irving, was conducting his most im portant experiments. Irving would pace across the silent rows of seats. Tall and angular with a gaunt face, he was always identifiable in the shadows by his peculiar, bent-legged gait. He would stop, twist his head to survey the action on the stage, or growl staccato directions to the hundreds of actors who gathered in clumps, in halos of limelight. Then he would fall into an upholstered chair, his arm thrown over the back, impatiently tapping his foot as a colored glass filter was adjusted over a gas jet, or a massive piece of scenery—a church wall or a garden cottage—was noisily moved by a small platoon of men in their shirtsleeves.

Slowly, astonishingly, the latest Lyceum production was taking shape onstage. It was nothing less than Goethe's famous story of the devil's bargain, *Faust*. "He is very exact in every detail," the famous American actor Edwin Booth explained of Henry Irving after they'd worked together in *Othello*, "and requires its elaboration to a nicety. You can easily imagine that the scene does not quickly reach perfection." The public knew Irving for his quirky, mannered characterizations, like Shylock, Hamlet, and Richard III. He was an expert at grand, haunted characters, and all of London anticipated his role of Mephistopheles. But the hundreds of performers and technicians at the Lyceum were awestruck by his mastery of the theatrical arts. The entire show had already been visualized inside the head of "the Governor," as his associates respectfully called him. Now, in the empty theater, Irving's vision was being translated to the cast and stagehands who would be entrusted to summon the magic for every performance. And so the hours passed, with whispers to the tight knot of designers and assistants who circled behind him and shouts to the players on the stage, as Henry Irving watched his *Faust* assembled, piece by piece.

Typically the rehearsals for a new show began with four or five hours each day, over six or eight weeks. Then the smaller scenes were slowly assembled on the Lyceum stage late at night and into the morning after the curtain was rung down on the current production. Finally, the previous show was removed from the theater and the new feature was completely installed. The company would endure a full week of endless work and adjustments as the Governor took charge. The process was exhausting and disorienting, a concentrated assault that denied the real world. In the darkness of the theater, the company's denizens lost track of the days turning into nights and then days again. Only when an exterior door rudely slammed open was the illusion destroyed, and a sudden blast of cold air or the rays of a winter sunset intruded into the sepulcher that was the Lyceum, temporarily upstaging the fantastic images and pure artifice that were being created on the stage.

Throughout the process, the officious man usually standing behind Irving—or seated in the next row, leaning over to answer Irving's question and then dash to the office to send a telegram—was his chief factotum, a tall, barrel-chested Irishman whose neatly trimmed red beard enhanced his special authority, like a Shakespearean king. As the "Acting Manager" of the Lyceum, he was responsible for pushing numbers back and forth on the budgets, arranging the schedules, writing letters, and smoothing over the personal relationships that were invariably neglected by an artist like Irving but were necessary for the mighty battle plans that would propel *Faust* to the stage.

Irving suddenly stood and squinted at the scenery, brushing back the long lock of hair that had fallen into his eyes. He was now completely satisfied with the precise mixture of gray, indigo, and olive green that had been daubed onto the curved glass filters. The actor had envisioned a specific surreal moonlight for the Brocken scene, and it had taken hours to find the blend of colors that would chill the naturally white-yellow glare of the gaslight. "That's it," he whispered to himself, examining the soft shadows that now surrounded the enormous papier-mâché snow-covered boulders and an outcropping of black trees on the blasted mountaintop. "Stoker?" The man with the red beard took two steps forward. Without looking, Irving knew that his Acting Manager was there, so he continued his question. "How many imps and goblins do we have?" Bram Stoker glanced down at a sheaf of notes in his hand. "Yes, Mr. Irving. We've designated thirty extras as imps . . . fifty extras as demons . . . fifty as witches . . ."

"Hmm . . . And yet," Irving interrupted with his flat theatrical drawl, "I suppose you can anticipate my thoughts, can't you? It's really about the sweep of motion, the action of a wave crashing against the shore." Bram Stoker nodded, returning to his notes. "I'll pull the additional costumes from stock, and give you over three hundred performers, all together." Licking a finger, he flipped to another page of scrawled notes. "Yes, I can make three fifty available for this scene." Irving nodded, telling him, "Make half of them witches." Bram Stoker pulled a short pencil from his vest and began a tally of supernatural beings.

Henry Irving was an international star, a spectacularly quirky, dark, lean actor who had become famous as a producer of remarkably innovative, lavish stage spectacles in London. Queen Victoria was a fan. In fact, Irving was England's first actor honored with a knighthood, which Victoria bestowed in 1895. His *Faust* was the perfect vehicle for his talents and was highly anticipated by London theater fans and London society. In one of the great twists of popular history, Irving is virtually forgotten today. When he is remembered, it is as a relic of the Victorian age, a quaint "Actor Manager" (meaning an actor and manager, as distinguished from Bram Stoker's title, "Acting Manager," responsible for the daily management of the theater). Irving dictated every detail of his stardom and adjusted history's great roles, like Richard III and Hamlet, to perfectly suit his taste for the mysterious and haunted.

Bram Stoker, the quiet red-haired Irish gentleman whom eminent Victorians remember for his dull devotion, who seemed to live his life in the shadows behind "the Governor," relentlessly adjusting his budgets and schedules, is forever enshrined for a bravado feat of authorship. He created one of the greatest characters ever imagined, who has only become more famous with each passing year.

Faust was being coldly calculated as a hit, a breathtaking spectacle that would leave London theatergoers agog and reaffirm Irving's preeminence. The actor was then at the height of his success, and the mighty Lyceum productions were supervised by the famous "Unholy Trinity" of the theatrical world: Irving, the star, producer, and creative force; Bram Stoker, responsible for the smooth running of its theater; and H. J. Lovejoy, a grand old man of London show business, who, as Stage Manager, supervised each production behind the curtain. The fourth part of the formula, and to many in the audience the most engaging element of the Lyceum productions, was Ellen Terry, the bright, golden-haired leading lady of many of Irving's shows. She was innocent when the leading actor was morose, beautiful and sympathetic when he was histrionic and mysterious. She won fans—particularly informed fans, like George Bernard Shaw and Oscar Wilde—who would have otherwise sniffed at Henry Irving's ordinary tastes. After Irving's marriage had dissolved, Terry was Irving's unofficial "leading lady" offstage as well.

Henry Irving had begun planning *Faust* by asking an Irish playwright, W. G. Wills, to turn Goethe's poem into a play according to Irving's specifications. The resulting script was a pastiche of the original tale in which Margaret's part was confined to a simple, virtuous innocence, Faust's part was deadened to a plodding scholar, and Mephistopheles—Irving's chosen role—became the sparkling, evil centerpiece. He was envisioned as a tall, lean devil who snarled with an evil lisp and hobbled with a limp. It was a role written to steal the show.

In the summer of 1885, Irving led a group of associates and designers to Nuremberg, studying the local atmosphere, picking up bolts of fabric that could be used for costumes, buying knick-knacks and properties. During their research trip, Irving proclaimed that the nearby town of Rothenberg had the right appearance; he wired Hawes Craven, his chief scenic artist, to come from London and join the group, and make sketches of the Rothenberg squares, streets, and countryside so that they could be reproduced on the Lyceum stage.

It was, by far, Irving's most expensive production, but as he had decided that it would be a "drawing" play, Irving rescheduled the opening to ensure that every detail would be perfect. Although a play, not an opera, this *Faust* had been scored with incidental music to be performed by a large orchestra, supporting all the action, in the tradition of Victorian melodrama. The scenery and costumes were elaborately built and painted to simulate etchings of medieval Germany.

During his plans, Irving decided that he would need an organ added to the Lyceum to furnish heavenly music for the church scene. Then a peal of bells was purchased for the angelic finale. A wooden trough for cannonballs was installed on a wall backstage; the sound of the balls rolling down a zigzag trough perfectly simulated a rumble of distant thunder. Special steam boilers were installed beneath the stage to generate the mist for Mephistopheles' entrances.

Then Irving turned his attention to a series of elaborate special effects. In the first scene, when Faust signs the devil's contract in blood, both Faust and Mephistopheles were to lean over an enormous book and the page would begin to glow with an eerie light, illuminating their features. Irving's technicians had concealed a series of batteries and bulbs inside the book. Similarly, Henry Irving experimented with small electric bulbs installed around the edge of Mephistopheles' hood, and dry cell batteries hidden within his full red cloak. The bulbs were arranged to give the demon's face a mysterious, ghastly glow even in the darkest scenes.

A far more elaborate effect was Valentine and Faust's sword duel. Mephistopheles directed the duel from afar. As the characters lunged toward each other, the devil's magic was realized in long, cracking sparks of blue lighting that hissed and jumped from sword to sword. The effect was accomplished by having metal plates mounted in the stage floor. These were wired to a fifty-cell Grove battery. Electrical contacts in the heels of the actors' shoes led to a wire concealed beneath the costumes and up to a special rubber glove with a small metal plate; this plate made contact with the sword. When the actors had their heels on the plates, the sparks leapt from sword to sword.

The electrical device was assembled by one of Thomas Edison's associates, his European agent, Colonel Gouraud. On opening night, the actor playing Valentine momentarily forgot his careful choreography, nervously grabbed the wrong part of the sword, and received a nasty ninety-volt shock.

———————

The Lyceum had been equipped for electric lights, but they were never used onstage during Irving's career, except for his unusual special effects. Onstage, electric lamps were considered too unpredictable, too limited, too cold. They seemed to turn actors a ghastly purple color. All of Irving's experiments with makeup and scenic colors were complemented by the golden glow of gaslight.

Ellen Terry always remembered the quality of light at the Lyceum. The brilliant, hissing open flames, in the footlight troughs or reflectors over the stage, glowed and flared on cue to accentuate the action onstage. That light, according to Terry, offered "thick softness with the lovely specks and motes in it, so like natural light." In fact, the glare of gas footlights provided an undulating layer of hot air, a glassy, almost perceptible wall that not only separated the audience from the magic, but also made everything beyond them seem more magical.

The rest of the formula was limelight, the intense beam of chemical light that had been introduced at the start of Irving's career, as if anticipating his selfish need for a spotlight. This was a focused, sputtering flame, produced when a cylinder of compressed lime was burned in a mixture of oxygen and hydrogen. It was fitting that Henry Irving's Mephistopheles would strut across the stage, illuminated by open flames and crackling, hissing embers. In this way, *Faust* was "modern" only in its slight variations on the Victorian formulas to which Irving was addicted. These included the melodrama (especially overwrought drama and sentiment, enhanced with musical accompaniment), the sensation scene (a lavish, incredible scene that was offered strictly to set tongues wagging), and the historical spectacle (filled with extravagant examples of taste and artistry but always negligent of real history). *Faust* had been adorned and bejeweled with special features, but the result was an evening top-heavy with artistic sensations.

Within a generation, these sorts of shows would collapse beneath their own weight.

Bram Stoker's principle job was to support all of Irving's plans, unobtrusively accommodating his indulgences. He later recalled the visit of an artist who watched from backstage during a premiere, noting the staff's fearless devotion to their boss and their hard work. The artist told Stoker, "I would give anything that the world holds, to be served as Irving is!" Stoker always remembered these words, realizing that this blind, selfless trust—serving Irving—was an important element of his duties.

But his second job was to ensure that the theater ran efficiently and productions were reined in to a responsible budget. In this way, *Faust* had raised the hair on the back of the Acting Manager's neck. As he watched preparations for the Brocken scene, just several nights before the December 19 opening, Stoker was becoming concerned.

Bram Stoker finally saw a partial rehearsal of the Brocken scene. Although it centered around Mephistopheles, Irving—as was his style—imperiously gave directions as he sat in the theater, leaving himself out of the action. He was never concerned with his own performance; he felt rehearsals were necessary to ensure everyone else's positions.

Stoker watched ten minutes of organized chaos. Set atop the moonlit mountaintop, the hundreds of extras screamed, cavorted, ran from side to side, jabbered, or shrieked on cue. "[With] all the supers and ballet and most of the characters being in dress," Stoker later wrote, "[it was] a wonderful scene of imagination, of grouping, of lighting, of action, and all the rush and whirl and triumphant cataclysm of unfettered demonical possession. But," he concluded with cautious understatement, "it all looked cold and unreal."

As the sun was coming up and rehearsals stopped, Stoker and Irving walked to Irving's dressing room and shared a meal of sandwiches. Stoker carefully explained his reservations, his deep baritone confined to a whisper. "After all, it might not catch on with the public as firmly as we had all along expected—almost taken for granted. Could we not be quietly getting something else ready, so . . . we should be able to retrieve ourselves?"

Irving listened carefully. It must have been a shock for him to hear his Acting Manager offer these concerns. He slowly shook his head.

Tonight, I think you have not been able to judge accurately. You are forming an opinion largely from the effect of the Brocken. As far as tonight goes you are quite right; but you have not seen my dress. I do not want to wear it till I get all the rest correct. Then you will see. I have studiously kept as yet all the color to that of grey-green. When my dress of flaming scarlet appears amongst it—and remember that the color will be intensified by that very light—it will bring the whole picture together in a way you cannot dream of.

By now, Irving had pushed himself out his chair, his theatrical bearing giving force to his words, his widening eyes dramatizing the anticipated wonder.

Indeed, I can hardly realize it myself yet, though I know it will be right. You shall see too how Ellen Terry's white dress and even that red scar across her throat will stand out in the midst of that turmoil of lightning!

———•◦•———

The Brocken scene was an astonishingly bold, even reckless, interpolation in *Faust*. The scene was completely unnecessary for the play. It contained no dialogue and did not further the story. It was pure, gratuitous spectacle, the demon's power made manifest in a theatrical fantasy. It was genius, it was madness, but it perfectly represented Irving's talents and tastes, playing directly to his public.

And Irving was completely right. His all-scarlet Mephistopheles costume was the first time that the demon had ever been pictured that way: Before 1885, the devil was usually dressed in black and red. Irving's Mephistopheles established this cliché, which was then adopted by popular culture.

Several nights later, on December 19, 1885, Stoker was standing at the back of the auditorium, watching with the opening-night audience.

The third act had just ended, wherein Mephistopheles' confrontation with Margaret in the cathedral reminded her that she was now a fallen woman, responsible for the death of her mother and brother. As Margaret cowered beneath the vaulted arches, the demon snarled a suggestion that she murder her child. Suddenly, the lights onstage shifted. The audience was no longer looking at the interior of the cathedral, but the exterior, and the dark figure of Mephistopheles was creeping down the steps, then loping and limping alone across the city square. The music reached a crescendo and the curtain fell to a burst of sustained applause.

After a brief intermission, the fourth act began when the curtain opened on the Brocken, Irving's artistic, snow-covered mountaintop. The stage was empty. A tall outcropping of rock, the mountain's summit, was on the audience's left, with shadowed pine trees in the background. A clouded moon glowed over the scene.

The orchestra began with a lush, dramatic score, anticipating the entrance of the characters. The audience heard a mysterious hubbub of voices and groans, a sort of supernatural chorus to accompany the music. Irving used an offstage chorus of more than forty singers. Suddenly, at a cleft in the rocks, Mephistopheles appeared in red, dragging Faust, in dark robes, to the top of the mountain. Lightning flashed. This was the work of bright chemical flames, ignited in the wings, to cast garish shadows on the rocks.

As the two main characters reached the rocky summit, a flock of witches flew over the stage. This was followed by a parliament of owls, whose darkened wings cast silhouettes across the pale moon. As the scene proceeded, "strange nameless beings and goblin specters, half men, half beasts, chattering imps, and winged fiends swarm out of the mountain sides with unearthly shrieks and cries and deep grave chants and songs."

Mephistopheles took a seat on the rock, as if resting on a desolate throne, as electric sparks surrounded him. Now dozens of witches, hundreds of witches, rushed onto the stage, surrounding the demon and filling the air with moans and shrieks. Mephistopheles watched the proceedings as a king would supervise his revels. The scene quickly turned into a chaotic celebration of loud howling and surreal dancing, the witches' filmy, gray-green garments swirling in the air. As Mephistopheles jumped to his feet, joining the celebration, red flames and mist began to surround the supernatural beings, as if the mountaintop were licked by fire.

Suddenly the dance stopped—the hundreds of supernatural figures froze, then melted into darkness at the edges of the stage. Faust turned away, appalled. He lifted his eyes to the background and saw a mystical vision of Margaret, dressed in a pure white robe, with a suggestive, bloody gash across her neck. The limelights illuminated her in a brilliant, shadowless glow at the edge of the roiling sky. Mephistopheles made a quick gesture, and the vision of Margaret disappeared. He was alone on the mountain with Faust.

The stillness drew a collective gasp from the audience. The demon took several steps forward in the dull, cold light, until he was standing at the highest point of the barren rock. He raised his hand dramatically. The thunder rumbled and roared, the orchestra screeched, and the mountain was transformed by shafts of fiery red light. The hundreds of witches and demons were returned to the mountaintop, twisting, gyrating, and then swarming to form a dense circle around the demon king. They fell to their knees in tribute. A rain of glowing sparks began to fall on the scene—Irving used baskets of gold tinsel, sprinkled from above, which showed flashes of red limelight—seemingly consuming the hellish characters in fire, as the curtain slowly descended.

After another brief interval the play resumed with the scene of Margaret in prison, having gone mad from her travails.

Author Michael R. Booth summed up the influence of Irving's Brocken:

Thus ended a scene, which in its combination of spectacle, mass force and power, grandeur, and nightmare, many reviewers said had never been equaled on the stage. The Brocken scene was one of the great spectacles of the nineteenth-century theatre, and probably the most extraordinary scene of its kind ever performed on the English stage.

But not every reviewer was charmed. Many noticed the extravagant, superfluous nature of the scene and were annoyed that it reminded them of an English pantomime. Henry James, the American author, who was then a sometime theater critic and a regular Lyceum first-nighter, found it all silly and coarse. "A mere bald hubbub of capering, screeching and banging, irradiated by the irrepressible blue fire, and without the smallest articulation of Goethe's text. The scenic effect is the ugliest we have ever contemplated. . . . It is a horror cheaply conceived and executed with more zeal than discretion."

Britain's greatest magician, David Devant, was just starting his career when *Faust* opened; he watched the "awesome" Brocken scene from the front, swooning at the perfect theatrical illusions. "A few nights afterwards, [I] was taken behind the scenes. I remember the awful shock of disillusion I got when I saw the labyrinth of canvas scenery and ropes, and the men in shirtsleeves working the lights."

Was it genius or was it madness? There's little question that Bram Stoker saw something more than the glow of Henry Irving's scarlet robes on December 19, 1885. The visualization of Walpurgisnacht; the image of the virginal victim in white, violated with a bloody wound on her neck; the powerful, hypnotic, devilish ruler of the underworld—all of this would be later played out in a thick manuscript. Five years after *Faust*'s premiere, Bram Stoker began plotting a novel that was published in 1897 under the title *Dracula*.

———•—•———

Who inspired the character of Dracula?

It's too simple to point at the antecedents in literature or history. It's deceptively easy to speculate that Dracula was inspired by an evil Transylvanian prince, or even by Stoker's magisterial boss, Henry Irving. The actual story is more complicated than that, and much more intriguing. Dracula is a pastiche of living historical characters—men who were surrounded by scandals and controversies, larger-than-life personalities who seemed to step from the mists of the nineteenth century and exert their influence, just as Stoker's vampire later seemed to materialize from the shadows of a Transylvanian castle and cast his spell.

As clues, *Dracula* left a bloody trickle, a trail leading backstage at the Lyceum and through the drawing rooms of Victorian London. There was even a distinctive splatter of crimson on American shores.

Two

THE BOY, "NATURALLY
SECRETIVE TO THE WORLD"

Bram Stoker's autobiographical prose suggests that the most insightful stories are the ones he has omitted. The picture of himself that he has painted, in rough, hesitant brushstrokes, seems to be one of a plodder, measuring his own life in terms of Henry Irving's. His most significant meeting was with Irving; his finest achievements were in service to the actor; his most treasured associations were the professional friendships formed backstage at the Lyceum, entertaining Irving's royal guests over cigars in a lounge, or at dinner after a sparkling performance. Somehow Stoker's family, marriage, son, and even the publication of his greatest work, *Dracula*, register as no more than shrugs in his brief autobiographical accounts.

After Irving's death, Stoker filled two volumes with his sincere recollections, *Personal Reminiscences of Henry Irving*, filled with his accounts of the great man: "When a man with his full share of ambition is willing to yield it up to work with a friend whom he loves and honors, it is perhaps as well that in due season he may set out his reasons for so doing."

At this point, a reader hopes to interpret the sentence ambiguously. Our estimation of Bram Stoker would rise if we could believe that their sacrifice, their teamwork and devotion, were mutual. But no, his point is clear. Stoker gave up everything out of love and honor for Henry Irving.

> Such is but just; and I now place it on record for the sake of Irving as well as myself, and for the friends of us both. For twenty-seven years I worked with Henry Irving, helping him in all honest ways in which one man may aid another—and there were no ways with Irving other than honorable. Looking back I cannot honestly find any moment in my life when I failed him, or when I put myself forward in any way when the most scrupulous good taste could have enjoined or even suggested a larger measure of reticence. By my dealing with him I am quite content to be judged, now and hereafter. In my own speaking to the dead man I can find an analog in the words of heartbreaking sincerity:

> *Stand up on the jasper sea,*
> *And be witness I have given*
> *All the gifts required of me!*

Despite Stoker's contention, these lines are not particularly heartbreaking. The verses are from "Bertha in the Lane" by Elizabeth Barrett Browning, a poem of a dying maiden's loneliness. Although Stoker omitted them, Browning's verses continued:

Hope that blessed me, bliss that crowned,
Love that left me with a wound,
Life itself that turneth round!

Personal Reminiscences presents a grand portrait of Irving, and a painful portrait of the author eternally in service, reticent in his own views, and apologetic to use ink and paper for anything but praise for the great actor. For example, when Stoker recounts their first meeting—Irving gave a dramatic recitation of a poem in a hotel drawing room—the performance so drained the actor that he concluded and "collapsed, half-fainting." Witnessing the performance so moved Stoker that he confessed, "I burst into something like hysterics." Presumably, this was a fit of uncontrollable tears.

And then, in his account, Stoker included a brief note of autobiography.

Let me say, not in my own vindication, but to bring new tribute to Irving's splendid power, that I was no hysterical subject. I was no green youth; no weak individual, yielding to a superior emotional force. . . . I was a very strong man. It is true that I had known weakness. In my babyhood I used, I understand, to be often at the point of death. Certainly 'till I was about seven years old I never knew what it was to stand upright. . . . This early weakness, however, passed in time and I grew into a strong boy and in time enlarged to the biggest member of my family.

Stoker's point was not to share personal recollections of his childhood but simply to endorse the actor one more time, proving

to the reader that his "hysterics" were no mere triviality. Bram
Stoker was habitually in service to Irving.

———•—

Stoker's early illness is a mystery, but those years of invalidism did
not seem to burden his later childhood. If he was coddled and pampered, he may have had extra time to hear his mother and father's
recitations by his bedside. His mother recounted rich Irish folk
myths—delicious horror stories—and his father detailed the latest
theatrical productions.

He was born Abraham Stoker, named after his father, in Clontarf, a quiet seaside town on the outskirts of Dublin. Little Abraham, later shortened to Bram, was the third of seven children.

His namesake, Abraham Senior, was twenty years older than
his wife, a civil servant who worked a monotonous job in the parliamentary section of Dublin Castle. Charlotte Thornley, his wife,
was from Sligo, on the northwest coast of Ireland. She remembered
the colorful stories of her Irish forbears, lived through the horrors
of the cholera epidemic that swept her hometown when she was
fourteen, and heard the scream of the Banshee when her mother
died.

The Stokers were a comfortably middle-class Church of Ireland
family—Protestant—living in Clontarf during the Irish potato
blight of 1845. Abraham Stoker's civil service job meant that the
family avoided the horrors of this famine, even if they shared the
economic calamity of the country.

After he regained his strength, Bram was a good student if
not an inspired one. His brothers were all achievers, and three became physicians. His mother was devoted to their education, and

she became a reformer, campaigning for government-supported schools for the deaf and the education of women in workhouses. His father spent frugally, but regularly indulged in pit seats at the Theatre Royal and watched star performers whenever he traveled. For his son, he replayed the great Edmund Kean's amazing performance in *A New Way to Pay Old Debts* and described the French magician Robert-Houdin's masterful "eye," taking in everything at a glance.

In 1863, following in his older brothers' footsteps, Bram entered Trinity College, at the time Dublin's renowned Protestant university. He had overcome and overcompensated for his early physical ailments. He was six feet, two inches tall, weighed 175 pounds, and excelled at sports: rowing, walking, running, swimming, and weight lifting. He also played on the rugby team.

His academic pursuits took a backseat, but he was invited to join The Phil (The Philosophical Society) and The Hist (or Historical Society, a parliamentary debate group). Stoker was an inspired debater, with an ability to think quickly on his feet. He was naturally shy, but he had learned to mix easily in university groups.

Abraham Senior retired from the civil service in 1865, which made the family finances shaky, especially with two sons at Trinity. Bram took a year off from school and worked for a year at Dublin Castle, where his father had worked. He later returned to school and graduated in 1871. He went on to earn a master's degree in mathematics. His mother and father decided that their pensions would carry them further if they lived abroad in France or Switzerland. They departed in 1872, leaving their five sons behind in

Dublin. Bram moved in with his older brother Thornley, who was a physician.

Bram Stoker had inherited his father's interest in the theater and even appeared in some Dublin plays—his acting roles seem to have been inspired by his fine, deep, assertive voice, which he found during debates at Trinity. He first saw Henry Irving perform at the Theatre Royal, Dublin, in 1867, when Stoker was nineteen and Irving was twenty-nine. Irving was touring with the St. James Company and played Captain Absolute in *The Rivals*, by the Dublin-born playwright Richard Brinsley Sheridan. As Stoker had seen other actors in this popular role, he was able to carefully assay Irving's "business," the clever little pauses or gestures that an actor would use to individualize a part.

Irving was already becoming known for his intelligent interpretations. Rather than bluster through a role, he imbued the part with subtleties, giving the impression that one could see the character thinking, reacting, changing intent, or avoiding a difficulty. It was a revelation to Stoker, a Captain Absolute "full of dash and fine irony, whose ridicule seemed to bite, an inoffensive egotist even in his love-making." After marveling at Irving's layered interpretation, Stoker was stunned that the newspapers failed to single out his hero for praise.

Four years later Irving returned to Dublin in a play called *Two Roses*. Again, Stoker was thrilled by his quirky Digby Grand and disappointed by the Dublin newspaper reviews. He volunteered to write criticism for the *Dublin Evening Mail*. It was an unpaid position, but his reviews gave him access to opening nights, put him at the center of theatrical news and gossip, and offered some prestige. He was writing, and readers were noticing what he wrote.

Bram Stoker checked the invitation in his hand, paused to remove his derby and button his coat, and then walked through the door at 1 Merrion Square in Dublin. It was among Dublin's largest residences, and the Saturday "at home" soirees were arranged grandly by the Wildes, with rooms lit by candle and tables of food prominently displayed. Stoker was guided from room to room by the sound of laughter and murmured conversation. Classical piano music reverberated from somewhere in the back of the house. The assortment of guests—artists, poets, professors, scientists, authors—were randomly scattered into tiny groups, but the hostess, Lady Jane Wilde, called Speranza by her friends, seemed to tie every conversation together by swanning from room to room, effortlessly offering clever introductions, witty and vaguely insulting bon mots, and an assortment of tea cakes and sandwiches. She was a tall, ungainly figure swathed in a Gypsy-inspired skirt and festooned with long sashes and dangling brooches.

Stoker was then working part-time as a reviewer and full-time as a clerk in the Petty Sessions, following his father's lead in civil service. The job was hardly the drudgery that the title might have suggested. Stoker did a good amount of traveling through Ireland and was highly regarded for his efficiency, earning regular promotions. But he had aspirations to a literary or theatrical career, writing short stories and submitting them to periodicals, and auditioning for theatrical roles in Dublin. At the Wildes' home in Merrion Square, he was able to rub elbows with the Dublin literati and any number of eccentrics who appealed to Speranza.

The Wildes were a famous, and famously odd, Dublin family.

The Irish poet William Butler Yeats, who knew the family around this same time, remembered the Wildes as "dirty, untidy, daring . . . very imaginative and learned." Speranza was her nom de plume; she had become infamous for writing inflammatory poetry, as well as articles espousing Irish nationalism and damning the British throne. Her husband, Sir William Wilde, was a small, angular man with a full gray beard. He was prone to monopolizing dinner conversations on myriad fascinating topics. He had been knighted for his services as an eye doctor to Queen Victoria; he was an expert in eye diseases, a student of Irish history and superstition, and an early, amateur Egyptologist.

The family had known its share of controversy. Lady Jane had given dramatic testimony in a treason trial. Before their marriage, her husband had fathered several illegitimate children, and after his knighthood he was accused of rape by one of his patients. These scandals were open secrets, bothering everyone in Dublin except, seemingly, the Wildes themselves.

Sir William and Lady Jane had two sons (a daughter had died in childhood). William Charles Kingsbury Wilde, known as Willie, was five years younger than Bram, and was a good student at Trinity who was talented beyond his aspirations. Their younger son, Oscar Fingal O'Flahertie Wills Wilde, was seven years younger than Bram. In 1871, he had just entered Trinity during Stoker's last year there.

Oscar Wilde inherited his father's penchant for conversation and his mother's tastes for humor and poetry—then bested both of them. He was tall, like his mother, with coarse features and a full face. His famous wit was being honed at the Merrion Square salon and his taste for stylish clothes and literary skills were being defined at Trinity, but he was not much longer for Dublin. In 1874 he won a scholarship to Oxford and, from there, went on to conquer London.

The Wildes became friends of Bram Stoker—who lingered longer in Dublin than their precocious son. Bram liked Willie and his father, and Lady Wilde took an interest in his government career (even if she condemned the Irish government), becoming a sort of surrogate mother. Stoker spent Christmas 1875 with the family. Sir William died the following year.

Oscar was too young, too flippant and mysteriously esoteric, to have ever been a close friend of Stoker in Dublin. But Oscar exhibited many of the achievements that Stoker had wished for himself, particularly his facile literary skills.

Over the course of his life, Stoker labored as a reviewer, a novelist, a poet and playwright, often with only middling success. He circled the periphery when famous, sparkling personalities met. Oscar Wilde, his bright young friend from Ireland, demonstrated brilliance in all of those fields. For many years, Wilde was the toast of London, always the very center of attention, even among the brightest luminaries.

Next to the Wildes' home was 18 Merrion Square, the tall brick residence of Joseph Thomas Sheridan Le Fanu.

Le Fanu was a celebrity in Dublin, a popular, prolific author who produced dozens of stories rich in Irish history, popular dramatic novels, and evocative, supernatural mysteries. He was a graduate of Trinity, having studied for the bar before becoming a journalist. One of his most successful novels, *Uncle Silas*, was published in 1864. Le Fanu's most remembered story, *Carmilla*, was first published in a periodical in 1872 and then in a collection of tales, *In a Glass Darkly*, which means it was being read and discussed in Dublin just shortly after Stoker left Trinity. Coincidentally, Stoker's first work of fiction, "The Crystal Cup," a fairy tale about a king's devotion to beauty, was published in a London periodical that same year.

Carmilla is a magnificent vampire story. In many ways, it set the standard for the genre: *Carmilla* drips with Gothic atmosphere and fascinates with vampire lore and repressed sexuality. As with many of Le Fanu's novels, the narrative is carefully framed as part of the casebook of an occult scientist and then told, in first person, by the story's protagonist, Laura. She explains how she was befriended by a mysterious girl, Carmilla, the victim of a carriage accident, who came to live with Laura and her father. She comes to haunt Laura's dreams with fearsome, late-night visits. Laura discovers that Carmilla is a vampire, an ancient countess named Karnstein. By the end of the story, the spell is broken when a vampire expert arranges to exterminate Carmilla, according to tradition, with a stake through her heart and a bloody beheading.

As a story, *Carmilla* is purely Gothic: suggestive and haunting rather than bold and sensational. The sexuality is apparent but coolly restrained. Le Fanu's twist on older vampire tales was his unmistakable lesbian theme, as the female vampire bites only other females, then seduces them as a lover.

It seems an astonishing missed opportunity, but there's no evidence that Bram Stoker and Sheridan Le Fanu ever met. When Stoker worked as a theater reviewer for the *Dublin Evening Mail*, Le Fanu was technically one of his employers—the newspaper's editor—but he was famously reclusive, avoiding most contact with strangers. After his wife's death in the 1860s, Le Fanu suffered guilt feelings regarding her mental breakdown, withdrew completely from his friends, and stopped writing. His Dublin neighbors named him the Invisible Prince, a man who waited until nighttime to stealthily enter or leave his dark mansion, avoiding any contact with society. He virtually became a haunted character from one of his own novels. After several years of grieving in solitude, he returned to writing and editing; he was editor of *Dublin University Magazine*. *Carmilla* was the author's last great hurrah. Le Fanu died the following year in Dublin at the age of fifty-eight.

Stoker followed Le Fanu's lead in a number of his later supernatural stories. *Carmilla*—the novella about a vampire created in Stoker's hometown, by Stoker's employer, in a house next to Stoker's friends, the Wildes—provided important inspirations for *Dracula*.

———

As a theater reviewer, Stoker would also have been familiar with the vampires that found success on the stage.

The Vampyre was the first piece of English-language vampire fiction. John Polidori's 1818 short novel was about Lord Ruthven, an aristocratic vampire who follows an acquaintance, Aubrey, across Europe, leaving in his wake a series of personal tragedies and mysterious deaths. At the end of the story, Lord Ruthven manages to wed Aubrey's sister and then quickly murders her by draining her blood and disappearing mysteriously into the night.

The book wasn't very good, but it had a famous genesis. Polidori, Lord Byron's friend, traveling companion, and physician, accompanied Byron to the Villa Diodati, on the shores of Lake

Geneva in Switzerland, for a summer holiday in 1816. They were joined there by a group of friends, including Percy Shelley and his fiancée, Mary Godwin.

The story of that literary group is well known: The guests were all inspired to try their hands at writing ghost stories. Authors Byron and Shelley failed with their efforts. But Mary Godwin began work on a weird story that was later published as *Franken-stein, or The Modern Prometheus*, under her married name Mary Shelley. Polidori took some notes abandoned by Byron and turned them into *The Vampyre*. The story achieved its initial fame when the credits were jumbled and it was mistakenly attributed to Byron.

Polidori's novel may have been forgotten completely had it not been turned into a popular French melodrama by Charles Nodier in 1818. Then a translation of the play made it back across the Channel, opening in London in 1820. The English version introduced the famous "vampire trap," a special piece of stage hardware allowing Ruthven to disappear in a flash when he was struck by lightning at the climax of the play. The vampire trap consisted of an opening in the stage floor, closed not with a large door, but by overlapping small rubber flaps. The actor playing Ruthven would dive headfirst through the stage, seemingly swallowed up by the earth as a blast of red flame indicated his hellish fate. The effect drew gasps from audiences and the "vampire trap" became a standard theatrical effect for a century.

The popularity of the melodrama led to a minor vampire craze through the mid-1800s, including *The Vampire Bride*, produced in New York at P. T. Barnum's American Museum, and another French play, *Le Vampire*, by Alexandre Dumas *père*. Dion Bouci-cault's version, produced in 1851, was also called *The Vampire*. In it, Boucicault included a sensational scene in which the victims of the vampire, pictured in full-length portraits, seem to come to life. They step from the paintings and warn the heroine of her fate.

Boucicault was a famous Dublin playwright and actor who had a long string of successful melodramatic plays. In his script, the vampire was a Welshman named Alan Raby; when Boucicault played the role, the vampire spoke with a thick Irish brogue. Boucicault was a charismatic, quirky Irish sprite on the stage, and it's difficult to imagine him as a monster. But Queen Victoria was a fan of the actor, saw the play, and praised Boucicault's haunting portrayal. When she returned to see the play a week later she changed her opinion, realizing that it was all "rather trashy." *The Vampire* was one of Boucicault's few flops.

Stoker met Boucicault at the Theatre Royal in Dublin, where the Irish playwright was a local celebrity. In the 1870s, Bram Stoker would have recognized a vampire as a creature primarily associated with the theater, since that's where the most popular vampires had managed to gorge themselves on box office receipts.

During his years at Trinity, Stoker had first encountered the poetry of Walt Whitman. More than likely, it was Edward Dowden, the noted Trinity professor and Stoker's mentor, who first recommended Whitman; Dowden was both a friend and a fan of the poet. Whitman's works were being avidly sought by the Trinity men for their controversial passages hinting about "robust love." The daringly homosexual passages were found in the "Calamus" group of poems in *Leaves of Grass*: "To tell the secret of my nights and days / To celebrate the needs of comrades." These verses earned praise as well as scorn from the students. In fact, most of Whitman's British readers had found only the 1868 William Michael Rossetti edition *The Poems of Walt Whitman*, which had omitted Whitman's poems that Rossetti deemed salacious.

Stoker, like Dowden, admired Whitman's bold, plain, manly phrases, imbued with honest sentiment. And both Stoker and Dowden were unafraid of the suggestive verses. Stoker later was given a copy of *Leaves of Grass* and was able to read the uncensored Whitman. Dowden defended the poet as having "never degenerated into anything lewd," but he also seemed to acknowledge the controversy by insisting that "no writer of eminence [has] not done injury."

Feeling a kindred spirit, Stoker impulsively wrote a long letter to the poet in 1872 but then thought better of his effort, locking the letter in a desk drawer. Perhaps the exercise of writing accomplished his immediate goal. Stoker had identified an artistic champion and then addressed Whitman as a confessor. Using his best Whitmanesque prose, he poured out his ideals ("How sweet a thing it is for a strong, healthy man [to address the] father, and brother, and wife to his soul"); his goals ("I would like to . . . talk to you as men who are not poets do not often talk"); and his shortcomings ("I am ugly but strong . . . naturally secretive to the world"). Stoker was well aware of the controversy generated by Whitman's poems ("I heard two men in College talking of you . . . reading aloud some passages at which they both laughed") but enthusiastically babbled his appreciation.

If the letter seemed untoward or desperate, it was particularly odd that, after reconsidering and tossing it aside, Stoker actually mailed it four years later. The original letter, coming from a recent Trinity graduate, may have seemed sweetly naive and ideal-istic. Years later, could Stoker really summon the same worshipful dreams?

The occasion for finally mailing the letter was a club event in 1876 at which Whitman's poetry was discussed. Stoker neatly de-fended him and, flushed with the success of his arguments, re-turned to his apartment to write Whitman, sending the original letter as well as a cover letter with even more confessions: "It is as truly what I wanted to say as that light is light. The four years which have elapsed have made me love your work four-fold...."

Whitman was tickled by young Abraham Stoker's impertinence and responded with praise for the letter, "so fresh, so manly." Whitman also inspired Stoker's long fascination with America; his poetry was often associated with American democracy and repre-sented an idealized, unadorned American culture.

It was Stoker's first experience with hero worship, and he suc-ceeded in that Whitman definitely remembered the name of his young correspondent. Whitman's poetry—later his friendship—would provide important inspirations.

Fortunately, another of Stoker's heroes returned to town.

In 1876, Henry Irving starred in *Hamlet*. As an important role reinterpreted by every great actor of his generation, Hamlet was perfectly suited to Irving's psychological touches. Stoker was work-ing in the civil service and still writing reviews. Now he was in a position not only to admire the performance but to offer, in a Dublin newspaper, the praise that Irving had deserved. Stoker's re-view, and a later article when he returned to see the show again, rhapsodized over Irving's modern characterization. The actor expressed an interest in meeting the critic (Stoker's reviews were not credited), so the theater manager arranged an introduction and a dinner.

"Thus it was on this particular night my host's heart was from the beginning something toward me, as mine had been toward him. He had learned that I could appreciate high effort. . . ." As a way of saying thank you to Stoker, Irving offered to recite "The Dream of Eugene Aram," Thomas Hood's dramatic poem of a murder and the murderer's conscience. It was typically a schoolboy's exercise, but Irving knew that he could take this simple work and twist it around his histrionic talents.

> So wills the fierce avenging Sprite,
> Till blood for blood atones!
> Aye, though he's buried in a cave,
> And trodden down with stones,
> And years have rotted off his flesh—
> The world shall see his bones.
>
> Oh, God! That horrid, horrid dream
> Besets me now awake!
> Again—again, with a dizzy brain,
> The human life I take;
> And my red right hand grows raging hot,
> Like Cranmer's at the stake.

By the conclusion, Stoker's reaction to "The Dream of Eugene Aram"—"something like hysterics"—must have provided the compliment Henry Irving was soliciting. When he theatrically re-gained his own composure, Irving went to his room and returned with a signed photo. The inscription betrayed how thrilled he was by Stoker's reaction, an actor gushing over his audience's good taste: "My dear friend Stoker. God bless you! God bless you!! Henry Irving, Dublin, December 3, 1876."

Thus began their relationship. Stoker craved Irving's attention, pleasing his artistic champion by crudely flattering. Irving would be needy, greedily gobbling the praise, and then, when feeling proud, carelessly ignoring his sycophant. Many years later, Stoker wrote of this meeting, concluding, "And the sight of his picture before me, with those loving words, the record of a time of deep emotion and full understanding of us both, each for the other, un-mans me once again as I write."

With "unman," Stoker had found a neat Victorian euphemism, rather than writing that Irving's photo still summoned tears.

Three

THE LEADING LADIES, "ONLY REAL FLOWERS"

A great actor can rehearse spontaneity and act happenstance. "The Dream of Eugene Aram" had been Henry Irving's showstopper for a long time. He had used it in 1870 to secure his job with Colonel Bateman, years before Stoker saw Irving's recitation in Dublin, and his little fainting act was something Irving had gradually refined over the years. Every performance needs a finale.

As a young actor, Henry Irving's first love was an actress named Nellie Moore, to whom he'd pledged his life. A series of jealousies resulted in Nellie leaving Henry for another actor; before they were reconciled she died of scarlet fever—backstage gossip reported that her death was the result of an abortion.

Heartbroken, Irving married Florence O'Callaghan in 1869. Florence was not an actress but the daughter of a respected military man. She initially pursued the young star, but after their marriage she felt impatient with his work and neglected at home.

Irving had been appearing in *Two Roses* at the Vaudeville Theatre in London but offered "Eugene Aram" on his benefit night— when the proceeds for a particular performance were offered to an actor as payment. In the audience was Colonel Hezekiah Linthicum Bateman, an American actor and theater manager who had taken over the lease of London's Lyceum Theatre in order to promote the acting career of his daughter, Isabel. He was impressed by Henry Irving's work and realized that the tall, young actor would make a wonderful leading man to show off Isabel's skills.

At the time, Henry and Florence had one son, with Florence expecting their second child, so the Lyceum offer was welcome, stable employment. But Irving and Bateman had trouble finding an immediate success, and Irving stumbled in several roles. Finally the young actor urged the manager to purchase Leopold Lewis's translation of a French melodrama, *Le Juif Polonais* (*The Polish Jew*). The English version had been named *The Bells*, after the sound of the mysterious sleigh bells that play on the mind of the murderer. *The Bells* was a taut, fascinating mix of psychology and melodrama, as if Alfred Hitchcock had stumbled back in time and landed on a dusty Victorian stage. The suspense built as the audience watched a murderer's mind unravel, much like Poe's "The Tell-Tale Heart," or indeed, Hood's "Dream of Eugene Aram." Irving tinkered with the story, building up the psychological tension of the lead character Mathias, the role on which he'd set his sights.

Ironically, *The Bells* did not have a part for Isabel Bateman.

The show opened on November 25, 1871, with virtually no help from the colonel; the costumes were borrowed and the scenery was assembled from old, badly painted backdrops in storage. The play is set at the home of an Alsatian burgomaster, Mathias. His daughter is about to be married, and the neighbors arrive to prepare for the wedding and watch a wild snowstorm outside the window. They begin discussing the mysterious murder of a Polish Jew.

Fifteen years earlier, the Jew had been murdered as he traveled through their village in his sleigh.

Mathias is troubled by the talk of the murder and seemingly haunted by the recurring sound of sleigh bells, a sound unnoticed by any of the other characters. The burgomaster has a vision of himself, from many years before—he held an ax as he crept up to the Jew in his sleigh, intent on killing him for his money.

Steeling his courage, Mathias arranges the wedding and congratulates himself for overcoming his guilt, but that night he is struck by a terrifying dream. He finds himself before a court, questioned by a mesmerist who forces him to reenact the murder. When Mathias awakes, his family is astonished to see him stagger into the room, wide-eyed, pulling at an imaginary noose. "Take the rope . . . from my . . . neck!" He struggles and dies.

The audience listened to *The Bells* quietly. The first scenes inspired little interest. The supernatural vision of the crime surprised, inspiring murmurs. By the time the curtain dropped on the third act—by the time they'd seen Mathias self-destruct from his gnawing secret and enact his own execution—they were dazed. Then gradually, slowly, they began to applaud, louder and louder, cheering, and calling Irving before the curtain. Pale and haggard, he took his bows with a wan smile that was ingeniously part Mathias and part Henry Irving, as if he were still awakening from the powerful narcotic of the role.

It was Irving's greatest night, the three acts that made his career. Many hours later, filled with congratulatory champagne and with the praise of his colleagues ringing in his ears—like Mathias's mysterious sleigh bells—Irving stepped into a brougham with his wife, Florence, to return home. That's when he noticed that Florence had watched the show without comment. When they were alone in the cab, she finally spoke. "Are you going on making a fool of yourself like this all your life?"

At that moment, the carriage was at Hyde Park Corner. Irving tapped on the door, signaling for the driver to stop. Without saying a word, he stepped from the cab, allowing his wife to continue alone. Irving strode into the darkness, never returned home, and never spoke to her again.

Indeed, Henry Irving did not have a part for Florence Irving.

———◦———

It was a different Florence, a Dublin beauty, who attracted Bram Stoker.

Florence Balcombe had auburn hair, pale eyes, and a classical profile. Like Irving's Florence, she was the daughter of a military man, and a resident of Clontarf, Stoker's birthplace.

Her first serious suitor was Oscar Wilde. They met in 1876; Wilde was twenty, back in Dublin after two years at Oxford. He was probably describing Florence when he wrote to a friend, "She is just seventeen with the most perfectly beautiful face I ever saw and not a sixpence of money." They shared a romance for almost two years. He made a pretty pencil sketch of Florence—he called her Florrie—and grandly presented it to her; for Christmas he gave her a gold cross engraved with both their names. The couple seriously discussed marriage.

Gradually their relationship cooled during Wilde's time at Oxford. His biographer Richard Ellmann suggested that Wilde may have been following the advice of his mother, Speranza, seeking to marry a wealthy heiress. Or he was following the advice of his doctor, if friends' reports are correct, and he was then being treated for syphilis. In 1878, Florence met Bram Stoker, and a quick court-ship followed. By the middle of that year they'd announced their engagement.

There's a strong possibility that Bram and Florence first met through the Wilde family, whom Stoker knew at this time. If so, Oscar may have felt an understandable sense of betrayal. Uncom-fortably, when Oscar and Florence discussed a final meeting to set-tle the end of their relationship, she suggested the home of Thornley Stoker, Bram's older brother. Neither Stoker nor Florence explained the details of their courtship, and more than likely Oscar Wilde romantically exaggerated his relationship with Florence, especially after it dissolved—his lost love seems to have inspired several poems. Wilde was genuinely dismayed to hear of her engagement and wrote to Florence suggesting that she return the gold cross, since she wouldn't be wearing it and he could be reminded of "the sweetest years of my youth."

Bram Stoker had always been something of a ladies' man: tall and handsome with a warm laugh and quiet, courtly manners. He was adept at the waltz. His career in the civil service represented a respectable salary for a new bride. Stoker was also pursuing his writing career, boasting of his aspirations and sending short sto-ries to periodicals. In 1878 he was just finishing his first book, which was not a work of literature but a sort of technical manual for his job, *The Duties of Clerks of Petty Sessions in Ireland*.

Stoker saw Henry Irving at least once a year, when Irving's tours brought him to Dublin, and at the end of 1877 he reminded Stoker of his plans to manage his own theater; he hoped that Stoker would consider giving up the civil service to work for him.

Henry Labouchère was an English journalist, diplomat, liberal politician, and member of Parliament. He also edited an influential weekly journal, *Truth*, and managed the Queen's Theatre in London. One of the leading actors there, Henrietta Hodson, became his mistress and later his wife.

Labouchère was an unabashed admirer of Irving and courted him for his Queen's Theatre. Labby (as his friends called him) realized that the Batemans of the Lyceum Theatre were holding Irving back, and he would produce better work without them. Labby wrote to Irving in 1878, first praising and then condemning his latest play, *Louis XI*: "Your acting is perfect. I never saw a more complete realization of an historical personage as set forth in a play. . . . The play has not taken because it is one of the worst and most undramatic plays ever written and because your company is below criticism. . . . Depend on it, no actor in the world can carry a bad play and a bad company. The better you act, all the worse do the duffers appear—there is a perpetual jarring contrast all through."

Irving resisted Labby's offer, but his fame presented an opportunity later that year. Irving had starred in a number of roles with Isabel Bateman, including Hamlet to her Ophelia, and Othello to her Desdemona. But, like Labouchère, he realized her limitations as a leading lady. After Colonel Bateman's death, Bateman's wife, Sidney, assumed management of the Lyceum. Irving petitioned for changes, including a new leading lady. Mrs. Bateman and her daughter, frustrated by Irving as well as their changed finances, finally gave up the lease on the theater in 1878 and moved their operations to Drury Lane.

Irving's instincts about Isabel Bateman were right. Although she had grown up in a theatrical family, she had very little taste for acting and later became a nun. Henry Irving secured the lease on the Lyceum Theatre and wired Bram Stoker to join him. Although Stoker suggested that he left Dublin to serve Irving's work at the Lyceum, his recent biographer, Paul Murray, has pointed out evidence of Stoker's ambition. Contemplating a writing career, Stoker had already been calculating a move to London.

Stoker and Irving began their furious preparations when they met in Dublin during Irving's next tour, and Stoker even moved up his marriage date so that he could bring his wife when he moved to London. He hadn't told Irving about his fiancée. When he arrived in Birmingham five days after the wedding, to meet Irving and return with his touring company to London, Stoker surprised his new boss by introducing a wife.

Florence Irving, Henry's wife, never discussed divorce. For many years, the couple communicated through chilly, restrained letters. She accepted money for her lifestyle, support for their sons, and tickets for Lyceum premieres, where she made polite appearances, seated in Irving's box, and then sneered about her husband's career to her friends. When he took those opening-night bows, he glanced up to see her, but they never met again. Henry Irving solved both of his problems—Isabel Bateman and Florence Irving—when he hired the respected Ellen Terry as his Lyceum leading lady.

Terry was an experienced theater professional, having been born into a theatrical family. She appeared with Charles Kean in Shakespeare when she was a child star in the 1850s. Like Irving, she had been unlucky in love, but it was not for a lack of trying. When she was seventeen she left the stage and married George Frederic Watts, a much older portrait artist who celebrated her beauty on canvas. They separated after only months. She then had a long affair with the architect and designer Edwin Godwin, which produced two children—Edith Craig, who became an actress, and Edward Gordon Craig, who became famous as a theatrical producer and designer.

These relationships inspired London gossip, but the public loved her too much to truly scorn her. After her affair with Godwin ended, she returned to the stage triumphantly as Portia in *The Merchant of Venice* and Olivia in *The Vicar of Wakefield*. She received a divorce from Watts and quickly married a character actor, Charles Kelly, but they soon separated.

Irving never went to see her Olivia; he didn't need to. He heard that she was wonderful. As a young actress, she had interpreted her parts with a tomboy swagger, but after her return to the stage she played her roles as a woman. Terry had a lovely voice, perfect profile, and luminous gray eyes. She was always magnificent in Shakespeare or with sentimental parts. She filled her scripts with scribbled notes, explaining reaction or emotion that she wanted to convey with individual lines, or the quicksilver changes of focus that she discerned in her characters.

Irving visited Ellen Terry at her home to discuss her engagement at the Lyceum, but that first discussion was so amiable, Terry so innocent, and Irving so politely indistinct that she didn't understand she was being offered a job until he followed up with a letter. By the time he introduced her to Bram Stoker, the deal had been arranged. Stoker always remembered that first meeting, in the winter of 1878, as Irving brought her through the dark passageway that led to the Lyceum offices. "Not even the darkness of that December day could shut out the radiant beauty," Stoker wrote. "Her face was full of color and animation, either of which would have made her beautiful. In addition was the fine form, the easy rhythmic swing, the large, graceful, goddess-like way in which she moved. . . . She moved through the world of the theatre like embodied sunshine. Her personal triumphs were a source of joy to all; of envy to none."

Stoker and Terry became like a big brother and sister (he was just a year older), laughing and teasing each other. She relied on him for advice about every element of the shows and her career, devotedly calling him "Mama." The Lyceum company adored her and indulged her at every opportunity. In *Hamlet*, the first Lyceum production to feature her with Irving, she played Ophelia and created a dazzling image when she entered in the fourth act cradling an armful of white lilies. Stoker recalled:

> Ellen Terry loves flowers, and in her playing likes to have them on the stage with her when suitable. Irving was always most particular with regard to her having exactly what she wanted. The property master had strict orders to have the necessary flowers, no matter what the cost. Other players could, and had to, put up with clever imitations; but Ellen Terry always had real flowers.

Years later, when the Lyceum company played in New York and encountered a blizzard, Stoker was determined to secure her roses for Terry's appearance in *Faust*. He located them "at famine price," five dollars for each bloom, personally bought a bouquet, and carried them back to the theater through the snow.

———

When she joined the company for *Hamlet*, Terry was surprised to find that Irving refused to rehearse her scenes. He left the characterization of Ophelia to her. She went to him and registered her complaint, but he brushed it off. "We shall be all right, but we are not going to run the risk of being bottled up by a gasman or a fiddler." That was Irving: imperious, diffident, and aching to trust the people around him.

Perhaps, too, he was trying to keep her just slightly off balance. Terry's neurosis was intact on opening night. As the curtain fell on the first performance, she had already left the theater confused and disappointed. She feared that she had done a poor job and, in turn, made Henry Irving look bad. She dashed into a cab without taking her bows. Irving received the cheers alone and then went to Terry's home to find her. They began an affair, insiders said, on that opening night of *Hamlet*.

———

Bram Stoker recalled Irving's relationship to Terry, officially, as "brotherly affection," which was a neat understatement. When traveling, they silenced gossip by staying in separate hotels, and for years they conducted themselves offstage with propriety, as devoted friends. They spent their days off together and shared vacations. Each had Jack Russell terriers, fat and spoiled; hers was Drummie and his was Fussie.

Edward Gordon Craig, Terry's son, later described his mother as one of those women who continually think they are "wretchedly weak," but who are always stronger than the men around them. Irving often boasted of her pathos, which he claimed was "nature helped by genius." He knew that she made him better; she softened his performances onstage and made him bearable to others offstage. Stoker's prose seemed unable to analyze her. Instead, he massed his compliments with superlatives—they elbow their way into the sentences and then spill over the page. She was, in Stoker's telling, more than a woman: "The natural style does not admit of falsity or grossness. . . . In her, womanhood is paramount. She has to the full in her nature whatever quality it is that corresponds to what we call 'virility' in a man."

———

In December 1879, a year into the new Lyceum management, Irving Noel Thornley Stoker was born to Florence and Bram. He was their only child, named for Bram's surgeon brother Thornley and, of course, Henry Irving. Irving also served as godfather—which was remarkable, since he had not attended the christening of his own second son. The family favored the name Noel. When he was older, he explained that he'd always avoided the name Irving because he resented the man who had monopolized his father's life.

It's easy to describe Florence Stoker as the long-suffering wife, and, indeed, the sheer mathematics of Bram's schedule demonstrates that he spent very little time at home. Stoker's biographer

and great-nephew, Daniel Farson, went one step further, speculat-
ing about an unhappy marriage, a vain, frigid wife, and a faithless
husband. But it's mere speculation, and memories of Florence, as
well as her surviving correspondence, show an engaging, insightful personality who delighted at being included in the social whirl,
proudly attended Lyceum openings and special dinners, and enjoyed parties with her husband—like Bram, she was a bit of a snob
when it came to celebrities.

When Bram was otherwise occupied, Florence sometimes attended social events with W. S. Gilbert, the acerbic playwright and
librettist who was half of the team of Gilbert and Sullivan. Gilbert
had already developed a strong distaste for Henry Irving, critical
of his bombastic productions. Bram Stoker received these comments with diplomatic silence. He and Florence were happy to socialize with Mr. and Mrs. Gilbert, and Gilbert was always willing
to chaperone the neglected Mrs. Stoker.

Another friend from their Dublin days had moved to London
by 1880. Oscar Wilde was sharing a house with the artist Frank
Miles, crafting his methodical assault on London society—witty
afternoon teas with the very best people, long dinner parties filled
with indulgent conversation, bright sparkling poems offered freely.
His formula included evenings at the theater, of course. At that
time Wilde was besotted with Lillie Langtry, the beautiful "Jersey
Lily" who was starting an acting career. Lillie had real gravita-
tional pull; she was the toast of society, celebrated by artists,
and the mistress to the Prince of Wales. Wilde was then a mere
satellite—a colorful, aspiring Irish playwright.

Wilde was drawn to the Lyceum's glorious productions and the
concentration of desirable society that filled the boxes. He also

found Ellen Terry, whom he christened "Our Lady of the Lyceum." This was the start of a long, sincere friendship. He was her fan. She was a fascinated friend, who became his fan. Wilde grandly offered his first play, *Vera; or, The Nihilists*, to Terry and Irving, sending them copies bound in red leather. Terry avoided responding and Irving politely refused; it was not a Lyceum production.

Wilde was more cautious—with Victorian social graces—in approaching the Stokers, remembering the awkward situations from their Dublin days. During *Othello* in 1881, when Irving and Edwin Booth alternated the roles of Othello and Iago, Wilde was drawn to the Lyceum. Newspapers observed him greeting friends in the box, leaning over to shake hands with admirers in the stalls, and talking with Bram Stoker in the lobby. If any awkwardness remained, it was evidenced in Bram, circling cautiously. For a while, he could still imagine himself as an equal to Wilde—a Trinity man with a writing career, who had fixed the theater in his sights—but Wilde's successes had already eclipsed his.

———·◆·———

Bram spent most vacations with the family, writing. He had never abandoned his literary career; he simply moved it to the side burner when Irving's needs at the Lyceum glowed red-hot. After *The Duties of Clerks of Petty Sessions in Ireland*, Stoker produced an array of titles. *Under the Sunset*, published in 1882, was a collection of dark, enchanted stories inspired, in part, by his mother's recollections of the Irish cholera famine. The book consists of fairy tales within a fairy tale—the fables gathered from a mysterious land, which exists only in dreams. It was dedicated to his son. A rumor among the Lyceum staff suggested that Stoker had paid

700 pounds ($3,500) to have the book printed; in other words, *Under the Sunset* was a vanity publication.

His following books included more traditional adventure novels: *The Snake's Pass, The Watter's Mou'*, and *The Shoulder of Shasta*. Modern critics feel that these works were hurriedly produced during Stoker's time away from the theater, primarily diversions from his work. Their romantic situations or adventurous spirit are in keeping with popular novels of the day, or the dramatic scripts for melodramas that were a part of Stoker's daily work. *The Snake's Pass* is set in Ireland. *The Watter's Mou'* uses Cruden Bay, Scotland, inspired by one of his vacations there. *The Shoulder of Shasta* is set in the American West for its exotic locale, after one of Stoker's American tours with Henry Irving.

The novels received mixed reviews. For example, the *Athenaeum*, a literary magazine, criticized the dialogue in *The Watter's Mou'*, suggesting that stilted phrases were better "adapted for the Adelphi stage than for a discussion between two Scotch lovers." That Adelphi remark would have been cutting to Stoker; the Adelphi had been infamous for cheap, "blood-and-thunder" melodramas, unlike Irving's more refined fare. Stoker was at his best describing local color, although—not surprisingly for a man who dealt with scripts—this sometimes turned into dialogue written in dialect: Irish, Scottish, American. Some critics found it all tedious and unnecessary.

The Shoulder of Shasta was also snubbed. "This story will not increase his literary reputation nor appeal to many readers. . . . This want of maturity and a sense of humor may be due to haste, for the book bears the stamp of being roughly and carelessly put together. Mr. Stoker can probably do much better than this," the *Athenaeum* concluded.

If the books were carelessly dashed off, it may be that Stoker was busy with his career. He trained for four years to become a barrister (a trial lawyer) and was called to the bar in April 1890. He never practiced law or tried a case. Perhaps he was readying himself for the time when he would no longer be working for Irving, or indeed, perhaps he felt a need to raise his status with Irving.

———·•·———

Voice recordings survive of Ellen Terry reciting "The quality of mercy" from *The Merchant of Venice* and Henry Irving performing "Now is the winter of our discontent" from *Richard III*. Both are from the last years of their careers. Their voices are stagy and affected, with the sharpened enunciation that was always necessary before electronic amplification. Terry's voice is powerful but lilting, filled with sincerity. Irving's voice gives evidence of his affectations: a quirky purr calls attention to itself.

Irving was distant, demanding respect. Terry admitted that he allowed few people to know him; she wondered if Stoker really understood his friend. Max Beerbohm, the English writer and caricaturist, who knew Irving for years, believed that the actor gave the appearance of "watching from a slight altitude. I think [he] wished to be feared as well as loved."

Despite being his costar, Terry had only slight influence over Irving. Her opinion was apparently always considered and often dismissed. Stoker recalled a time when Irving had interpolated a new line into *Much Ado About Nothing*, a silly joke to close the scene:

BEATRICE: Benedick, kill Claudio!

BENEDICK: As sure as I'm alive, I will!

Irving was following a centuries-old tradition of bettering Shakespeare's lines: During Irving's early years onstage, the Bard was regularly rewritten, twisted, and tortured. Terry protested, "almost to tears." She held every word of Shakespeare sacred and felt that this addition was wrong. Her reverence reflects the attitude of modern theatrical audiences.

It was Irving's theater, and Irving persisted, of course. Stoker dutifully agreed with the boss: "To my own mind Irving was right. . . . Modern conditions, which require the shortening of plays, necessitate now and again the concentration of ideas. . . . It may be interesting to note that this [new line] was not, so far as I remember, commented on by any of the critics."

Like everyone around Irving, Ellen Terry came to suffer. She was denied a number of excellent parts because—just like poor Isabel's experience with *The Bells*—every artistic decision was made by Irving and for the benefit of Irving. Her devoted fans, especially George Bernard Shaw, resented the limitations. The cult of Terry came to praise the greatness she'd achieved under duress and to grumble about the greatness that had been denied her.

But for her part, Ellen Terry never complained; she threw herself into each role and adored Irving, seeming to tolerate every one of his faults. She also understood the rules of an egotist. Terry once explained to her son, "Were I to be run over by a steamroller tomorrow, Henry would be deeply grieved; would say quietly, 'What a pity!' and would add, after two moments' reflection: 'Who is there—er—to go on for her tonight?'"

Many shows were dependent on extras to fill the stage; they called them "supers," short for supernumeraries. Most managers paid them sixpence a night; Irving paid one and sixpence (18 pence) and then raised that to two shillings (24 pence). It was a handy job, a little extra money, for theater porters, workmen, soldiers on leave, or other friends. Supers could work for an hour each night to make extra cash for their beer. Stoker was watchful for people who were working only as supers—he considered them loafers.

One of Irving's most famous effects, for a show called *The Lady of Lyons*, involved a platoon of troops, four abreast, marching past an open window and door. As the scene played out, the hero pledged himself to the army and rushed out to join the brigade. Astonishingly, the troops marched, and marched, and marched throughout the long scene, and then through the curtain calls. Irving used 150 men; they stomped across the stage at an even pace, and into the wings, then turned and ran in the opposite direction, behind the backdrop, to join the line as it marched in from the other wing. In this way, the procession of supers was truly endless.

The Cup was an 1881 play, a script by Alfred Lord Tennyson, Britain's poet laureate. It was set in ancient Greece at the Temple of Artemis. Neither the play's pedigree nor its learned exoticism was lost on Irving, who consulted archivists at the British Museum and contracted his finest scene painters to re-create the great temple. The mysterious ceremony, the centerpiece of the show, was supplemented in typical Lyceum largesse with one hundred vestal virgins, who supported Ellen Terry in the role of Camma.

Florence Stoker was recruited as one of the beautiful virgins.

Perhaps she considered it a lark or as an attempt to ingratiate herself with her husband's associates. There's no question that she was pretty enough to be onstage and professional enough to be entrusted with the role. She was given a colorful costume and directed in the choreography—a fantasy pagan ceremony that Irving invented for the occasion. When Oscar Wilde heard that his dear Florrie would be making her debut onstage (standing behind his revered Ellen Terry), he sent Terry a package with two floral headdresses. His letter shimmered with intrigue.

> I wish you every success tonight. . . . I send you some flowers, two crowns. Will you accept one of them, whichever you think will suit you best? The other, don't think me treacherous . . . please give to Florrie *from yourself.* I should like to think that she was wearing something of mine the first night she comes on the stage, that anything of mine should touch her. . . . You won't think she will suspect? How could she? She thinks I never loved her, thinks I forget. My God, how could I?

If the note seemed unnecessarily furtive or conspiratorial, this was probably Wilde's idealism. Within the London theatrical world, his personal theatricality was in ascendance. When he later became a grand hero, and the most condemned of villains, the Stokers would have to learn how to accept him on their own terms.

Four

THE ACTING MANAGER, "DISAGREEABLE THINGS"

F ussie had been completely spoiled by Henry Irving. "I have caught them often sitting opposite each other at Grafton Street [Irving's flat], just adoring each other!" Ellen Terry wrote. "Occasionally Fussie would thump his tail on the ground to express his pleasure." The dog dined with Irving and stayed with him at hotels; the hotels that wouldn't accept him were crossed off the tour itinerary. Fussie accompanied the company to theaters, wandered off whenever he wished, and created any amount of trouble. He went missing on trains, boats, and carriages and then inspired frantic searches.

But he was careful to stay off the stage when his master was on it; even Fussie knew his place. Irving loved the limelight even more than he loved his little dog. However, Fussie became confused at a charity performance in New York, where Irving and other actors were performing short scenes. When Irving stepped offstage and put on his coat, the dog assumed that the show was over—this was how it worked at the Lyceum—and he promptly trotted across the stage to find the stage door. Unfortunately, actors John Drew and

Maude Adams had just started their domestic scene. Drew watched the fat little terrier screech to a halt, and their eyes locked.

"Is this a dog I see before me?" Drew began to extemporize, reaching his hand out slowly, to lure the pooch. "His tail towards my hand? / Come, let me clutch thee. . . ."

Bram Stoker had even less success when he appeared on the Lyceum stage.

He volunteered as a super for one of those famous crowd scenes. In 1880, Irving offered a spectacular version of Dion Boucicault's 1852 play *The Corsican Brothers*. One of the most popular Victorian melodramas, it offered a little bit of everything: a ghost, a sword duel, revenge, and elaborate settings. When it first premiered, it was one of Queen Victoria's favorite shows, and it became famous for its weird ghost materialization; a special sliding trapdoor, called the Corsican Trap by theater professionals, allowed the ghost to glide across the stage and, at the same time, rise through the floor.

Best of all, the play offered two wonderful roles for Irving, as twin brothers Fabian and Louis de Franchi. A series of doubles, trick costumes, and traps allowed him to magically disappear from one scene and appear in the next, playing both parts.

Irving's Lyceum was infamous for its mishmash of popular crowd-pleasers—like *The Corsican Brothers*—and serious classics, like Shakespeare. Adding to the critics' disdain, Irving treated them all alike, filling the stage with lavish, sometimes gratuitous, artistry. In *The Corsican Brothers*, one scene included a masked ball in an opera house. Irving used the full depth of his stage, filling it with boxes like a real theater, with the entire set carefully arranged in perspective. When the curtain was raised, the audience at the Lyceum saw a different theater, which appeared to be an even larger one looking back at them!

The setting required hundreds of extras to fill the boxes and prance across the stage, playing revelers at the masked ball. Bram Stoker kept a rack of domino masks and slouch hats in his office so that anyone unoccupied (or any special guests) could be quickly costumed and shoved onto the stage. On one night, Prime Minister Gladstone, who was visiting backstage, took part in the scene.

At a different performance, Stoker donned a mask and a hat with a long plume to become part of the crowd in the opera house. A group of clowns had been booked for the masked ball to add color to the festivities. When they spotted Stoker onstage—their boss—they couldn't resist the temptation of involving him in their comedy. "They seized me and spun me around and literally played ball with me, throwing me from one to the other backwards and forwards." They rushed him down the footlights, hurtled him back and forth, but wouldn't let him get away. At the end of the scene, Stoker escaped their clutches and reeled into the wings, breathless and dazed.

The next night, when he returned to the stage, the results were even more embarrassing. Attempting to avoid the clowns, Stoker drifted upstage—far away from the audience. Irving was finishing his scene downstage, near the footlights. The actor delivered his final line and then dramatically turned on his heel to take his exit. Approaching Stoker in his costume, the actor's stern expression crumbled and he began to laugh. Fortunately, he was turned away from the audience, so they couldn't see him lose his composure.

Bram was confused and followed his boss into the wings like a hurt puppy. "Stoker, it was you!" Irving let loose a guffaw. "Don't you remember how we arranged the scene?" Irving reminded his Acting Manager how they had used small children in adult costumes at the farthest edge of the stage, to increase the apparent size of the set. This part of the scenery had similarly been built in miniature, a trick of forced perspective. Stoker had inadvertently been standing with these children. Because he was over six feet tall, it gave the impression of a giant milling around the stage. Irving had spotted the transgression and was wondering who could have ruined his scene when he recognized his Acting Manager behind the mask. "You looked fifty feet tall!" Irving told him, wiping tears from his eyes.

Bram Stoker smiled glumly. Fortunately, Irving was laughing.

The story should have been a prophetic warning to Stoker. At the Lyceum, he held his job with a delicate balance of flattery, loyalty, and honest competence. But the calibration was continually being adjusted. When trying too hard to please, it was dangerously easy to be drawn into the wrong setting and ruin Irving's carefully crafted illusions.

Irving would be watching.

The Lyceum became famous for a number of important productions. *The Merchant of Venice* opened in 1879, with Henry Irving as a surprisingly ennobled, introspective Shylock and Terry repeating her success as Portia. *Faust* was the long-planned sensation of 1885 and was revived for future seasons. Irving's elaborate *Macbeth* opened three years later. This was the actor's favorite role—he found the mixture of the supernatural, murder, and royal grandeur irresistible. Irving's new Macbeth was not the bold villain of previous actors but darker, self-doubting, and agitated.

Irving avoided the cliché of Scottish tartan and dressed in the armor of prehistoric kings. Ellen Terry offered an equally fascinating Lady Macbeth—not traitorous, not scheming, but desperately trying to gratify her husband, and naive about his potential evil. The play was the result of two brilliant actors, but again, not a collaboration. When Terry was praised for her choices, she admitted to a critic that she'd never had a chance to discuss her character with Irving.

For the role, Terry wore a wig of deep red locks and was dressed in glittering, bejeweled robes that felt mysteriously Middle Eastern. Oscar Wilde, a fan of *Macbeth* and Terry in particular, noted that "Lady Macbeth seems an economical housekeeper and evidently patronizes local industries for her husband's clothes and the servant's liveries, but she takes care to do all her own shopping in Byzantium." Terry was memorialized as Lady Macbeth in a portrait painted by John Singer Sargent; she wore her iridescent gown and held a gold crown in a death grip.

Henry Irving's first royal command performance was in 1889, before Queen Victoria at Sandringham. The performance was a special challenge for the Lyceum technicians, who supervised building a special twenty-foot-wide stage and scenery that was scaled down to fit. Henry Irving refused any payment for expenses. The Lyceum was closed for that night, and Stoker took charge of a special train car to Sandringham, with a group of actors and technicians—seventy-six people in all.

Irving presented *The Bells*, and then the courtroom scene from

The Merchant of Venice, which was a fine showcase for Ellen Terry. After the show, Irving and Terry quickly removed their costumes and makeup and dashed down the hall to meet Her Majesty, who complimented them on the production and presented them with jeweled mementos emblazoned with her initials. Irving and Terry then shared supper with the Prince and Princess of Wales. It had been the Queen's first opportunity to see Irving perform, and he later returned for two more command performances.

Bram Stoker didn't overhear the Queen's conversation. "For the rest of the company, supper was prepared in the Conservatory," he reported later, suggesting where he ended up. Stoker accepted the hierarchy of the evening without comment. "The heads of departments and workmen were entertained in the Housekeeper's room or the Servant's Hall, according to their degrees."

At one of those later command performances, Stoker felt flattered that Victoria conveyed a message, allowing him to send a telegram from Windsor Castle to the press. As Irving and Terry were ushered into another audience with Her Majesty, the Acting Manager dashed to the telegraph room at Windsor and composed a brief story congratulating his boss. He had learned to savor the warmth from reflected glory.

Bram Stoker had earned a reputation of knowing everything that happened at the Lyceum. He was a stickler for organization and decorum, which served him well through his career. He supervised the theater with an iron hand—sometimes literally. One evening during a performance, a lit torch onstage brushed against a piece of scenery, setting it afire. A stagehand quickly saw the problem and stomped out the flame, but a young man in the audience also noticed the fire and dashed from his seat. Stoker saw his panic and was determined to prevent the audience from overreacting. He threw his shoulders back and marched down the aisle, grabbing the man by the throat and turning him around. "Go back to your seat, sir!" he growled. "It is cowards like you who cause death to helpless women!"

Henry Irving would habitually shrug off requests by saying, "Ask Stoker." In this way Stoker's duties gradually expanded to handle vendors, favors, and employees. Bram Stoker would arrive at the Lyceum during the day, attending to the daily finances and schedule. He replied to correspondence. (At the end of his career, he estimated that he'd written over half a million letters.) He then changed into eveningwear and attended performances, supervising the ushers and hosting guests. After the curtain dropped, when Irving was still energetic and talkative, he accompanied his boss on late-night suppers.

When tours were arranged, it was Stoker scurrying around with railway schedules and tickets, pasting labels inside of train car windows to signal where the Lyceum company should congregate, herding them from carriages to the hotel, and scheduling the scenery to be shipped to the auditoriums. When renovations were made at the Lyceum, Stoker was there to see that Henry Irving's wishes were turned into paint, upholstery, and plasterwork.

Those were his daily duties. Stoker was much prouder when he was called upon for his creativity. He was often asked to write speeches or articles for Irving expressing the actor's views on his art or career. Irving was a good extemporaneous speaker, but he was a much smarter actor; he always wanted to work from a script. He trusted Stoker's insights and literary skills to deliver clear, dependable manuscripts that would satisfy these audiences and burnish his reputation. "He always took precautions with regard to speeches and interviews," Stoker later wrote. "On occasions where he had to speak quasi-impromptu . . . he learned the speech by heart. When he could have anything before him, such as at dinners, he would have ready his speech carefully corrected, printed in very large type on small pages. . . . This he would place before him on the table."

Bram Stoker was also asked to read plays, offer his advice to the Governor and Terry about roles, and suggest edits. In this capacity, he had the opportunity to consult with such authors as Arthur Conan Doyle, Alfred Lord Tennyson, and Thomas Hall Caine on planned scripts.

Thomas Hall Caine is generally forgotten today, but he's a fascinating character and had an important influence on Bram Stoker. Caine was a popular Victorian novelist. Although he was born in England, his family was from the Isle of Man, and he spent much of his childhood there. Caine was six years younger than Stoker, but their early lives had many parallels. Just as Stoker began a correspondence with Walt Whitman, Caine wrote confessionary letters to the poet and painter Dante Gabriel Rossetti, who was living in London. (It so happened that Rossetti's brother had published Whitman's poetry in an English edition.) Caine later served as Rossetti's secretary and nurse. And, like Stoker, Caine saw a production of Henry Irving's *Hamlet* and wrote a long, effusive review, which earned him a meeting with the actor and inspired their lifelong friendship.

When Caine saw Irving one night in Liverpool, Irving said casually, "Bram is going to join me," and this was the start of another important friendship. Stoker and Caine shared their literary dreams, swapping stories and plans for books and plays. Hall Caine went on to write dozens of books. His novels became immensely more successful than Stoker's early efforts, bestsellers for the late Victorians. These included *The Deemster*, *The Manxman*, *The Bondsman*, *The Christian*, and *The Prodigal Son*.

Irving tried, for over twenty years, to coerce Caine into writing a script for him, and Caine came very close with several efforts, including a life of Muhammad, a melodrama called *Home, Sweet Home*, and a retelling of the Flying Dutchman saga. But something always interfered. In the case of Muhammad, the Lord Chamberlain's office, who licensed plays, objected before the script was completed, as Muslim subjects would be offended by a depiction of Muhammad. For *Home, Sweet Home*, Irving listened carefully to the plot but objected to playing the character because he was too tall, telling Caine, it appears seriously, "There is no general sympathy on the stage for tall old men." (When Irving later played a sad old man in a different play, he did it stooped over or slouched in his chair.)

Caine attended Irving's first night at the Lyceum and was often hosted at the theater. He stayed with the Stokers in London and delighted in Bram's company, later describing him as "the big, breathless, impetuous hurricane of a man." Holding out for a play, Irving once told Stoker how much he admired Hall Caine's imagination, convinced that he would "write a great work of weirdness some day." Ironically, it was his own Acting Manager who wrote the greatest book of "weirdness," and when *Dracula* was published, the novel was dedicated to "Hommy-Beg," Manx slang for "Little Tommy," which was Thomas Hall Caine's childhood nickname.

———•—•———

Henry Irving was not really sociable. But he was good at *acting* sociable, playing the gracious, genial host. This was particularly easy with the help of Bram Stoker behind the scenes: arranging the guest lists, contacting the caterer and designer, welcoming the guests, and then writing out Irving's elegant, literate toasts on a menu card, handing it to the actor, and standing quietly behind him. The Lyceum hosted a number of extravagant dinners. For example, the hundredth performance of *The Merchant of Venice* was followed by a feast for 350, filling the stage with tables of bright china, cut glass, fresh flowers, and the very best of London society. Specially printed copies of the play were provided to each guest. When Irving toasted the monarch, an unseen boys' choir provided a ghostly accompaniment of "God Save the Queen." The decanter of port was passed. Cigars were offered. Oscar Wilde stood to recite a sonnet that praised Ellen Terry's Portia.

> . . . *The sober-suited lawyer's gown you donned,*
> *And would not let the laws of Venice yield*
> *Antonio's heart to that accursed Jew—*
> *O Portia! take my heart: it is thy due:*
> *I think I will not quarrel with the Bond.*

Most Lyceum dinners, much smaller affairs, were held in the Beefsteak Room. This magical, out-of-the-way little dining room was inspired by an old legacy, dating from 1735, of actors and theater technicians at the original Covent Garden. The eighteenth-century lunch group, who called themselves the Sublime Society of Beefsteaks, later convened in the room at the Lyceum. When Irving took over the lease of the theater, Bram Stoker discovered the old, wood-paneled Beefsteak dining room, restoring it while Irving was away on a vacation.

It was no longer a club; it just offered all the pretensions of one. The Beefsteak Room was another opportunity for Stoker to organize and socialize, and for Irving to preside. It seated only thirty-six people. There was no room for the actors and crew of the Lyceum; they smelled the roasting meats, walked past the locked door, and heard the hum of conversation and the tinkle of crystal, mindful of their lowly standing. Only special guests of the Lyceum would be invited to the inner sanctum. After a performance they trudged up a back staircase to the small Gothic dining room decorated with theatrical memorabilia.

Before dinner was served, the door would open and Henry Irving would arrive, sometimes still in costume, welcoming his guests. Dinner was deliberately simple and unstuffy: roast chicken, grilled steaks, and potatoes. That just added to the unconventional atmosphere, for the Beefsteak Room was a rite of passage for London society, the place to be seen. Stoker, Lovejoy, and Irving presided over it all like lords at the castle. Oscar Wilde frequently petitioned for an invitation and was welcomed by his friends; his lilting laughter echoed through the hall. It's easy to see that the Beefsteak Room was an opportunity for Irving to prolong the performance and costar with a new group of celebrities.

In his recollections of Irving, Stoker reserved more than twelve pages of small type to list over a thousand celebrities, literary figures, royalty, and nobles who were guests at the Beefsteak Room. The list is a ridiculous exercise in name-dropping; clearly Stoker prized this part of his duty and appreciated the exclusivity imposed by Irving's little dining room.

As successful as the Lyceum productions were in London, Henry Irving's tours were responsible for financing their operations. Starting in 1883, they made eight tours of America. Irving had been warned that American audiences would be difficult. They were not. Americans loved the English actor and his melodramatic productions.

Stoker fell in love with the broad countryside, the big cities, and the rough-around-the-edges politicians, authors, cowboys, and showmen who became fans of the Lyceum. These were, to English sensibilities, deliciously theatrical personalities. Mark Twain became a good friend, later visiting the Lyceum and Stoker in London. They met William "Buffalo Bill" Cody, the Wild West entrepreneur and showman. Irving and Stoker also socialized with four presidents: Chester Arthur, Grover Cleveland, William McKinley, and Theodore Roosevelt.

Part of the charm of America, for Stoker, was a country filled with Irish immigrants and proudly lacking a class system. The tall Irishman who was Irving's Acting Manager was almost as exotic, to Americans, as the famous English actor. Much to his surprise, the press was interested in what he had to say. He found himself at the center of interviews and receptions.

On their second trip to America in 1884, Irving and Stoker

were able to meet Walt Whitman, who was then visiting his friend Thomas Donaldson in Philadelphia.

They arrived at Donaldson's home and as Stoker and Irving stepped into the parlor, admiring a painting, they noticed Whitman, seated on the opposite side of the room. "Great shaggy masses of grey-white hair fell over his collar . . . I knew at once who it was," Stoker later wrote. But Donaldson rushed into the room to make the introduction. "Mr. Irving, I want you to know Mr. Walt Whitman," he proudly said.

Stoker had offered a copy of *Leaves of Grass* to his boss, so the actor was familiar with Whitman's work. Irving grinned and offered his hand to the poet. As they chatted, Donaldson maneuvered Stoker into position. "Bram Stoker," he casually announced to Whitman. Whitman noticed the name instantly, leaning forward.

"Bram Stoker—Abraham Stoker, is it?" Whitman purred. Stoker was thrilled to see the poet's bright blue eyes twinkle with recognition. They shook hands "as old friends," recalling their correspondence of nearly a decade earlier. Quickly, the spotlight shifted from the guest of honor, Henry Irving, to Stoker, who was remembered as the charming Irish boy who had poured out his self-confessions and his love of poetry.

Irving and the poet chatted amiably; he said that Whitman reminded him of Tennyson. Although Whitman had not met Britain's poet laureate, he was tickled by the comparison and flattered to hear this. When Stoker drew his chair close, Whitman was curious about mutual friends in Dublin. "To me he was an old friend," Stoker recalled, enthralled with their conversation. "I found him all that I had ever dreamed of, or wished for in him:

large-minded, broad-viewed, tolerant to the last degree, incarnate sympathy, understanding with an insight that seemed more than human."

Whitman asked his friend to promise that he'd visit his Camden, New Jersey, home on any future visits. Stoker gave his word and returned to see Whitman on two additional trips.

———•+•———

Ellen Terry resented the way that Irving could treat Stoker as a servant, depending on him for menial tasks and carelessly dismissing him from important decisions. Hall Caine saw Stoker's life as being the "absorption of one man's life in the life of another," and regretted how often Stoker was forced to do "disagreeable things . . . assuming the responsibility, taking the blame, accepting the blow."

Even worse, by the mid-1880s Irving had surrounded himself with a layer of sycophants—his personal secretary, Louis Austin, press agent Austin Brereton, and journalist Joseph Hatton. They were engaged to take notes for a projected book about his American tours, to publicize the tour and write speeches for their boss. At the end of the 1884 tour, Joseph Hatton's book *Henry Irving's Impressions of America* was published in Boston. It's an indulgent book, worshipfully celebrating Irving's celebrity. Hatton reduced Stoker to brief appearances, generally playing the part of the officious stuffed shirt, puzzled by Irving's wit or the company's amusement. Adding to the sense of competition, after the next tour of America, Stoker gathered materials for his own lecture, "A Glimpse of America," which was later published as a pamphlet. A recipient of hospitality wherever he went, Stoker pointed out that

"Americans have no princes of their own, [so] they make princes of whom they love."

The Acting Manager was confused and irritated by Irving's buzzing satellites. They were a drain on the Lyceum budget and a continual threat to his position. The new men understood this, which made them all the more resentful. They saw Stoker as a clumsy sycophant.

Irving was part of the problem. He seemed to take some pleasure in this teasing, setting up tests for the men around him and dropping hints about loyalty. Louis Austin was asked to write Irving's speeches for Harvard University and for a farewell banquet in New York. When he brought the manuscript and recited it for Irving, it "made him tearful," according to Austin. He had noticed Stoker's own draft for the speech on Irving's table, but the Governor waved it off. "Poor old Bram has been trying his hand, but there isn't an idea in the whole thing." Austin, unable to resist the temptation to put another nail in the coffin, told his boss, "I should be very much surprised if there was."

For a Christmas party during the 1885 American tour, Louis Austin wrote some satirical verses, lampooning his Lyceum cohorts. When it came time for Stoker to pick up the paper and read the poem written for him, the first line, "I'm in a mortal hurry," drew gales of laughter. It was a perfect caricature; Stoker was known for his fever pitch, and Austin's efficient lines turned him into a buffoon. Austin reported that the poem left the Acting Manager "in a rage of jealousy because I had done something successful." Years before, it would have been Stoker who was called upon for witticisms after the evening's drinks. Now he had to read a speech written by another.

It was unfair of Irving to dismiss his associate as "poor old Bram," but there's no question that the actor knew how to play to his audience. Louis Austin sneered at Stoker's literary aspirations, writing to his wife, "His first effort in literature, that marvelous book [*Under the Sunset*] neither you nor I nor anybody else could understand . . . never had and never will have the smallest return."

Bram Stoker's family vacations were the only times he was away from the theatrical world. In the summer of 1890, Bram, Florence, and Noel spent three weeks in the Yorkshire village of Whitby. It was a quiet, misty port that had become popular as a Victorian resort town, steeped in gray medieval history. A series of 199 stone steps led from the red-tiled fishing village to St. Mary's Church. High on the east cliff, overlooking the town, was the crumbling skeleton of a Benedictine abbey, which added a haunted, Gothic element to the panorama. Lewis Carroll, Charles Dickens, and Wilkie Collins had all spent time writing at Whitby. If Stoker thought that the colorful little fishing port might provide inspiration for a novel, he was right.

Stoker seemed to be turning over several ideas in his head; a novel, which was later titled *Miss Betty*, was a sweet adventure romance, set in eighteenth-century London. Another idea, which Stoker had begun to outline as four separate sections, was a tense horror story. Something about the wild Whitby landscape made this seem especially interesting, and Stoker got down to work.

While Florence and Noel visited local shows or were hosted at teas, Bram donned his comfortable clothes and stalked the town, asking about its history, writing down inscriptions from the gravestones, talking to the local fishermen, translating Yorkshire dialect into a sort of dictionary, and researching at the dusty Whitby Library. In London, he'd already begun notes for a new novel. When he started, he didn't have a name for the character. His early notes were labeled, simply, "Vampire." It was at the Whitby Library, reading a book about middle-European history, that Stoker found the name that sounded right: *Dracula*.

Five

THE VAMPIRE, "I AM DRACULA"

T he elements of the story have become tightly interwoven into popular culture, but the plot of the original novel *Dracula* still surprises with unexpected twists.

The first page contains a dry little paragraph in which the author establishes the epistolary tale: "How these papers have been placed in sequence will be made manifest in the reading of them." It is Stoker's reassuring throat-clearing to lull the readers into his fiction.

Then the first four chapters take us directly to Transylvania, according to "Jonathan Harker's Journal (Kept in Shorthand)." Harker has been following the travel instructions of a Count Dracula, working his way into Eastern Europe. A former solicitor's clerk who has just taken his examinations and received word that he's a "full-blown solicitor," Harker has been sent to "explain the purchase of a London estate to a foreigner." He travels through Budapest and Bistritz, keeping a travelogue and noting the colorful meals that he's been served and the local dress of the peasants.

The journey becomes more haunting as he proceeds toward Transylvania. When Harker is about to leave for the Borgo Pass, his hosts at an inn become concerned about his travels. An old lady warns him that his journey will take place on the eve of Saint George's Day, a day with supernatural connotations. She places a rosary with a crucifix over his neck, "for your mother's sake."

During his ride in the coach, Harker notices "an endless perspective of jagged rock and pointed crags . . . in the distance . . . snowy peaks." Here Stoker's descriptions of the landscape are purely imaginative; he never set foot in Transylvania and his mountain range is an exaggerated caricature of the Borgo Pass. But the Carpathians of *Dracula* are analogous for the increasing nightmare of Jonathan Harker's journey. At the pass, a mysterious driver and a carriage arrive to take him to Dracula's castle.

When Jonathan Harker arrives, Dracula greets him at the great door by saying, "Welcome to my house! Enter freely and of your own will!" Dracula's greetings are oddly jumbled; he tells Harker he is "welcome" three separate times, and then offers an innocuous and cheery greeting, that Harker should "Come freely. Go safely; and leave something of the happiness you bring!" Then he finally introduces himself: "I am Dracula."

He is described as "an old man," tall, thin, pale, clean-shaven except for a long white mustache that covers a set of red lips and sharp white teeth. His nose is thin and aquiline, with arched nostrils; his hair is "thin around the temples" but full and long. His eyes glow red. His breath is rank and horrifies Harker when Dracula passes close to him.

Still, the Count presents himself as a genial, if oddly unpleasant, host and he is anxious to talk in English to his new guest, share stories about his country, and hear about the property he is about to purchase in London: Carfax Abbey in Purfleet. The solicitor's clerk has helpfully taken Kodak photographs of the abbey for the new owner—a surprisingly modern twist in the cold depths of Transylvania.

Harker notices that Dracula's castle is dusty and neglected, although a fine small library is at his disposal, including English guidebooks and railway schedules that the Count has been studying. Dracula will not eat, drink, or smoke in front of Harker, making various excuses, but he serves his guest dinner and sits with him, offering friendly conversation.

But something seems wrong. Harker notices that there are no servants present. Dracula has evidently been making his dinner, clearing the plates, arranging the bedclothes, and—on one night—carrying his guest to bed, undressing him, and folding his clothes into a neat bundle. This domestic Dracula presents an unpleasant and unexpected image, especially as Harker begins to hear the rules of the mysterious castle. Dracula is absent for most of the day, and he forbids Harker from entering certain rooms, from writing unauthorized letters, or from sleeping anywhere except the room assigned him. Harker comes to realize that he's a captive, and Dracula inexplicably demands that he stay in Transylvania for a month.

A peculiarity of the castle is that there are no mirrors in it. As Harker endeavors to shave, holding his own small shaving glass up to his face, he suddenly realizes that Dracula is in the room behind him, although he did not see his reflection in the mirror. Surprised, Jonathan nicks his chin with the razor. Dracula reacts to the blood, lunging for Harker's throat, but when he notices the rosary he quickly recoils, cautioning his guest against such careless accidents. Dracula picks up the mirror, saying, "This is the wretched thing that has done the mischief," and tossing it out the window.

One evening, Harker has an astonishing revelation. He is peering out of his window and looks down the castle wall, where Dracula's room must be. Dracula's window opens and the old man crawls completely out of the room and proceeds down the castle, facedown "with his cloak spreading out around him like great wings." Dracula moves "as a lizard moves along a wall," until he disappears.

———+·+———

When Jonathan Harker defies Dracula's warning and sleeps outside of his room, he discovers that he's reduced to a sort of stupor, a dreamlike state, watching everything through half-closed eyes. He is approached by three tempting and beautiful women, who laugh among themselves and discuss how "he is young and strong; there are kisses for us all." The first bends over him, licking her lips and lowering her head until he feels her breath and teeth against his throat, providing an unexpected thrill.

Suddenly Dracula appears in the room, furious, snarling, and pushing the women away. "How dare you cast eyes on him when I had forbidden it? . . . This man belongs to me!" The women protest, pointing out that they will now "have nothing." Dracula offers them a wriggling cloth sack with something inside, and they eagerly carry it away. Harker is horrified by the thought that the sack contains a living child.

Dracula's courtly manner and obsequious attention to Jonathan Harker has now been erased. He boldly asks Harker to write three letters to his friends, postdating them weeks in advance. The letters are to explain that he's left the castle and that he is returning home from Bistritz. Harker studies the dates that Dracula suggests to him and concludes in his journal, "I now know the span of my life."

Meanwhile, the mysterious Count has busied himself with preparations for his journey, and a troupe of Gypsies arrives to pack a number of large wooden boxes onto carts. Harker tosses letters down to the Gypsies, attempting to convince them to post them, but Dracula intercepts the letters, returning them to Harker's room. He arrogantly burns the letter to Harker's fiancée, Mina, bothered that it's been written in shorthand so that he cannot understand it. The following evening, as Harker looks out his window, he notices Dracula leave down the castle wall once again, this time wearing Harker's own traveling suit.

Harker's dire situation leads him to boldly explore the Count's room, which adjoins a graveyard. There a stack of large, coffin-like boxes have been filled with a layer of earth. In one of the boxes, Harker finds the body of the Count, with his eyes open but without a breath or heartbeat—apparently newly dead. The next day Dracula comes to his room, explaining that he will be leaving Transylvania and Harker will be free to leave on the following day. That night, Harker searches the Count's room again and finds him in his coffin, but now "the mouth was redder than ever, for on the lips were gouts of fresh blood, which trickled from the corners of the mouth and ran over the chin and neck." Dracula seems bloated, sated, "like a filthy leech." When a group of local workmen, Szgany and Slovaks, arrive with their wagons to carry away Dracula's wooden boxes, Harker finds himself trapped again within the castle, awaiting his fate with the three deadly women. He writes of his resolve to scale the wall and escape, and then head back to England.

These first four chapters of the novel form a perfect Gothic tale of sensuality and danger, leaving the reader, quite literally, with a cliffhanger. The earnest Jonathan Harker's account of Eastern Europe, starting as a travelogue, ingeniously supports Stoker's reality. When Dracula enters the tale, he is a strange, fascinating, if fussy old nobleman, offering genuine hospitality and conversation. By the end of Harker's diary pages, the Count has been transformed into a murderous, blood-soaked monster lying prostrate in a coffin, seeming to sneer at his guest's fevered realizations.

Now the narrative shifts abruptly to Mina Murray's journal and correspondence. She is Jonathan's fiancée in England and awaits his return from his business trip to Transylvania. An assistant schoolmistress, Mina eschews the thought of the "New Woman" but still exhibits a modern, enlightened sensibility. She is learning shorthand and typing to help Jonathan in his career as a solicitor.

Mina's letters are exchanged with her school friend Lucy Westenra, a beautiful and coquettish young lady. They are planning a holiday together in the resort town of Whitby on the Yorkshire coast. Lucy writes, excitedly, that she has had three proposals of marriage in one day! The first is from a young physician and the proprietor of a lunatic asylum in London, John Seward. The second is from a gallant American cowboy and adventurer, Quincey Morris. But she refuses both and accepts the proposal of a third, her true love, Arthur Holmwood, the heir to the title Lord Godalming.

Dr. Seward's journal (kept via phonograph recordings on wax cylinders) notes his disdain at being refused, but he also includes the first notes of an unusual patient, R. M. Renfield, fifty-nine years old, who seems "morbidly excitable." A few short letters reveal that all of Lucy's suitors—Seward, Morris, and Holmwood—are old friends; Seward and Morris congratulate Holmwood on his engagement and good-naturedly commiserate about their lost love.

The ladies meet in Whitby, where Lucy arrives with her mother. Their holiday is ruined by various concerns: Mina finds that Jonathan's letters to her have mysteriously stopped, raising concerns about his safety. In Whitby, Lucy returns to an old habit of sleep-walking, and her fiancé, Arthur, is delayed in joining her, as his father, Lord Godalming, is seriously ill.

Mina records some of her conversations with an old Whitby sailor, Mr. Swales, who is described as "nearly a hundred." He is argumentative and difficult; he sniffs about the inscriptions on the tombstones, and the notion of resurrection. Mr. Swales is one of Stoker's typical, colorful, "dialect" characters, and Mina's journal, improbably, quotes long paragraphs of his monologue, so packed with Yorkshire slang as to be nearly indecipherable.

But Whitby proves to be mysterious. The novel now includes a long article from *The Dailygraph* that offers an account of a derelict ship, the *Demeter*, from Varna, which ran ashore at Whitby. The captain's body was found lashed to the wheel, a crucifix tied to his hand. The ship was otherwise empty, with a load of large wooden boxes filled with earth. According to the article, when the wreck was brought ashore, an immense dog or wolf leapt from the bow and ran away on the beach.

The captain's log was examined and it told a horrific story. The crew was haunted by the notion that a dark stranger was aboard; members of the crew disappeared mysteriously, and the ship seemed engulfed in fog throughout the journey. In the last log entry, the captain vowed, "I shall baffle this fiend or monster, for I shall tie my hands to the wheel when my strength begins to fail, and along with them I shall tie that which He—It!—dare not touch. . . ."

Lucy and Mina attend the funeral of the *Demeter*'s captain, which is marked by a sad procession of ships up the harbor. At night, Mina finds that Lucy has been sleepwalking again. In the middle of the night, Mina leaves the flat to find her, in her white nightdress, on their favorite seat near the ruined abbey. As she approaches, Mina notices a dark figure leaning over Lucy. Mina calls her friend's name; the dark figure lifts its pale white face and stares at Mina, but by the time she runs to her, Lucy is alone again, reclining languidly across the seat. Mina pins a shawl around her friend's neck and escorts her back to their room. The next morning, when Mina finds two small punctures on Lucy's neck, she assumes that the injury was caused by her own carelessness with the pin.

A letter from a convent hospital in Budapest offers Mina news of her fiancé. Sister Agatha of the convent, writing for Jonathan, explains that he's had "some fearful shock . . . in his delirium his ravings have been dreadful." Mina instantly goes to Budapest, to find him slowly recovering from his horrors. There he entrusts her with his notebook, the diary of the nightmares at Castle Dracula, telling her he never wants to hear the contents. Unexpectedly, Jonathan asks her to marry him as soon as possible, and the ceremony is performed that afternoon, with Jonathan in his hospital bed.

———•—•———

Dr. Seward keeps busy with his patient Renfield, who has become increasingly agitated. Renfield collects flies and spiders and is observed eating the flies, obsessed with the thoughts of devouring life. He suggests that his "Master" is coming for him. When Renfield escapes from the asylum, he runs to Carfax Abbey, the property adjoining Seward's home and asylum. This is, of course, the old abbey that Dracula has just purchased, where the mysterious boxes of earth have now been delivered.

Arthur Holmwood, concerned about Lucy's health, contacts Dr. Seward, who puzzles over the symptoms and, in turn, wires his professor, Dr. Abraham Van Helsing, in Amsterdam, asking him to come to London to consult.

At this point in the novel, the reader realizes that all of these characters, places, and events are being tied together into one story. Dracula has arrived at Whitby precisely when Harker's fiancée, Mina, was visiting there. He seduces Lucy exactly when Mina is called to Jonathan. He is moving into a property next to Dr. Seward in London, precisely when Lucy is put in Dr. Seward's care. He is exerting an influence over Renfield, increasing his madness, just as Seward contemplates the case. It would all be ridiculously coincidental were the novel not so infused with a weird supernatural quality. There seems to be a deliberate, diabolical force focusing on this small group of people.

⸺•⸺

The next chapter details the battle for Lucy's life, told principally through Dr. Seward's diary. Van Helsing is a wise European professor who is intrigued by Lucy's malady and charmed by the young lady. When Lucy's mysterious nighttime illness returns, the two doctors recognize symptoms of anemia and prescribe an immediate blood transfusion. As they are deciding which of them is to donate blood, her fiancé, Arthur Holmwood, arrives and volunteers for the procedure. This immediately restores Lucy's health for several days. But her malady returns, requiring repeated transfusions from her three suitors as well as Van Helsing. The Dutch doctor seems secretly to be coming to conclusions about a diagnosis, and he wires for a package of garlic flowers from a friend in Haarlem. He spreads them around Lucy's room and arranges a wreath of the pungent flowers around her neck. This, he assures her, will provide a good night's sleep.

The next morning, Lucy's mother reports that she had checked on her daughter during the night and, overcome with the odor of the flowers, offered fresh air. She foolishly opened the window and removed the flowers from Lucy's neck.

When Van Helsing hears of Mrs. Westenra's mistake, he breaks into tears, raging against the powers of evil. He and Seward enter Lucy's room to find her pale, waxen, and near death once again. Now the novel combines her fate with a climax of tragedies: Lucy's mother dies from a weak heart; she is terrified when a wolf crashes through Lucy's bedroom window and a bat enters the room. (The wolf, we later learn, was borrowed from the London Zoo by a mysterious stranger.) Arthur's father, Lord Godalming, succumbs to his long illness and dies. And Peter Hawkins, Jonathan Harker's boss and law partner, dies in Exeter, leaving Jonathan and Mina heartbroken. Finally Lucy dies, weakened by her latest nighttime bout with anemia.

These deaths form a tragic climax in the middle of the novel, signaling the dark tragedy that has descended on all the characters. Lucy provides a suspiciously beautiful corpse, and Van Helsing seems to anticipate more difficulties, telling Seward, "We can do nothing as yet. Wait and see." But Seward assumes that, with Lucy's death, these mysterious episodes are now finished. He closes his diary with the word "Finis."

Stoker was anxious to incorporate factual details, and he consulted his brother Thornley about medical science—head injuries—using that information later in the novel. But the episodes with Lucy are jarringly naive about narcotics, anemia, and blood transfusions. Transfusions, in particular, were a novel procedure at that time. Proof of Stoker's unfamiliarity is the fact that his multiple, frantic transfusions are described only vaguely—these details would have made a horrific and gripping subject for Dr. Seward's diary. To a modern reader the transfusions sound wrong, as blood typing was not then recognized; it was discovered in 1901 and came into practice a decade later. The doctors' procedures in the novel, using any available man as a donor without checking blood type, would have been disastrous.

Arthur Holmwood, unaware that other men provided transfusions, tells Van Helsing and Seward that although they had been only engaged, he believes "the transfusion of his blood to her veins had made her truly his bride." The doctors decide, for Arthur's peace of mind, to not tell him of the other donors. This commingling of blood as a surrogate for sex—both holy and unholy unions—becomes an important motif as the story proceeds.

Now the novel includes a chilling article from the *Westminster Gazette*: the neighborhood of Hampstead, near Lucy's grave, has been haunted by sightings of a "bloofer lady" (presumably children's slang for "beautiful lady"). This mysterious woman is attracted to small children playing on the heath; when the children are later found, they are in a weakened condition with small tears or wounds on their throats. Van Helsing finds this article and groans sadly, "Mein Gott! So soon!"

The Dutch doctor has been studying Lucy's letters and diary entries from before her death in an effort to solve the mystery of her illness. He visits Mina and Jonathan Harker in Exeter. Mina surprises him with a typewritten account from her husband's journal—his horrific discoveries in Transylvania. She also relates how she and Jonathan, on a visit to London, saw a strange man in Piccadilly. The man was staring intently at a beautiful girl with a large hat, and Mina remembered him as "tall, thin . . . with a beaky nose and a black moustache and pointed beard [with] big white teeth [and lips] so red," his teeth "pointed like an animal's." Jonathan was mortified to see him, murmuring, "It is the man himself!" and explaining to Mina that the Count has grown younger since arriving in London.

Dr. Seward resumes his diary to record Dr. Van Helsing's musings on Lucy's fate. The two men decide to investigate, and they sneak into Lucy's tomb one evening, opening the coffin. Her body is gone. They observe a mysterious figure, dressed in white, returning to the cemetery and carrying a sleeping child. The figure disappears and the doctors rescue the child. The next day they enter Lucy's tomb again, finding her body in the coffin. She is now "more beautiful than ever," with her lips "redder than before; and on the cheeks was a delicate bloom." Van Helsing also notices that her canine teeth are now pointed. He decides that this vampire, having proven herself to be one of the "un-dead," must be destroyed.

Arthur Holmwood and Quincey Morris arrive to assist with the expedition, and they are taken to the cemetery at night. The men are shocked to see the vampire Lucy on her nightly hunt. Lucy now has a cruel face, fiery eyes, and lips reddened by fresh blood. Van Helsing holds up a crucifix, and Lucy snarls, dashing back into her tomb.

The four men return the next day, hiding in the cemetery and then entering the crypt with Van Helsing's special toolkit. Dr. Seward's diary carefully records the excruciating procedure. Van Helsing places the tip of a thick, three-foot-long wooden stake against Lucy's heart and then instructs Arthur, Lord Godalming, to pound it securely in place. Steeling his resolve for this horrific deed, Arthur dutifully swings the hammer and the stake pierces her body. Lucy opens her eyes, writhes, screams, and contorts. Her teeth gnash until her lips bleed. Blood wells around the stake and spurts from the wound. When the task is done, the men look back at the body. Lucy is once again saintly and beautiful in death, with "a face of sweetness and purity." Arthur and Quincey leave the tomb, and Van Helsing and Seward finish the grisly job, sawing off the top of the stake, cutting off her head, and stuffing her mouth with garlic. Finally, they seal the coffin and lock the door of the crypt.

———— • ————

Mina and Jonathan arrive in London, staying at Dr. Seward's home and asylum. Now the entire group of vampire hunters has been assembled: the Harkers, Seward, Arthur Holmwood, Quincey

Morris, and Dr. Van Helsing. Jonathan has arrived from Whitby, where he has been researching the shipment of Dracula's boxes and reveals that Dracula's lair is in the abbey next to Seward's home. Meanwhile, Mina and Jonathan busy themselves by transcribing all of the journals, including Dr. Seward's phonograph cylinders, typing everything carefully and arranging the manuscripts in chronological order so that everyone can share the accounts. As readers, we are given the perspective of witnessing the assembly of the book that we are reading. Indicative of Stoker's fascination with records, accounts, and schedules, the manuscript provides vital clues for the characters, and they carefully study the collected information.

Van Helsing explains the rules of vampirism and the history of the ancient Count Dracula, their foe. The wise Dutch doctor has armed himself with garlic, crucifixes, and a package of consecrated host from a priest in Holland. Dracula, he explains, is bound to his coffins of native soil. Van Helsing plans to find all of the coffins and destroy them.

Here Bram Stoker must be given credit for ingeniously defining vampire mythology. The vague superstitions, expressed in earlier books, had to be clarified and expanded for *Dracula*. Stoker borrowed from everywhere. The bloody procedure for driving a stake through the heart was explained in *Varney the Vampire*, a popular "Penny Dreadful" novel from 1845, as well as Le Fanu's *Carmilla* from 1872. The use of garlic to repel a vampire was taken from folklore. But the inability of a vampire to cause a reflection was actually exaggerated from an old Transylvanian superstition, and Stoker was the first to apply it to vampires. Similarly, Dracula's difficulty in crossing running water and his need to sleep in consecrated native soil were Stoker's inventions. In the novel, Van Helsing points out the vampire's weakness during sunlight, but this bit of mythology was exaggerated in later movies—now it's assumed that sunlight will destroy a vampire. In fact, in Stoker's novel, Dracula appears several times in the sunlight.

Perhaps Stoker's most important contribution was the rule by which a vampire's victim, once dead, becomes a new vampire. This is evidenced in Lucy's fate, and it also endangers Mina. The idea of a spreading contagion imparted an exciting level of danger and morality to the story.

At this point in *Dracula*, the band of protagonists forms a sort of family at Seward's residence. The diaries include accounts of breakfasts or dinners together, where the players compare notes and plan their strategy, forming a "board or committee." Mina becomes a sister/wife/mother to them all, impressing the men with her bravery and determination. She has a "man's brain . . . and a woman's heart," according to Van Helsing. The men, in turn, are often brought to tears, wallowing in Victorian bathos, recalling Lucy's fate, Mina's selflessness, or Dracula's threat.

Having read about the mysterious patient, Renfield, Mina now asks to visit him. She and Dr. Seward find him unexpectedly rational and intelligent. The patient has similar conversations with Arthur Holmwood and Quincey Morris, impressing them with his sophistication as he begs to be set free.

The men search the abbey, take inventory of the boxes, and realize how many must have been moved to other locations: Dracula has planned several lairs around London. Jonathan bribes a workman and finds a house in Piccadilly, another residence that Dracula has purchased under the name Count de Ville.

Dracula's activities across London are neglected in most adaptations of the story. The locations of his homes and business connections suggest a number of inside jokes intended for friends. The Piccadilly house was near Hertford Street, the location of Bram's brother George Stoker's medical practice. Another house, in Chicksand Street, was near the site of the Jack the Ripper murders. It was also near a favorite East End social club sponsored by Baroness Burdett-Coutts, a supporter of Henry Irving and a friend of Stoker's. The baroness is also acknowledged with the information that Dracula's bankers in London were Coutts and Company.

During these expeditions to find Dracula's whereabouts, Mina has been left at the house, and the reader recognizes the significance of her troubled nights of sleep: Dracula has been paying her sinister visits. A clock begins ticking; will the men find the vampire and exterminate him before Mina succumbs?

———•◆•———

Seward and Van Helsing are called to Renfield's cell; he's suffered a mysterious blow to his head and a broken neck. Van Helsing trephines the patient's skull to relieve the pressure, and Renfield confesses that Dracula has been visiting him, sending him bits of life to fulfill his obsessions. He confirms to the doctors that Dracula has been influencing Renfield's erratic need for blood and is now visiting Mina. Renfield refers to the vampire as his "lord and master."

At the point in the novel, readers are treated to the dramatic scene where the vampire hunters encounter Dracula and Mina. The vampire is discovered in Jonathan and Mina's bedroom, forcing her to drink blood from an opened vein in his breast. The men push Dracula back, until a shadow passes in front of the moon and he dissolves away again, "nothing but a faint vapor."

Mina's assault presents the most horrific view of Dracula, whose snarling warning indicates both revenge and carnal desire. Mina recognizes that she is now "unclean." The implication is that this bloodlust has befouled her marriage to Jonathan. When Van Helsing attempts to correct this situation the next day, touching a piece of the holy wafer to Mina's forehead, the Host burns her flesh, leaving a prominent red scar that enshrines her shame.

The men discover that Renfield has died from his final encounter with Dracula, and the enraged vampire has "made hay of the place," destroying their carefully assembled manuscript of notes and diary entries. Fortunately, another copy of the manuscript has been preserved in a safe. Again, Stoker memorializes the manuscript that we're reading, and we can trace its importance as the key that can give insight into Dracula's secrets.

———

The following day, the men begin their important process of extermination. They break into the abbey, opening each coffin and sprinkling bits of crushed Host, sanctified wafers, to prevent the vampire from returning to these resting places. Then they proceed to Dracula's house in Piccadilly, hiring a locksmith to break in, and similarly destroy these coffins. There they find evidence that Dracula had purchased two additional houses. Godalming and Morris proceed to those addresses, taking inventory of the missing coffins and sanctifying them.

Mina, however, has noticed Dracula leaving Carfax Abbey and sends a telegram to the men in Piccadilly, warning them. Dracula enters the house and bursts in on the men. They attempt to capture him, even slashing at him with a knife, but he escapes them by lunging through the window and running for the stables. As he does, he stops to offer his final warning: "You shall be sorry yet, each one of you. You think you have left me without a place to rest, but I have more. My revenge is just begun! I spread it over centuries, and time is on my side."

In the morning, Mina has an ingenious idea. She summons Van Helsing and asks him to hypnotize her, realizing that her alliance with Dracula has imparted a sort of psychic connection. Under hypnosis, she identifies the sensation of lying in a coffin—Dracula's last remaining coffin—and the sound of a creaking sailing vessel, about to weigh anchor. Proceeding to the docks, they find that one ship, the *Czarina Catherine*, has just left for Varna and other locations up the Danube. Questioning the dockworkers, they find that a mysterious man, dressed in black and wearing a straw hat, booked passage and brought one large, coffin-shaped box with him.

His departure does not solve the problem. Van Helsing points out that Dracula must be found and destroyed, forever removing the stain—the curse—from Mina before she becomes doomed. They plan to travel overland, reaching Varna before the vampire. Mina insists on traveling with them, and she makes the men promise that they will destroy her if she becomes a vampire. Mina even insists that the men read the service for the Burial of the Dead for her— the vampire hunters take solace in this simple, beautiful ritual.

The following day they all travel by train and await the arrival of Dracula's ship. Here Mina's hypnotic trances are used to the group's advantage, for they ascertain that Dracula is still aboard the ship, still hearing lapping waves. They board a train to Galatz, but they are too late. The cargo of Dracula's box has already been consigned to a local agent, and it has disappeared.

The chase is guided by Mina's supernatural abilities as well as her logical deductions, carefully analyzing his route and the modes of travel. The group splits apart and Mina travels with Van Helsing. When they reach Dracula's castle, Mina makes a psychic connection to her three vampire "sisters," who call to her from the castle. Van Helsing protects her by placing her within a holy circle, and then he methodically finds the graves of the three vampire brides, destroying them with stakes through their hearts.

Mina and Van Helsing leave the castle, awaiting the men. Sunset approaches, and the pair watch from the rocks, aiming their rifles, as a band of Gypsies bring the Count's coffin into the pass. Jonathan, Quincey, Godalming, and Seward ride up to the group and dash toward the cart. There is a fierce battle with the Gypsies, who defend their cargo. Quincey is stabbed, but Jonathan manages to pry open the coffin lid, exposing the vampire. Jonathan wields his knife, decapitating the vampire. Quincey Morris plunges his dagger into Dracula's heart, and as the sun sets, the vampire's body seems to crumble into dust. As Quincey Morris draws his last breath, he is relieved to see that the stain has been removed from Mina's forehead.

A short postscript from Jonathan Harker concludes the novel. He proudly writes that his and Mina's first child, named after Quincey Morris, was born just a year after Morris's death. Returning to Transylvania several years later, they recalled the terrible events. Now Dracula's castle is but a "waste of desolation." Kindly

Dr. Van Helsing suggests, "We want no proofs, we ask none to believe us!" vowing that young Quincey Harker will someday understand the bravery of his mother and the important sacrifice of the
men who loved her.

———•—•———

Stoker originally included a more elaborate finish, three paragraphs in which Dracula's castle was destroyed by a sudden earth-
quake and crumbles in front of the heroes just after the Count
is destroyed. The image would have been in keeping with the repeated claims of the novel—that, besides the written accounts, no
actual evidence remains of the events. Stoker deleted these paragraphs, perhaps suspecting that they offered too unrealistic and
sensational a climax.

Critics have debated a more curious inconsistency. Several of
Stoker's own rules for vampires were inexplicably violated within
the novel. For example, Dracula is killed according to the rules of
Emily de Laszowska Gerard, not the rules of Van Helsing. Dracula's death seems confusingly inexact and has been debated since
the book's publication. Some writers have suggested that Stoker
anticipated the phenomenon exploited by Hollywood forty years
later—leaving a loophole for a possible sequel. More than likely,
Stoker had confused his own rules by the end of the book and
these discrepancies were oversights of the author.

Similarly, Stoker's novel suffers from some now-famous inade-
quacies. The band of men, who at times seem to collapse in pathetic tears, or populate a grail romance, or ride off in a Western
potboiler, become virtually indistinguishable from one another as
the novel proceeds, and Mina becomes more prominent. Stoker's

use of dialect is tedious and becomes especially annoying and un-realistic when set within the frame of diary entries and letters. Often the action of the novel seems to slow in order to accommo-date the thick, working-class accents of the old sailor, the zoo-keeper, or the dockworker. Each character who offers a diary or letter seems to quote Van Helsing's broken English with the same awkward, halting phrases.

But there's no question that *Dracula* is also Stoker's finest novel. It enshrined the vampire and formalized his world of the super-natural. Perhaps Stoker's most remarkable achievement was com-posing a novel called *Dracula*, while writing almost nothing about Dracula. Stoker left it to everyone else—a century of readers—to fill in the mysterious characterization.

Six

THE VOIVODE, "RAGE AND FURY DIABOLICAL"

Bram Stoker never spoke about the origins of *Dracula*. According to Noel, his father laughingly suggested that the novel was inspired by a nightmare after a "surfeit of dressed crab."

The joke must have saved Stoker a great deal of explanation. Remaining evidence shows an author who combined a wide variety of sources and inspirations from his research—he planned and wrote the book for at least six years. *Dracula* was not only Stoker's most famous work, but also a labor of love. Between his tours and the politics and responsibilities at the Lyceum, Irving returned to his novel again and again to adjust the story and rearrange the plot. Dracula, one of the most surprising and horrific characters in literature, must have become a comfortable old friend to Bram Stoker.

Stoker's notes—his research and outlines for the novel—were sold by his wife, Florence, after his death and are now in the collection of the Rosenbach Library in Philadelphia. From these notes, the evolution of the novel is apparent.

The earliest dated page is from March 8, 1890. Henry Irving was then in London performing in *The Dead Heart*. This was a melodrama set during the French Revolution, with an especially interesting cast, including Squire Bancroft (an old actor-manager who had appeared with Irving and officially retired from the stage four years earlier) and Edward Gordon Craig (Ellen Terry's son, in his first professional performance). Terry agreed to play the part of his mother—she couldn't resist the temptation of acting with her son—but she realized that the part was "uninteresting," especially after her success as Lady Macbeth. Irving, of course, had a substantial role; he fought a duel and was then marched to the guillotine.

In his March 8 note, Stoker was still struggling with character names and situations. He was planning the book as a series of letters, first told with correspondence to a law society: "Letter to Aaronson from Count—[from] Styria asking to come or to send trustworthy law[yer] who does not speak German. . . . In this series of letters is told visit to Castle."

Here Stoker later inserted the phrase "Munich dead house." He toyed with setting an early incident, during the lawyer's travels, at a Munich mausoleum. The page continued:

People on train knowing address dissuade him. Met at station. Storm. Arrive old Castle. Left in courtyard. Driver disappears. Count appears. Describe old dead man made alive. Waxen color. Dead dark eyes. What fire in them. Not human, hell fire. Stay in castle. No one but old man but no pretence of being alone. Old man in walking trance. Young man goes out. Sees girls. One tries to kiss him not on lips but throat. Old Count interferes. Rage & fury diabolical. This man belongs to me I want him. A prisoner for a time. Looks at books. English law directory. Sortes

virgilianae. Central place marked with point of knife. Instructed
to buy property. Requirements consecrated church on grounds.
Near river.

"Sortes virgilianae" was a term for predicting the future by
choosing random words in books; perhaps this was how the Count
would be plotting his move across Europe.

It's surprising how Stoker's brief phrases efficiently map out the
book that we now all recognize. These are indeed the early chapters of *Dracula*. Of course, early in 1890, the author didn't have
the names for Hawkins, the solicitor in England; Count Dracula, the haunting, aristocratic vampire; or Jonathan Harker, the
hapless lawyer who is sent to meet the Count and becomes the protagonist in the story. Styria (later part of Austria) was the setting of
Le Fanu's *Carmilla*, suggesting that Stoker had quickly, carelessly
picked this locale as a home of vampire folklore.

Stoker's notes are especially fascinating for the names and
places that he had not yet discovered.

———·•·———

Researchers have speculated that Stoker's knowledge of Transylvania came from Arminius Vambery, a Jewish-born adventurer from
Hungary. Vambery had a precocious skill for languages and was a
natural adventurer; as a young man he disguised himself as a der-
vish and traveled from Constantinople to Samarkand—the first
Western European to report on this fabled city of the Silk Route.
When he came to London, his speeches on Eastern European culture made him an instant celebrity. He defended English interests
in the Middle East and criticized Russian influence; nearly a cen-

tury after his death, the Russian government released files that showed he had been engaged as an agent for the British government.

Vambery would have been familiar with the traditions, languages, and landscape of Transylvania. Even more intriguing, he dined with Irving and Stoker at the Beefsteak Room, where he regaled them with stories. For example, when Stoker asked if he ever feared death during his travels through Tibet, Vambery thrilled his hosts with his daring: "Death, no. But I am afraid of torture. I protected myself against that, however. I always had a poison pill fastened here, where the lappet of my coat is now. This I could always reach with my mouth in case my hands were tied. I knew they could not torture me, and then I did not care!"

Another of Vambery's remarks, to Empress Eugenie, is more revealing. When she was surprised that he had walked so much, yet started his life lame, confined to crutches, he told her, "Ah, Madam, in Central Asia we travel not on our feet but on the tongue." In fact, Vambery was always a fantastic self-publicist.

Coincidentally, Vambery dined with Irving and Stoker on April 30, 1890, just nine days before Stoker's first written notes for the vampire novel. Since the earliest notes mention neither Dracula nor Transylvania, it seems unlikely that Vambery whispered these magical names during his evening at the Beefsteak Room. When Stoker met Vambery again, two years later, he had already found the essential information on Transylvania.

In the finished novel, Vambery receives a tribute from the learned Abraham Van Helsing: "I have asked my friend Arminius of Buda-Pesth University to make his record; and from all the means that are, he tells me of what he has been. He must, indeed, have been that Voivode Dracula who won his name against the

Turk. . . ." But even here, Stoker's account of Dracula has been cobbled together from a few books and enhanced with a great deal of fiction. The name Arminius simply lends credibility.

It was another visitor to the Beefsteak Room, the explorer Henry Morton Stanley, whose presence seems to haunt Bram Stoker's early notes.

Stanley had been born out of wedlock in Wales in 1841. He took his father's name of Rowlands, and spent much of his childhood in a workhouse. At eighteen, he went to America to start a new life, first settling in New Orleans and adopting the name Stanley from a man who treated him as a son. There he managed to shake his British accent. He fought for both the Confederate army and then the Union army in the Civil War, finally becoming a journalist for New York newspapers and earning a reputation for his intrepid travels in search of a story. The *New York Herald* gave him the assignment to locate the long-missing David Livingstone, who had disappeared while exploring Africa. After a long, perilous adventure, Stanley found him on the shores of Lake Tanganyika in 1871, greeting him with his famous, and probably fictitious, British understatement, "Dr. Livingstone, I presume?"

Stanley's explorations, including his later search for the source of the Congo River, were described in his books. His adventurous life was famous in Victorian London, but his heroism was accompanied by controversy: misrepresentations of his adventures, hints of a homosexual scandal, and episodes of cruelty toward African natives. Stoker noticed his unusual features when they first met at a special Garrick Club dinner with Irving in 1882 and described him as a sort of shell of a man, a mysterious presence who quickly took everything in but was careful to release only occasional, measured flashes of light.

> [Stanley] had a peculiar manner, though less marked than later years. He was slow and deliberate of speech, the habit of watchful self-control seemed even then to have eaten into the very marrow of his bones. His dark face, through which the eyes seemed by contrast to shine like jewels, emphasized his slow speech and measured accents.

Stoker met him several times after that. Their last meeting, according to Stoker, was at a special lunch on June 26, 1890, about four months after he started the notes for his novel.

> At that time Stanley looked dreadfully worn, and much older than when I had seen him last. . . . He was darker of skin than ever; and this was emphasized by the whitening of his hair. He was then under fifty years of age, but he looked nearer to eighty than fifty. . . . There were times when he looked more like a dead man than a living one. Truly the wilderness had revenged upon him the exposal of its mysteries.

As developed in the novel, the Count becomes a figure that virtually defies description, but Stoker's first written notes, an "old dead man made alive," with a peculiar hell fire in his eyes, and—in the novel—a long, drooping white mustache, matched the author's description of Stanley. Before the character appeared in the novel, he had managed to acquire the traits of other influential men.

Stoker's notes from around the same time included a preliminary list of sixteen different characters—no names yet. Three were lawyers and one was "Lawyer's clerk" who "goes to Styria." (Stoker actually began to write "Germany," then crossed out the first words and wrote "Styria.") The characters also included a "Mad Doctor," "Mad Patient," "Philosophic historian," "Lawyer's shrewd, sceptical sister," and a "Detective inspector." The list suggested a sort of detective story or mystery.

The author followed with a series of memos with plot ideas. One memo listed characteristics of the vampire: "No looking glasses in Count's house. Never can see him reflected in one—no shadow? Never eats nor drinks. Carried or led over threshold." Another suggestion showed that Stoker was planning on introducing modern technology, including the portable camera: "Could not codak [Kodak] him—come out black or like skeleton corpse."

A plot point, "Doctor at Dover Custom house sees him or corpse," suggested that Stoker originally planned for Dracula's arrival at Dover, the most logical port from continental Europe.

Another memo mentioned a "dinner party at the mad doctor's" that consisted of thirteen guests. Each guest was asked to contribute to a strange story, adding their own incidents as the story proceeded around the table. "At the end the Count comes in."

And then, he began work on two important pieces of paper that defined the novel. The first was a list of characters, which Stoker labeled "Historiae Personae." The page had deletions, changes, and alterations. It was obviously a page that Stoker returned to again and again as the plot developed. Here, for the first time, the names began to appear that we recognize as characters in the novel. "Doctor of madhouse . . . Seward." "Girl engaged to him, Lucy Westenra." "[Law] clerk, Jonathan Harker." "Fiancee of the above, pupil, teacher Wilhemina Murray (called Mina)." The central character's name was still undecided. Here Stoker labeled him "Count Wampyr."

Harker was a name taken from an associate at the Lyceum. Joseph Harker was a freelance scenic painter who was often brought in to work with Hawes Craven and William Teblin on backdrops for Henry Irving's shows. Harker was working at a scenic dock at Her Majesty's Theatre, he later recalled, when Stoker strode in one day, casually mentioning that he had "appropriated my surname" for a character. There was no explanation why. Harker was thirty-five years old and may have reminded Stoker of the young lawyer he had invented for his novel.

Other characters in the "Historiae Personae" were still being developed. "A German Professor, Max Windshoeffel," later became Van Helsing. And "a Texan, Brutus M. Moris," became Quincey Morris.

"A painter, Francis Aytown," represented Stoker's attempt to include a sequence in which Dracula's portrait cannot be represented on canvas.

Then, a sheet initially dated March 14, 1890, transformed the structure of the novel into four separate sections or "books," echoing the structure of a four-act play at the Lyceum. The first book, "Styria to London," detailed the adventure at the Count's castle. "Tragedy" told the story of the Count's arrival in England and the transformation of a young lady into a vampire. With "Discovery," the suspicion fell on Dracula, and the Texan was sent back to the

Count's homeland to search for clues. "Punishment" began with a dinner of thirteen, a sort of vigilante committee who returned to Styria to find the Count.

The page showed numerous deletions and additions; it was obviously a worksheet as Stoker was adjusting the story.

———•—•———

Stoker's joke about "dressed crab" may have been more than a social expedience, simple chitchat about his book. If *Dracula* really was inspired by a single nightmare, Stoker's notes from the spring of 1890 suggest what was in that nightmare. There is a single incident at Dracula's castle that was repeated in early notes and was then readjusted by the author, even after the book's publication.

From March 8: "Young man goes out. Sees girls. One tries to kiss him not on lips but throat. Old Count interferes. Rage & fury diabolical. This man belongs to me I want him. A prisoner for a time."

And then again, from March 14: "Arrive the Castle. Loneliness, the Kiss. 'This man belongs to me.'"

"This man belongs to me" are the first words that Stoker "heard" from his Count, and the first words he recorded, even before the character had a name. Stoker repeated the phrase "Belongs to me," or a variation, five more times during the course of his notes, indicating that it was a key moment in the story.

The scene with the vampire brides seemed to be unnecessary to the plot, but it was recorded in early notes and sailed through directly to the novel, complete with the Count's simple pronouncement. Jonathan Harker was threatened by the lascivious vampire brides, who approached him with their teeth bared. Then Dracula interrupted them. With his one remark, Jonathan was both saved and imperiled by Dracula, who claimed him as his own prize.

When the first American edition of the book was published, by Doubleday in 1899, there was an addition to the text, presumably made by Stoker, that only accentuated this point.

In the first British edition, after Harker's initial meeting with the brides—"This man belongs to me!"—he later overhears Dracula whispering to the women, outside his door. The vampire tells them, "Wait. Have patience. Tomorrow night, tomorrow night is yours." In 1899, the line was changed to, "Wait! Have patience! Tonight is mine. Tomorrow night is yours!" It's the only clear hint that Dracula bites and draws blood from another man. This scene is a curious twist on Le Fanu's *Carmilla* and has invited a century of speculation about the author's intentions.

Bram Stoker's favorite place for writing had been Cruden Bay, in Scotland. But he found a similar respite in Whitby. The port town was the perfect mixture of Old World and New, and he immediately recognized that it should be the place where his Count arrives in Western Europe—the ragged, colorful medieval town that would serve as a physical and emotional transition to London.

In July 1890, Bram, Florence, and Noel visited Whitby, and Stoker found several books in the local library that became important sources. *An Account of the Principalities of Wallachia and Moldavia* was written by a former British consul to Bucharest, William Wilkinson, and published in 1820. Transylvania was not a part of the book's title, but this province figured in the book, separated by Wallachia and Moldavia by the Carpathian Mountains. In Bram Stoker's time, Transylvania was part of the Austro-Hungarian Empire.

Wilkinson's book was probably where Stoker first encountered the names Dracul and Dracula, the names applied to father and son rulers in Wallachia in the fifteenth century. Wilkinson himself seemed to jumble the roles of father and son, and Stoker's later account of the historical Dracula is a similar pastiche taken directly from Wilkinson. But Stoker was attracted to a footnote that explained, "Dracula in the Wallachian language means Devil."

An article on Transylvania, "Transylvanian Superstitions," seemed to confirm the setting for Stoker's story. The article on superstitions was written by Emily de Laszowska Gerard and published in *Nineteenth Century* magazine in July 1885. Gerard was an Englishwoman; she married a Hungarian cavalry brigade commander who had been stationed in Transylvania. Her article described a colorful, backward, and deeply superstitious area of Eastern Europe where centuries-old traditions of ghosts, werewolves, and vampires were still accepted by the population.

Transylvania's deep traditions of the supernatural made this land an ideal setting for Stoker's story. Even the name, which translates as "The Land Beyond the Forest," sounds like a mysterious fairy tale. Gerard's article included mentions of Saint George's Day eve as the witches' Sabbath; the Sholomance, a demonic school in the mountains where the Devil supposedly teaches his disciples; and the belief that it is "unlucky to look in a glass [mirror] after sunset." These were all elements that later figured in Stoker's mythology. Stoker also made careful note of Gerard's instructions for killing a vampire: "Vampire or nosferatu: to kill vampire drive stake through corpse or fire pistol shot into coffin or cut off head and replace in coffin with mouth full of garlic, or extract heart and burn it and strew ashes over grave." Gerard later incorporated "Transylvanian Superstitions" into a book published in 1888, *The Land Beyond the Forest*, although there is no evidence that Stoker was aware of this book.

In refining his own mythology, Stoker ignored the advice about shooting a vampire; this would be far too ordinary for his purposes.

———

We can see the transition in Stoker's notes. A sheet labeled "Book 1, Chapter 1" has notes about "Count Wampyr," but the name Wampyr was later crossed out and Dracula was inserted. By the last note on the page, it seemed as if Stoker was writing "Dracula" at his first stroke, without hesitation.

———

Similarly, his "Historiae Personae" showed a dramatic explosion of ink, as if Stoker's newest discoveries left evidence of a celebration. The name was written into the margins and Wampyr was crossed out. Stoker added the new heading, three times, across the top of the page, as if convincing himself: "Count Dracula, Dracula, Dracula." He had not yet decided upon the title of book, but he was clearly enamored with this dark, simple name. On the same page, Whitby was woven into the plot, and Transylvania was the setting for the first and last part of the novel; often it was put in place of the deleted "Styria."

Like a detective, Stoker prowled the streets of Whitby, noting any scenery, local color, or recent history that might be of use in his novel. He chatted with local fishermen about their recollections and talked to a coast guard named William Petherick, obtaining details of a Russian ship, the *Dimetry*, that had run ashore at Whitby Harbor. He drew maps of the coastline; he took note of wind conditions and wrote descriptions of the countryside and buildings; he copied down information from tombstones so that he could invent local residents with the proper surnames. Stoker even compiled a long dictionary of Yorkshire slang—attesting to his love of writing in dialect—so that he could make his Whitby sailor wheeze and whine with the proper slang words. One long passage in his notes details the appearance of the town at nine a.m., with "sheep and lambs bleating . . . band on pier, harsh waltz . . . Salvation Army in street off Quay, neither hearing each other, we hearing both." Later he used these details, at exactly this time of day, in the novel.

As he continued gathering material, he consulted over a dozen additional books. These included *Magyarland* by "A Fellow of the Carpathian Society," *Round About the Carpathians* by A. F. Crosse, *The Golden Chersonese and the Way Thither* by Isabella L. Bird, *On the Track of the Crescent* by Major E. C. Johnson, and *Transylvania: Its Products and Its People* by Charles Boner. These were filled with information about the area, the dress of the inhabitants, food, traditions, and language. A curious source was *The Theory of Dreams*, by Robert Gray. While Stoker used very little from this book, he realized that the quality of unusual dreams and clairvoyance would be an important element of his plot.

Before plotting all the chapters, Bram Stoker's skills as Acting Manager were utilized to meticulously plan a timeline for his story. He started with blank calendar pages, filling in dates starting in the month of March. Then he noted key events in the novel opposite the run of dates. For example, the first entry is on March 16: "Dracula's letter to Hawkins (dated 4 March old style)." After correspondence to and from Transylvania—allowing time for each letter—Jonathan Harker leaves London on April 25, "8:[30] p.m." and arrives at Paris on the following day, "5:50 a.m. Leave Paris 8:25 p.m. Arrive Munich 8:35 p.m." The travel schedule was arranged with guidebooks and railway schedules, ensuring accurate times.

The novel takes place between March 16 and November 6, in one calendar year. Researchers have noted, from the days and dates as well as several events during the course of the book, that Stoker was probably using 1893 as his model. This suggests that he was in the process of plotting his novel in 1893, copying dates out of a current calendar. But Stoker's dating isn't flawless. Certain statements within the novel seem to contradict this year. For example, at the conclusion of the book, Jonathan Harker wrote that it has been "seven years" since the events. This was impossible if the events took place in 1893 and the book was published in 1897. More than likely, Stoker used a current calendar to plan his novel, but then adjusted the story as was convenient, avoiding the suggestion of any specific year.

For all of his work on the novel, it's curious which elements seemed to elude the author's plans. Stoker never set foot in Transylvania, and his description of the cragged cliffs and imposing Gothic castles are essentially imaginary. The Borgo Pass, a link between Wallachia and Transylvania, looked remote and forbidding on a map. In fact, the landscape is one of rolling hills and grass-covered mountains.

Similarly, Stoker's London is a busy metropolis with very little definition. The Count moves from house to house, from his abbey in East London to the docks on the Thames, but city landmarks disappear into the fog of the story. Dracula is described as being enamored of the new city, but the author had, long ago, grown bored with it. For these reasons, the single great setting in Stoker's novel is the one that most readers forget: Whitby. This little port, the transition between Transylvania and London, is carefully and colorfully described.

Van Helsing, a central character in the book, is named very late in the author's notes. He apparently first took shape as an assortment of characters, including a detective, a physical research agent, and a German professor.

Renfield, the lunatic who falls under Dracula's spell and begins eating flies, never appears by that name in his notes. The character is called "Flyman" early in his notes, Stoker's placeholder for the character, and the name was decided upon at the last moment, appearing only in the finished manuscript. Stoker seems to have first named him Renfold, and finally as Renfield.

Stoker worked on the novel during two trips to Cruden Bay in 1893 and 1896. The contract for the book was signed in 1897, to be published by Archibald Constable and Company in London. Even then, Stoker had not yet decided upon a title; his initial contract labeled the book *The Un-Dead*.

———•—•———

Then there is the problem of the voivode.

The name Dracula became one of the most insidious and enigmatic hints in literary history. It was a fortuitous result of Bram Stoker's afternoon at the Whitby Library. In Wilkinson's book, *An Account of the Principalities of Wallachia and Moldavia*, a footnote reads: "Dracula in the Wallachian language means Devil. The Wallachians were, at that time, as they are at the present, used to give this as a surname to any person who rendered himself conspicuous either by courage, cruel actions, or cunning."

Unfortunately, Wilkinson's explanation made a number of errors, which were translated into Stoker's book. He compounded a father-and-son ruler and misunderstood the intended meaning of Dracul. Obviously, the notion of "Devil" must have been appealing, and "courage, cruel actions, or cunning" also seemed to complement his character. In the novel, Van Helsing commented authoritatively on the history of the old ruler, but this brief history was basically fiction, designed to incorporate Stoker's brief facts and lend credibility to the novel. The noted *Dracula* researcher Elizabeth Miller has demonstrated how Van Helsing's account was completely drawn from Wilkinson's book and four other sources, as noted in Stoker's papers, and then stitched together with assumptions. For over fifty years these historical references lurked within the novel, awaiting discovery.

Several authors made the connection in the late 1950s and 1960s, researching the original Dracula and citing his horrific tortures as inspirations for the novel. Stoker's first biographer, Harry Ludlam, claimed in his 1962 book that Stoker had consulted "fifteenth century manuscripts," one of which spoke of Dracul "as a 'wampyr.'" (Such a manuscript, with this reference, has never been found.) Grigore Nandris, in a 1966 article, claimed that portraits of the real Voivode Dracul must have been used by Stoker to describe his white-haired Count with the long mustache.

A fascinating 1972 book, *In Search of Dracula*, written by Raymond T. McNally and Radu Florescu, finally tied the fictional Count to his historical predecessor. In their telling, the real Dracula proved to be every bit as notorious as Stoker's later literary villain.

Vlad (the father of Dracula) was a Wallachian military commander who, in 1431, was awarded a special chivalric order, the Order of the Dragon, by Sigismund, the Holy Roman Emperor. This marked his devotion to the emperor and his battles against the Turks. To enshrine the honor, Vlad proudly added the name Dracul, meaning "dragon."

His son, later known as Vlad Tepes, was probably born that same year. When he became a ruler, he adopted the name Dracula, meaning "son of Dracul." Curiously, these sobriquets had positive connotations for the father and son, although Stoker's sources had indicated the opposite.

Young Vlad and his brother spent part of their childhood as prisoners of the sultan of Turkey, political blackmail to ensure his father's cooperation. When Vlad was finally returned to Wallachia as a young adult, he found that his father had been murdered.

Vlad reigned as voivode on three separate occasions, over a span of seven years, battling fiercely with the Turks as well as the Hungarians. During that time, he was infamous for his horrific displays of power. In 1457 he reportedly invited his enemies, the noble families, for an Easter feast, and then killed the elders by having them impaled on tall upright spikes. Several years later, when the Turks were led by the sultan to attack his castle, they found it surrounded by a virtual forest of impaled victims. It was an effective deterrent. The sultan considered his enemy not only bloodthirsty but also psychotic, and he withdrew his troops. His nickname, Vlad Tepes, translated to "Vlad the Impaling Prince."

Dracula was killed in battle in 1476. According to tradition, his head was carried back to Constantinople as a prize for the sultan.

To weave together the narrative for their 1972 book, McNally and Florescu made several assumptions. They speculated that Arminius Vambery told Stoker about the Voivode Dracula, and then directed him to several books in the British Museum that explained his reputation and atrocities. Similarly, a footnote in Wilkinson's book could have directed Stoker to the seventeenth-century *Generall Historie of the Turkes* by Richard Knolles, which included an account of Dracula's gruesome execution of twenty thousand victims. Altogether it was just too tempting a story—a ruler known for murderous cruelty, nicknamed "Devil," or "Dragon," and situated in Transylvania. Readers of *In Search of Dracula* became convinced that Stoker must have carefully read the history of this middle-European voivode and then concealed much of the history within his text.

Coincidentally, it was the intrepid McNally and Florescu who then unearthed the evidence that began to unravel their theory. While researching a later book on Dracula, they visited the Rosenbach Library in Philadelphia to see a fifteenth-century pamphlet about Vlad Tepes. An archivist there helpfully mentioned that if the authors were interested in Dracula, they might like to see Bram Stoker's original notes, which were in the library's collection but had not yet been cataloged.

Of course, the authors were thunderstruck. They deciphered Stoker's handwritten notes, which first recorded the dates of its composition and his research. McNally and Florescu then used Stoker's notes in preparing their books *A Clutch of Vampires* (1975) and *The Essential Dracula* (1979). Perplexingly, the dates and sources within Stoker's notes made it apparent that he never had more than a scant knowledge of Vlad Tepes.

There are many small details that attest to Stoker's limited research. For example, Stoker assigned the wrong allegiances to Dracula. In the novel, his character explains that he is a "boyar" (an aristocrat) when, in fact, Vlad Dracula struggled against the boyars. Stoker's villain claimed to have been related to the Szekely, when the actual Dracula was a Basarab, from Wallachia. Even the setting of Transylvania was wrong. The historical Dracula lived in Wallachia, on the outskirts of Transylvania, and had a castle at Poenari.

More telling, Stoker never incorporated the bloodthirsty reputation, his tortures, his impaling, the name Vlad, nor the nickname Tepes (Impaling Prince). In fact, Stoker has Van Helsing say that Dracula was "in life a most wonderful man. Soldier, statesman and alchemist . . ." Could the meticulous Stoker have researched this character and then not used the historical information?

Researchers now generally accept that Stoker was never aware of more than the name and several historical facts. He had not read of the voivode's career or his reputation. After their first book, McNally and Florescu revised their opinions; in 1997, Florescu delivered a paper that concluded, "The connection between the historical Dracula and the novel . . . beyond the title, is limited to four short references from a single book."

Dracula scholar Elizabeth Miller has carefully examined the evidence and soberly concluded:

> [Stoker's] research seems to have been haphazard (though at times fortuitous) rather than scholarly. What he used, he used "as is," errors and confusions included. . . . While it is true that the resurgence of interest in Dracula in the early 1970s is due in no small measure to the [McNally and Florescu] theories about such connections, the theories themselves do not withstand the test of close scrutiny.

In fact, it now seems that the Dracula of Stoker's novel had merely the name of the fifteenth-century ruler, but echoed the characteristics of nineteenth-century celebrities, which added to his haunting and mysterious qualities. Dracula was drawn from a handful of dangerous and damaged personalities. Bram Stoker knew them all.

Seven

THE NOVELIST, "DREADFUL"

A s the character of Dracula became enshrined in popular culture, it came to summon distinct, particular images—Bela Lugosi's hypnotic, menacing presence, in a dark opera cape with the high collar; or Christopher Lee's hissing, dissolute Count, part animal and part aristocrat, as he threatens with blazing bloodshot eyes and bared teeth. The novel surprises modern readers by offering almost none of that.

As author and researcher Leonard Wolf points out, Dracula appears on only sixty-two of Stoker's 390 pages, and many of those appearances are incognito—as the coach driver for Jonathan Harker, as the dog that dashes from the *Demeter*, as a bat that threatens at Lucy's window. He is given only a handful of speeches, and there are only two or three opportunities for us to witness his full powers.

Deep in the novel, as the characters discuss the problem in mythic terms and with vague, romantic ideals, the concept of Dracula becomes so abstract that it actually seems a shock to have him burst into a room. As much as Stoker's change of title—from the original *The Un-Dead* to *Dracula*—seems like false advertising, it also becomes his advertising masterpiece. Our anticipation of Dracula, the flapping bat or the swirling mist that circles and never quite arrives inside the novel, becomes the intrigue that keeps readers turning pages.

Even the Count's appearance remains indistinct and debatable. Jonathan Harker describes him as an old man with white hair and an aristocratic, aquiline nose. By the time Dracula arrives in London, he is presumably gorged on blood and rejuvenated, with a sharp dark beard and a "high" nose, long nostrils, and lips that suggest an animal, like a bat.

It was the later incarnations of vampires that created the verb "vamp." The word implies, from actors like Theda Bara to Robert Pattinson, a delicious combination of seduction and threat. By contrast, Stoker's original character is always repulsive, foreign, and unappealing. When he finally overpowers Mina in her bedroom, it is a horrible, aggressive act, with none of the teasing sexual appeal that Broadway and Hollywood later discovered lurking inside Dracula's coffin.

On May 18, 1897, about a week before Stoker's book was officially published, the author arrived early at the Lyceum Theatre for his own experiment.

The Acting Manager, dressed in a dark suit, steeled his nerves and quickened his pace as he turned the corner onto Burleigh Street. It was unusual for him to be approaching the Lyceum stage door with the bright morning sun. When he saw the Lyceum at this hour, it was usually on the way out, after a long, bleary evening of rehearsals with Irving. Bram Stoker pushed open the stage door, turned and checked with Lovejoy, the stage manager, in the wings, and then glanced across the wide Lyceum stage, nicely swept clean and arranged with a small pattern of tables and chairs. Everything was in place. Stoker pushed through the metal pass door and strode up the aisle and into the lobby. There, the ushers were putting out the signboards on the pavement, announcing the special morning program. A neat stack of crisp, white programs had already been arranged on a marble table. Bram Stoker leaned over to examine the printing. *"Dracula, or the Un-Dead.* First Time."

As Henry Irving's Acting Manager, Stoker had calculated his new character's potential value for the stage; in the past, vampire melodramas had always sold tickets. He knew that even if the vampire proved evasive to the vampire hunters, he would have to lock up Dracula—wrap him in copyright law—to ensure that he didn't escape into the commercial world of the theater.

The process of securing rights to a theatrical production—as dictated by the Lord Chamberlain's office—involved a public performance. The Lyceum had produced a number of these copyright performances, including one for Tennyson, *The Foresters.* It was a necessary part of the theater business. These public shows were not creative exercises but legal necessities, allowing an author to stake his claim to a work and prevent other adaptations. The play for these purposes might be a play in name only: little more than a public reading. The cast might hold scripts in their hands, wander to and from the chairs, exit into the wings, or improvise their own actions to accentuate the words.

Certain necessities would be in place. Gaslights would be turned on. Bits of scenery would be placed on the stage, a few stock backgrounds, a door, a table, and a bundle of props, as needed for the action. To make it an official performance, programs would be printed and a bill posted, but the copyright show was usually scheduled at an inconvenient time and for only a single performance.

This was precisely the case with Stoker's new play, which started promptly at ten a.m. The admission, one guinea, was prohibitively high, designed to discourage an audience. Lyceum records show that only two tickets were sold—no doubt to a couple of theater stalwarts who had taken notice of the special show. The rest of the audience, no more than a handful of spectators sprinkled throughout the stalls, consisted of the cleaning crew, a few friends, and fellow actors. Stoker paced in the back, his usual place during most of Irving's plays, although this production promised exceptional opportunities for pacing.

Fortunately, Stoker's script survives; it was filed with the Lord Chamberlain's office as the contents needed to be approved for decency. While we don't know who watched from the seats, the script allows us to imagine the herky-jerky formality of this one-time production. It was Bram Stoker's only effort to put *Dracula* on the stage, and the only time the Count was dramatized during the author's lifetime.

Stoker's finished script may not have been expected to be a work of art, but the Acting Manager, busy with the publication of his novel and tending to Irving's business, had found the time to assemble only a rough cut-and-paste job, using galleys from the novel and additional lines to stitch the pieces together. The finished script shows evidence of being hurriedly assembled, with long speeches taken directly from the novel and very little effort to dramatize any of the events. In the places where Stoker was forced to write material, the results were deflating and ordinary.

The show opened with a quick overture from the pit, a few musicians who had been recruited to make it feel like a show. The curtain was raised on a smattering of nervous applause from the tiny audience. An actor walked onstage, bowed slightly, and stood behind the lectern.

For this version of *Dracula*, there was no opportunity to provide the rolling travelogue of Transylvania, none of the moonlight niceties that Henry Irving would have fussed over for his own productions. Stoker's script began with the actor playing Jonathan Harker arriving at an imaginary castle door, pounding an imaginary knocker, and calling out loudly. That morning, there couldn't have been much acting. The actor bent over the script, poised on the lectern, reading his lines.

> JONATHAN: Hi! Hi! . . . Well, this is a pretty nice state of things! After a drive through solid darkness with an unknown man whose face I have not seen and who has in his hand the strength of twenty men and who can drive back a pack of wolves by holding up his hand . . . to be left here in the dark before a ruin. Upon my life I'm beginning my professional experience in a romantic way! Only passed my exam at Lincoln's Inn before I left London, and here I am conducting my business. . . .

Dracula arrived. The second actor entered through the imaginary door and slid up to the lectern. He was forced to introduce himself with a series of perfectly ordinary lines that made him sound inappropriately befuddled. His opening lines had been adapted from the book and, as in the book, he welcomed his guest three times.

On that sunny morning at the Lyceum, there was none of the successful, menacing atmosphere that made Stoker's Transylvania so successful.

COUNT DRACULA: Welcome to my house! Enter freely and of your own will.

> *(Stands immovable till Harker enters, then advances and shakes hands.)*

Welcome to my house! Come freely! Go safely! And leave something of the happiness you bring!

HARKER: Count Dracula?

COUNT DRACULA: I am Dracula and you are, I take it, Mr. Jonathan Harker, agent of Mr. Peter Hawkins? I bid you welcome Mr. Harker to my house. Come in the night air is chill and you must need to eat and rest.

> *(Places lamp on bracket and stepping out carries in luggage.)*

HARKER: *(Trying to take luggage.)* Nay, sir, I protest.

COUNT DRACULA: Nay sir, the protest is mine. You are my guest. It is late, and my people are not available. Let me see to your comfort myself.

Stoker squinted at the scene and groaned. Barely five minutes into the play, and the script had revealed itself as a crashing bore. Stoker straightened his vest, turning away from the stage and walking impatiently from one aisle to the next. As a solicitor (like his hero Jonathan Harker), Stoker reminded himself that this was not art. It was a legal necessity. At this point, *Dracula* simply had to be endured.

Irving reportedly wandered through the auditorium shortly after he arrived at the Lyceum. He stood briefly at the back and then offered a one-word criticism: "Dreadful." It was said just a bit too loudly, leaving no doubt about the great actor's disdain for these awful proceedings. He turned and pushed his way through the pass door, returning to his office.

No doubt another interested spectator that morning was Ellen Terry, who walked into the auditorium, delicately took a seat, and listened politely for as long as she could. Her daughter, Edith Craig, had been asked to play Mina. It was a wonderful bit of casting, especially since the Mina of the novel had clearly been inspired by Terry, Stoker's coworker. Edith was in her late twenties, just starting her acting career. She was appearing each night in a small part in *Madame Sans-Gêne*, the current Lyceum comedy costarring her mother, with Henry Irving taking the part of Napoleon. In fact, most of *Dracula*'s cast consisted of character actors from *Madame Sans-Gêne*, with other roles filled out by young actors.

Jonathan Harker was being played by Herbert Passmore, who had worked in the touring company of the Lyceum and was featured in *Madame Sans-Gêne*; Dracula was T. Arthur Jones, a character actor with an aristocratic demeanor who was also appearing each night. The part of Van Helsing was taken by Tom Reynolds, a balding, round-faced comedian with the Lyceum, who went on to a long career in London.

VAN HELSING: Brave lad! A moment's courage, and it is done. This stake must be driven through her. It will be a fearful ordeal—be not deceived in that—but it will only be a short time, and you will then rejoice more than your pain was great, and from this grim tomb you will emerge as though you tread on air. But you must not falter when once you have begun. Only think that we, your true friends, are round you, and that we pray for you all the time.

ARTHUR: Go on. Tell me what I am to do.

Of course, that morning there was only talk, no dramatic vampire killing or bloody special effects. As the production proceeded, the endless script exhausted the actors and exasperated Stoker. It was filled with speeches clipped directly from the galleys of the book. That morning, the play reading took over four hours—a sign that the actors had adopted a breakneck pace and dry, mechanical recitation. When Stoker's script was given a second reading, exactly one hundred years later at a London pub, the reading took a full six hours.

The conclusion of the play arrived with a dull thud. Having been reduced to a few perfunctory lines, it offered none of the daring chase or supernatural resolution from Stoker's climactic sunset over Castle Dracula. According to the script, Van Helsing and Mina watch as the action continues:

(Gypsies and horsemen draw near.) . . .

(Horsemen fight with Gypsies and Morris and Harker throw box from cart and prise it open. Count seen. Fades away as knives cut off his head. Sunset falls on group. Morris is wounded and Harker holds up his head.)

The script doesn't explain how this battle could have been staged, or combined with Mina's furtive glances, or the revelation of the scar disappearing from her forehead. In fact, these events couldn't have been enacted that morning—just a few lines from the lectern and a few pantomime gestures. The curtain slowly descended to the sound of a few people applauding.

It was finished.

———•—•———

When Stoker's play had been approved by George Redford, the examiner of plays in Lord Chamberlain's office, Redford offered that it was a "very remarkable dramatic version of your forthcoming novel," and he found nothing "unlicensable" in it. In fact, there was a great deal in Stoker's cut-and-paste play that should never have been approved for a London stage, including Jonathan's attack by the three vampire brides, Lucy's extermination by driving a stake through her heart, Mina's drinking of Dracula's blood in her bedroom, and Dracula's final beheading. Redford must have carelessly approved the play because of his long professional relationship with Stoker, understanding it would never be produced in this form.

The copyright performance had been a humiliating ordeal for Stoker, especially for his friends who had been introduced to his new novel by this tedious performance. There are almost no written memories of the morning. Stoker never spoke of it. More than likely, it was treated as mere busywork.

Whatever Bram Stoker had wished for *Dracula* onstage, the copyright performance was his first and last effort to turn it into drama. After the single Lyceum production, there was no effort made to rewrite the play or produce it in any form. The author must have lost interest or viewed the project as untenable. If he had hoped to impress his boss, Henry Irving, with this new story, *Dracula, or the Un-Dead* was a distinct failure.

Fortunately, the book received more attention.

———•◦•———

With its publication on the twenty-sixth of May 1897, the novel may not have been a hit, but it was a definite success.

W. L. Courtney, in the *Daily Telegraph*, wrote a long and insightful review, offering praise for Stoker's style.

> Never was so mystical a tale told with such simple verisimilitude. We are not allowed to doubt the facts because the author speaks of them as mere matters of ascertained truth. Such is Mr. Stoker's dramatic skill that the reader hurries on breathless from the first page to the last, afraid to miss a single word. . . . Though the plot involves enough and to spare of bloodshed, it never becomes revolting, because the spiritual mystery of evil continually surmounts the physical terror. Nevertheless, no part of the book is so good as the opening section. The reason is obvious . . . the local colouring [is] quite as important as the central incidents. When you are transported to an unknown region everything is possible.

The *Spectator*, similarly, remarked on the ordinariness of the modern setting.

The sentimental element is decidedly mawkish. . . . The up-to-dateness of the book—the phonograph diaries, typewriters and so on—hardly fits with the medieval methods which ultimately secure the victory for Count Dracula's foes.

But the *Pall Mall Gazette* adopted exactly the opposite opinion.

Mr. Bram Stoker lays the main scenes of his tale in England and London, right up to date, with the typewriter, the phonograph, the Pall Mall Gazette, the Zoo, and all the latest improvements complete. That is the way to make a horror convincing. The medieval is well enough in its way, but you don't care what sort of bogeys troubled your ancestors all that way back. . . . There are slight discrepancies, possibly, and the mechanism which helps the characters out is once or twice rather too obviously mechanism, but that is inevitable. There is a creep in every dozen pages or so. For those who like that, this is a book to revel in.

The *Athenaeum* thought that Stoker's approach was "too direct and uncompromising" and that the book "was wanting in the constructive art as well as in the higher literary sense."

The early part goes best . . . but the want of skill and fancy grows more and more conspicuous. The people who band themselves together to run the vampire to earth have no real individuality or being. The German [*sic*] man of science is particularly poor and indulges, like a German, in much weak sentiment.

The first American edition was published just two years later. The *Wave*, a San Francisco newspaper, provided a uniquely negative review, detailing the book's "degeneracy."

> Here is a man who has taken the most horrible theme he could find in ancient or modern literature [and] has then gone on to carry the thing out to all possible lengths. The plain horrors were enough, perhaps, but the author goes farther, and adds insane asylums, dissecting rooms and unnatural appetites galore. No detail is too nauseating. In the first seventy pages, there are four cases of deaths caused by the preying of human vampires, one murder, one suicide, one lunatic with homicidal mania and a habit of eating flies, one somnambulist, one shipwreck, extent of fatalities not fully reported, one death by hysterical fright. Pleasant, isn't it?

But most American reviewers were swept up in the sheer exhilaration of thrills. The reviewer from the *Detroit Free Press* remembered the congenial Bram Stoker from his visits with Henry Irving's company, expressing honest astonishment that Stoker had penned such a weird, successful novel.

> And Bram Stoker wrote it!
>   Think of him.
>   He—a great, shambling, good-natured, overgrown boy— although he is the business manager of Henry Irving and the Lyceum Theatre—with a red beard, untrimmed, and a ruddy

complexion, tempered somewhat by the wide-open full blue eyes that gaze so frankly into yours! Why, it is hard enough to imagine Bram Stoker as a businessman, to say nothing of his possessing an imagination capable of projecting Dracula upon paper.

One suspects that Stoker's British associates had been similarly surprised, even if they were too polite to admit it.

———————

Over the years, commentators have noted how different *Dracula* is in scope and ability from Stoker's other works. There's no question that it was his finest book, perhaps confusingly so. In 1927, the American fantasy author H. P. Lovecraft wrote to his friend Donald Wandrei:

Have you read anything of Stoker's aside from *Dracula*? . . . Stoker was absolutely devoid of a sense of form, and could not write a coherent tale to save his life. Everything of his went through the hands of a re-writer and it is curious to note that one of our circle of amateur journalists, an old lady named Mrs. Miniter, had a chance to revise the *Dracula* manuscript (which was a fiendish mess!) before its publication, but turned it down because Stoker refused to pay the price which the difficulty of the work impelled her to charge. Stoker had a brilliantly fantastic mind, but was unable to shape the images he created.

Mrs. Miniter was Edith Dowe Miniter, an American author of a 1916 novel, *Our Natupski Neighbors*. There's no reason to believe that Lovecraft's comment is anything more than gossip—and no reason why Stoker would have sought a young American author to revise his book. The discovery of Stoker's notes has effectively demonstrated that Lovecraft was wrong. Stoker composed the book himself. The notes also demonstrate why *Dracula* was his most successful book—it was carefully considered and revised over the course of seven years.

A century of critical analysis has pulled *Dracula* to pieces, hammering virtually every possible theory, psychoanalysis, or motivation into the vampire's corpse in an attempt to explain Stoker's masterpiece. It's a sad fate that even Dr. Van Helsing would not have prescribed.

Part of the difficulty has been a need to psychoanalyze Stoker himself—his quiet stoicism and his erratic literary career just frustrates scholars. So, he has been explained as a proponent of Irish home rule, a misogynist, a latent homosexual, a vengeful employee, an anti-Semite, or someone morbidly afraid of syphilis—or even better, a sufferer from syphilis. It is the doppelgänger. It is Freud. It is a grail romance. It is *Macbeth*. It is a twisted Oedipal fantasy.

The marvel of *Dracula* is that there are so many mythic themes—psychosexual, religious, cultural, fairy-tale—integrated into the vampire myth and brightly polished throughout Stoker's novel. There is truly something for everyone. A modern reader, examining the original criticisms, may be struck with how the book's erotic content went virtually unnoticed. This is a surprise for the late Victorian age, a period of fussy prudes who should have been decrying *Dracula*'s suggestiveness. Perhaps their prudery allowed them to overlook it, and our "sophistication" allows us to fixate on it. By a modern standard, this might be the novel's most surprising deception. Dracula is about sex—and here scholars are free to debate the particulars of that sex. As the Victorian prudes tingled, they were deceived into thinking the tingle was caused by horror. Today we know better.

The question still remains whether Bram Stoker himself understood the eroticism that he had hardwired into his story—this is usually the jumping-off place for later psychoanalysis of the author. As we'll see, that answer isn't clear.

It's a good story, well told. It scares the hell out of you. It causes nightmares. Did anything more ever need to be said?

A popular author like Arthur Conan Doyle, the creator of Sherlock Holmes and a professional associate of Bram Stoker, seemed to instantly understand the novel's genius and wrote to him.

> I think it is the very best story of diablerie which I have read for many years. It is really wonderful how with so much exciting interest over so long a book there is never an anticlimax. It holds you from the very start and grows more engrossing until it is quite painfully vivid. . . . I congratulate you with all my heart for having written so fine a book.

But perhaps the most pleasing comment for Bram Stoker was supplied by his mother, Charlotte Stoker, who was then in poor health in Dublin. It was Charlotte's supernatural stories from

Sligo, related when Bram was a small boy, that first inspired his literary career, and after reading *Dracula*, she wrote two letters offering praise.

> [It is] a thousand miles beyond anything you have written be-
> fore and I feel certain will place you very high in the writers
> of the day[;] the story being deeply sensational, exciting, and
> interesting. . . . No book since Mrs. Shelley's *Frankenstein* or
> indeed any other at all has come near yours in originality, or
> terror[;] Poe is nowhere. I have read much but I have never met
> a book like it at all in its terrible excitement[.] It should make a
> widespread reputation and much money for you.

Her powers of prognostication were nearly perfect, and few critics of 1897 who read *Dracula* and then endorsed it with the usual polite words had Charlotte Stoker's foresight.

Eight

THE MURDERER,
"MORBIDLY FASCINATING"

B ram Stoker may have had dinner with Jack the Ripper.

At the very least, it's possible that he served as a host to two suspects in the case, Richard Mansfield and Francis Tumblety. Curiously, Stoker addressed this connection to the Jack the Ripper crimes only in vague terms, hinting that the famous murders of "Saucy Jacky" were inspirations for Dracula's terrors.

The 1901 Icelandic edition of *Dracula* contained a new introduction by the author. He used the opportunity to continue the conceit of the letters and diary entries, insisting that the protagonists were personal friends of his.

The reader of this story will very soon understand how the events outlined in these pages have been gradually drawn together to make a logical whole. . . . I have let the people involved relate their experiences in their own way; but for obvious reasons, I have changed the names of the people and places concerned. . . . The events are incontrovertible, and so many people know of them that they cannot be denied. This series of crimes has not yet passed from the memory, a series of crimes which appear to have originated from the same source, and which at the same time created as much repugnance in people everywhere as the murders of Jack the Ripper, which came into the story a little later. . . .

The introduction is signed "B.S." and dated from London, August 1898.

First, the fiction: Stoker's casual dating of the events plays havoc with the time frame in the novel. Although events within his story suggest that the setting was 1893 or later, his suggestion that Dracula's crimes preceded Jack the Ripper's indicates that the events could not be later than 1888. Of course, his careful discussion of dates is nothing more than a bit of legerdemain—more of his earnest assurances about the truth of the story. But the hint about Jack the Ripper is fascinating, for the crimes that gripped London, the apparently random and rapid murders that swept through the East End, occurred less than two years before Stoker began composing his book.

The connection is not an obvious one. *Dracula* is remarkably crime-free. The murders seem to trouble a small group of people in Transylvania, and then a small circle of vampire hunters in London. Only Dracula's shipboard terrors or Lucy Westenra's nocturnal assaults rate newspaper coverage, and even then, Lucy's assaults seem a mere curiosity in the *Pall Mall Gazette.* Unlike the Jack the Ripper case—which was played out in lurid headlines, letters to the editor, and the shouts of newspaper boys—Count Dracula's bloodlust manages to avoid publicity.

So it's fascinating that Stoker made a decisive, fictional connection between his villain and the famous serial killer. And it's equally interesting that he never discussed his real connections to the case. The controversy stirred the Lyceum Theatre, and Bram Stoker discovered that the suspects were part of his professional circle.

"Modern" is, admittedly, in the eye of the beholder. Bram Stoker once praised Henry Irving as the "modern master of lighting." By today's standards, it seems to be a confusing distinction. Irving's use of gaslight and limelight was refined and precise, but much of his work involved pushing this old technology along, devoting men, equipment, and hours to try to conquer the limitations of long-established Victorian systems. At the end of his career, Irving's own developments—however meticulous and artistic—were being supplanted by genuinely modern work with electric lamps, as pioneered by producers like Steele MacKaye and David Belasco. The Lyceum Theatre, in fact, had installed electric lighting in the 1880s, and bright clusters of electric lamps illuminated the hallways and lobbies. But electricity, Irving felt, was never suitable for the stage, and for his entire career he appeared in the warm, attractive glow of gaslight.

If Irving was a "modern master," it's only because we can recognize him bumping against the limits of technology during the course of his career. He becomes a transitional figure between the Victorian and Edwardian eras.

Similarly, *Dracula* is a novel that bumps against old-fashioned Victorian storytelling, the loud death throes of the classic Gothic novel. In *Dracula*, readers find many of the old clichés: a mysterious nobleman, a faraway castle, an obsession with Victorian purity, and a plot woven together from a bundle of letters and diary entries—the way Mary Shelley did in *Frankenstein* or Wilkie Collins did in *The Woman in White*. Reviewers noticed these old-fashioned trappings in *Dracula*. "It is odd that . . . one of the most curious and striking of recent productions should be a revival of a medieval superstition, the old legend of the 'werewolf,'" W. L. Courtney noted in his *Daily Telegraph* review.

> There are two things which are remarkable in the novel [*Dracula*]—the first is the confident reliance on superstition as furnishing the ground work of a modern society; and the second, more significant still, is the bold adaptation of the legend to such ordinary spheres of latter-day existence as the harbor of Whitby and Hampstead Heath.

When the critic from the *Spectator* scoffed at the "up-to-dateness" of the book, noting that Stoker had included references to typewriters, phonographs, or the underground, it was a similar comment on the timelessness of the story.

Actually, the "up-to-dateness" is the novel's most powerful twist, and the most jarring aspect of this otherwise-Gothic tale. *Dracula* begins in a deliberately foreign and timeless way, deep within the unknown (and invented) world of Transylvania. But then, the story suddenly shifts to more familiar territory. When the vampire invades Whitby, he is perfectly at home amid the windswept coast, the Georgian streets, and the ruins of the old abbey. Whitby forms a halfway point between ancient and modern societies. And then, horrifyingly, relentlessly, Dracula comes even closer. He inhabits several homes in London, entering the modern age. He moves within a sophisticated society, bringing an ancient, neglected curse to the modern metropolis. His power allows him to haunt all classes and indiscriminately infect any era. If the reviewer from the *Spectator* winced when Dracula invaded fin-de-siècle London, that was precisely what Bram Stoker had intended.

Dracula was modern, but by no means unique. This distinctive mix of ancient horror in a modern setting had been anticipated in one of the great horror stories of Victorian England—Stevenson's *Strange Case of Dr. Jekyll and Mr. Hyde.*

———•———

In 1886, during the time Stoker and Irving were occupied with their production of *Faust*, Robert Louis Stevenson published his short novel *Strange Case of Dr. Jekyll and Mr. Hyde.*

The story is told through the eyes of Dr. Jekyll's professional associates, and positioned as a sort of mystery. Mr. Hyde, a small, repulsive man with a criminal demeanor, has been tied mysteriously to the respected Dr. Jekyll, even to the point where Jekyll's attorney, Mr. Utterson, notices that Hyde is the beneficiary of Jekyll's will. But Jekyll refuses to discuss Hyde. The doctor becomes more and more reclusive and suffers mysterious bouts of illness. On one occasion, his friends notice a transformation in his appearance, which horrifies them. When Jekyll disappears and his laboratory door is locked, his friends break into the room. There they find Hyde's body, dead on the floor, dressed in Jekyll's oversized clothing.

A note from Jekyll's friend, and Jekyll's own written confession, explain his crimes. A passionate researcher, the doctor had developed a drug to demonstrate man's dual nature. Once he took the drug, it transformed him into Mr. Hyde. Hyde became his alter ego, the evil side of his personality. Gradually the drug overcame the doctor, and his transformation became unpredictable. When Jekyll realized that Hyde's personality had overtaken his own, he committed suicide.

In the book, Jekyll's transformation to the cruel, animalistic Mr. Hyde is not the work of an ancient spell or enchantment, but purely a state-of-the-art achievement of medicine—a special formula developed by a man of science. Just as Jekyll is a part of London's respected upper class, Hyde instantly descends to the disreputable areas of the city, where he moves comfortably.

> Aware of the great field of lamps of a nocturnal city . . . the figure [Hyde] haunted the lawyer all night . . . to see it glide more stealthily through sleeping houses, or to move the more swiftly, and still the more swiftly, even to dizziness, through wider labyrinths of lamp-lighted city, and at every street corner crush a child and leave her screaming.

The novel describes only two crimes committed by Edward Hyde, but other offenses are suggested: conversations stop short before the characters detail these crimes. In this way readers were forced to think the very worst of Hyde and imagine the instincts of an animalistic man let loose in London's crime-ridden areas— crimes that could not be discussed in polite society or, indeed, within a book.

Stevenson suggested savagery, but Stoker wrote of it; the comparison earned *Dracula* condemnation from the critic of the San Francisco *Wave*:

[The] fault is the lack of artistic restraint. Stevenson, the century's greatest artist in fiction [used] a theme like this one—in *Dr. Jekyll and Mr. Hyde* . . . where the horror is suggested, hinted at, written around except for the one moment of the climax when it is brought home.

———•✦•———

Jekyll's effete self-analysis, his learned desire to explore the various elements of a man's personality, and Hyde's savage and irrepressible villainy, were irresistible roles for an actor. There was a long tradition in the theater of the dual part, and Henry Irving himself had established his career with two meaty dual roles: in *The Lyons Mail* and *The Corsican Brothers*. Irving himself might have been the ideal actor to play *Jekyll and Hyde* onstage, although Stevenson's story offered neither the melodramatic nor the historical sweep that Irving always craved. Coincidentally, in later years, when Henry Irving's son H. B. Irving became an actor, he made *Jekyll and Hyde* one of his most popular features, along with reprising some of his father's favorites.

The opportunity was left to an American actor, Richard Mansfield, who read Stevenson's book and realized the potential of the part. He quickly commissioned a writer named Thomas Russell Sullivan to develop the story into a script.

Mansfield was a popular actor who found his early successes in London before establishing his career in America. Critics debated his abilities. In some roles he was ideally suited; in others he seemed mechanical and ineffective. He was short of stature with thinning hair and could be unappealingly cold in his characterizations. One critic, John Ranken Towse, called him "imperious, willful, self-centered, and indocile. He was a terror to his managers."

But Mansfield's portrayals of Jekyll and Hyde were a decided hit. His script took liberties with Stevenson's short novel and, like most later adaptations, added a love interest for Dr. Jekyll. Instead of playing him as a solid man of science, Mansfield's Jekyll was a young man "conscious of a dreadful fate impending," according to the *New York Times*, and his Hyde exhibited "a fiendish brutality." Towse felt that Mansfield was deficient in the part; instead of playing Stevenson's energetic, quirky, evil little man, Mansfield was a grotesque "nightmare of goblin hideousness." He inserted a scene in which Hyde was supposedly haunted by the invisible ghost of one of his victims, an opportunity for some scenery-chewing in the great tradition of melodrama. A photographic portrait with Mansfield in both roles doesn't inspire confidence. His Hyde shows only a coarse grimace.

Audiences came to see Mansfield's wonderful transformation scenes, in which Jekyll was transformed into Hyde—this was the expected tour de force. The actor accomplished it without any special effects, although contemporary reviews suggest that Mansfield may have utilized directional lighting, or even colored lighting, to alter the appearance of his makeup, which was arranged in complementary colors. This trick of colored lighting was later repeated when Fredric March starred in the 1931 film.

The show opened in Boston in May 1888 and quickly moved to

New York. Mansfield had taken the trouble to secure the rights from Stevenson, but because Stevenson's book was not copyrighted in America, he found that an unauthorized play, *Dr. Jekyll and Mr. Hyde*, produced by Daniel Bandmann, was opening in opposition. Both shows raced to London, attempting to win that promising market.

Mansfield enlisted the help of Henry Irving, whom he had met at the start of his career in London and then again in America during the Lyceum company's tour. Irving offered the Lyceum stage to Mansfield; the Lyceum company would then be on tour in Scotland. Irving also calculated that Bandmann would need the Opera Comique in London for his own *Dr. Jekyll and Mr. Hyde*. Irving secured the Opera Comique "for extra rehearsals," cleverly delaying Mansfield's competition. In this way, Mansfield was able to hold his competition at arm's length while appealing to lawyers that he alone had the rights to Stevenson's work.

Stoker advised the actor on the program, schedule, and business plan at the Lyceum, and Irving lingered in London long enough to watch Mansfield's rehearsals. Irving had his doubts; he reported to his stage manager, Lovejoy, that the American company would "want looking after," as the production seemed incredibly disorganized. Mansfield, in turn, complained in a letter that the Lyceum staff was unprofessional and difficult.

> The men are slow to obey and argumentative, and full of importance and the conviction that they know it all, or least, much better than we do. . . . Scenery which has arrived at St. Louis or Grand Rapids at four in the afternoon, and been used without a hitch at eight in the evening, required [at the Lyceum] all Thurs-

day night, all day Friday, and a scenic rehearsal which lasted from eight yesterday evening until two this morning!

Since the Lyceum company was well known for their professionalism and rapid scene changes, it's easy to understand that Mansfield had made enemies at the theater. The stagehands might have been deliberately dragging their feet in protest of the American upstart.

Mansfield's *Dr. Jekyll and Mr. Hyde* premiered at the Lyceum on August 4, 1888. William Winter, the theater critic and friend of Mansfield, attended the premiere and thought Mansfield was slightly off his game from "nervous excitement."

He acted with intrepid spirit and, generally, with amazing vigor. . . . Jekyll was invested with poetic sentiment; Hyde as embodied as loathsome and venomous, [and] very awful. . . . [Mansfield] did not win the public heart; hearts are not won by horrors, but he made it clear that he was a unique actor and one entirely worthy of high intellectual consideration.

Privately, Winter offered sharper critiques, telling Mansfield there was too much of "Jekyll's misery, and misery never was popular, on stage or off." He also advised the actor, "I wish you would get a new wig." The London production received positive reviews, although the *Times* found the usual quibbles with his acting:

As Dr. Jekyll, Mr. Mansfield does not strike one as an actor of remarkable resource; as Mr. Hyde, however, he plays with a

rough vigor or power which, allied to his hideous aspect, thrills
the house, producing a sensation composed of equal measure of
the morbidly fascinating and the downright disagreeable.

Ultimately, the play was not remembered because of the unhappy man of science, the grimacing villain, or the actor's histri-
onics. The Mansfield *Dr. Jekyll and Mr. Hyde* became a legend just
nights later, when an incredible event, "the morbidly fascinating
and the downright disagreeable," suddenly intruded. It was the
real Mr. Hyde, London's most notorious murderer.

On Monday, August 6, 1888, Martha Tabram was drinking in
White Swan pub on Whitechapel High Street in the notorious
East End of London. Tabram was thirty-nine years old, one of
the area's regular prostitutes, and she had spent the evening
winding her way from pub to pub in the company of another
prostitute, Mary Ann Connelly, and two unidentified clients
who wore soldiers' uniforms. Just before midnight the ladies and
their soldiers separated, and Tabram was last seen leading her
client up George Yard.

At 4:50 a.m., a workman was starting his day; as he walked out
into George Yard, he noticed the body of a woman on a landing.
He called to a constable, Thomas Barrett, who noticed that the
body was lying in a pool of blood. A local doctor was called to examine the body and discovered thirty-nine knife punctures all
over the lady's body, neck, and abdomen. The cuts suggested that
two distinct knives had been used. The *Illustrated Police News* reported the crime on August 18:

The wound over the heart was alone sufficient to kill, and death must have occurred as soon as that was inflicted. Unless the perpetrator was a madman, or suffering to an unusual extent from drink delirium, no tangible explanation can be given. . . .

Testimony suggested that Tabram's murder had taken place between two and four-thirty a.m. The police called an inquest and soldiers housed at the Tower of London and Wellington Barracks were reviewed and questioned, but the crime went unsolved.

Today it's still debated whether Martha Tabram was actually the first victim of Jack the Ripper, or whether her murder preceded Jack's actual crimes. The number of wounds was extraordinary, and to many researchers this murder has suggested the first step of an important crime spree.

Weeks later, on August 31, at twelve-thirty in the morning, another local prostitute, Mary Ann Nichols (known to the locals as Polly), was seen leaving the Frying Pan, a local pub. She walked to a local lodging house but was put out because she didn't have four pence for a bed that night. She drunkenly boasted that she'd soon have the money and wandered out into the street. At two-thirty a.m., she was seen by a friend, lazily watching a fire at a dry dock and leaning against a wall. Just over an hour later, a local cart driver noticed a woman lying on her back in the road, about half a mile from where Nichols had last been seen alive. Her clothes were disarranged and her upper body was still warm. Blood oozed from a wound at her neck.

An examination revealed that her throat had been savagely cut from left to right, with the windpipe, gullet, and spinal cord sliced through. Her abdomen had been slashed open, with a number of small stab wounds, including cuts on her body. Residents nearby never heard a disturbance and could offer no clue to the mystery.

The murderer struck again in the same area, on September 8. Prostitute Annie Chapman was spotted in conversation with a dark man in a deerstalker cap. The man asked her, "Will you?" and Annie replied, "Yes." It was five-thirty a.m. Within half an hour, her body was found by a workman, lying next to a fence. Her face was bloody and her throat had been deeply cut. Her stomach was cut open and she was disemboweled, with her intestines, uterus, and bladder completely removed. The examining physician esti mated that the specific knife-work required anatomical knowledge and could not have been accomplished in less than fifteen minutes.

The press took notice of the savage, apparently random nature of the crimes, which seemed the work of a madman. Unfortunately, the East End was rife with crime, and murders were not uncommon. It took Jack the Ripper to demonstrate the murder rate by committing crimes that were out of the ordinary.

———

News of the crime spree filled newspapers and fueled debate by the authorities and the public. Analyzing the victims, London coroner Wynne Baxter later made a sensational judgment, setting the tone for a century of speculation:

> The injuries were made by someone who had considerable ana-
> tomical skill and knowledge. His anatomical knowledge carries
> him out of the category of a common criminal, for that knowl-

edge can only have been obtained by assisting at post-mortems or by frequenting the post-mortem room. Thus the class in which search must be made, although a large one, is limited.

Of course, an experienced surgeon could hardly be expected to be a murderer. Baxter's suspicions perfectly suggested Stevenson's novel or the current play at the Lyceum: a kindly, respected "Dr. Jekyll" was leading a mysterious double life, consorting with criminals in the East End.

On September 11, a letter appeared in the *Star*:

> You, and every one of the papers, have missed the obvious solution of the Whitechapel mystery. The murderer is a Mr. Hyde, who seeks in the repose and comparative respectability of Dr. Jekyll security from the crimes he commits in his baser shape.

Mansfield's play ended on its announced schedule on September 29. The next night, the Whitechapel Murderer struck again with astonishing violence.

On September 30, 1888, at about twelve-thirty a.m., prostitute Elizabeth Stride was seen chatting with a man; fifteen minutes later, a witness watched an argument between two people on the street, in which the man apparently threw the woman to the ground. At one a.m., Stride's body was found. Just forty-five minutes later, prostitute Catherine Eddowes's mutilated body was found about six streets away. Both women had their throats slashed. Catherine Eddowes had also suffered slashes to her cheeks, ear, and nose, and she had been disemboweled. In a passageway about a third of a mile away, the police discovered a bloody rag and a portion of Eddowes's bloodstained apron. On the wall was a chalked message: "the Juwes are The men That will not be Blamed for nothing."

Meanwhile, the press had become aware of a letter, apparently sent from the murderer, written in blood-red ink:

> *Dear Boss, I keep hearing the police have caught me but they won't fix me just yet. . . . Keep this letter back till I do a bit more work, then give it out straight. My knife's so nice and sharp I want to get to work right away if I get a chance. Good luck.*
>
> *Jack the Ripper*

On October 3 an accusation appeared in a letter in the *Daily Telegraph.*

> The perpetrator is a being whose diseased brain has been in-flamed by witnessing the performance of the drama of *Dr. Jekyll and Mr. Hyde,* which I understand is now wisely withdrawn from the stage. If there is anything in this, let the detective con-sider how Mr. Hyde would have acted, for there may be a system in the demonic actions of a madman in following the pattern set before him.

The following day, the *Pall Mall Gazette* continued that thought.

> Possibly the culprit is [a doctor, who] has seen the horrible play, lives in Bayswater or North London . . . goes out about 10 p.m. straight to Whitechapel. Commits deed. Home again to break-fast. Wash, brush up, sleep. Himself again, Dr. Hyde.

A popular Jack the Ripper myth has persisted that Mansfield was forced to withdraw his play because of the controversy generated by his portrayal of Hyde and even may have been questioned by the police. In fact, a week after the double murder, he acknowledged the "continued and great demand," bringing back the play in repertory for several nights a week. A few days later, as the inquests into the murders proceeded, Mansfield publicized a benefit show for October 10, raising money for the poor women of the East End. For the benefit, he announced the London premiere of his comedy *Prince Karl*. The murderous *Dr. Jekyll and Mr. Hyde* would never have suited this purpose.

Bram Stoker was monitoring the controversies swirling around the Lyceum productions and advised Mansfield against introducing a new play at his benefit, which would come across to critics as a "bid for favor" and reduce the importance of the play—sound show business advice, which Mansfield ignored.

Henry Irving returned from his vacation and saw a performance of *Dr. Jekyll and Mr. Hyde* at the Lyceum, afterward taking the actor to dinner at the Garrick Club. Mansfield grumbled about the disappointing box office and complained of the "tremendous strain imposed . . . by the acting of such painfully difficult parts." It was a naive and arrogant conversation to offer the great Henry Irving. Irving listened and then responded drily, "Ah, yes, interesting. Very. But Mansfield, my boy, if it isn't wholesome, I wouldn't do it."

Richard Mansfield should have laughed. Instead, he sulked.

Overall, *Dr. Jekyll and Mr. Hyde* was only a moderate success for Mansfield in London, and the play's problems stemmed from his acting and his carelessness as a producer, not from controversy. If anything, the Whitechapel murders prolonged interest in the play. Years later Mansfield privately blamed Henry Irving—he had become hypersensitive to Irving's criticisms and irrationally imagined that Irving was pulling strings behind the scenes to engineer his failure in London. He ended the season in debt to Irving—rent and other expenses—for over 2,000 pounds ($10,000). William Winter, who knew both Mansfield and Irving, felt that the American actor's paranoia and failure to take responsibility were his shortcomings.

———••———

Bram Stoker recorded that Mr. and Mrs. Mansfield dined at the Beefsteak Room in the Lyceum during a return visit to London; this must have been after Mansfield's marriage in 1892. The actor played *Jekyll and Hyde* throughout his career and introduced a number of important plays in America, including George Bernard Shaw's *Arms and the Man* and *The Devil's Disciple*, as well as the first American production of Henrik Ibsen's *Peer Gynt*.

Today, Mansfield is remembered not for his work in the spotlight, but the spotlight of suspicion that briefly illuminated him in the Ripper case. He was never really a suspect so much as a confusing footnote to the story.

The suspect, it's now been revealed, was Francis Tumblety.

Nine

THE SUSPECT, "DISTINGUISHED PEOPLE"

Despite the speculation, the East End murders didn't end when Mansfield finished playing in *Dr. Jekyll and Mr. Hyde.* Several teasing letters arrived at the Central News Agency and the Whitechapel Vigilance Committee, and researchers still debate whether these letters from "Jack" were authentic or manufactured by reporters to fuel the sensational story. The last letter, delivered on October 16, 1888, arrived with a box containing half a human kidney. "I send you half the Kidne I took from one woman, prasarved it for you tother piece I fried and ate it was very nise. . . ."

Jack's final murder was the most spectacular. Mary Jane Kelly was twenty-five years old and had attempted to stop prostitution, living with Joseph Barnett in a small room in the area. When Barnett lost his job, she returned to walking the streets to earn their rent. Friends recalled that she'd been frightened by the Whitechapel murders; she had Barnett read her the latest revelations from the newspaper and had planned to leave London.

After a night on the streets, Mary Kelly emerged from her small room in Miller's Court at about eight on the morning of November 9, 1888. A friend passed her in the street and asked why she was up so early. Kelly said that she was sick from "the horrors of drink." About two hours later she was seen at the Britannia public house, imbibing with some other people. Forty-five minutes later her landlord told his associate, Thomas Bowyer, to knock on her door and ask her for some of the long-overdue rent. There was no response, but Bowyer noticed a broken pane of glass in the window, so he pushed back the curtain and peered into the room. He first saw two lumps of flesh piled on the bedside table, and then he recognized Kelly's mutilated corpse sprawled across the bed.

When the police arrived and entered the room, they discovered a scene more the "work of a devil than of a man." Mary Kelly's throat had been savagely sliced open, her face was hacked beyond recognition, and her body had been meticulously sliced up, with various organs and body parts carefully arranged around the bed or piled on the nearby table. Her clothes had been burned in the fire grate.

The official report suggested that she had been murdered some time around two a.m, belying the witnesses who saw her on the streets the next morning. The distinctive Jack the Ripper murders apparently ended with this bloody climax—there's never been a good reason proposed for the crimes, or any reason why they stopped. Of course, the case has become infamous and inspired endless speculation and theories—but nothing more than speculation. A definitive solution is probably lost to time.

———— ·•· ————

Dracula was dedicated "To My Dear Friend, Hommy-Beg," Manx slang for "Little Tommy." That was Stoker's friend, the novelist Thomas Hall Caine.

Ironically, the powerful force of Stoker's vampire has imparted a curse on Caine, the same way that Jack the Ripper imparted a curse on Mansfield, virtually obliterating a successful career and turning him into a footnote—or, more properly, a line of dedication.

Thomas Henry Hall Caine was born in Cheshire in 1853. His father, a shipsmith, was from the Isle of Man, and when little Tommy was five he was sent to the island to stay with his grandmother, where he was indoctrinated into the Manx language and folklore.

He returned to his family in Liverpool, an undersized, odd little boy with wide dark eyes and red hair. He was always a bit of a loner and an intellectual. Before he was ten years old, he lost two of his sisters, one to "water on the brain" and one to whooping cough, and he developed a dread fear of disease—made all the worse when cholera swept though Liverpool in 1866.

Caine was apprenticed to the office of an architect and slowly developed a talent for writing. When he was still a teenager he returned to the Isle of Man, reveling in the hospitality of his aunt and uncle, and accepted a job as an assistant schoolteacher. When he returned to Liverpool, two years later, it was with the resolve to write a novel or a play. In 1874, when he was twenty-one, he first met Henry Irving, then a young touring actor attempting the role of Hamlet. Caine was writing theater criticism for the Liverpool newspaper and contributed an article, "Irving's Influence on the Theatre of His Day," which led Caine to lecture on Irving's performance in *Hamlet*. Their meeting formed a parallel to Irving's later meeting with Stoker—another young writer, this time in Dublin, who also publicized the actor, pledged his friendship, and fell under his spell.

That same year, 1874, Caine met a curious character, a self-proclaimed "American Doctor" named Francis Tumblety, who had set up shop in Liverpool and offered herbal cures that, he claimed, were authentic secrets of the American Indians. Caine's preoccupation with his health drew him to Tumblety in search of cures, and they immediately formed a friendship.

———·•·———

Dr. Francis Tumblety was clearly something of a quack. He was apparently born in 1833 in Canada, the youngest of eleven children, and named after his father, Frank, who was an Irish immigrant. When the boy was still young the family moved to Rochester, New York. A boyhood friend remembered him as selling books and papers on the packet ships, boarding as the ships approached the Erie Canal and offering his wares. He was "a dirty, awkward, ignorant, uncared-for, good-for-nothing boy" who traded in equally dirty merchandise. Evidently he sold nasty pornographic booklets and pictures to passing crew and passengers.

When he was seventeen he left Rochester, then turned up in Detroit, Toronto, and Saint John, New Brunswick, practicing as a doctor. He probably had received no training at all, except for some work at a local drugstore. Tumblety boasted that he was the "electric physician of international reputation" and promoted himself with pretentious newspaper advertisements or by walking about town with an imperious manner in outlandish, elaborate clothing. He usually favored some mysterious combination of military uniforms, bright-colored trousers, boots with spurs, a breast filled with medals, and headwear with plumes. He wore a long brush mustache that, some portraits show, was sometimes twisted and waxed to ridiculous, long horizontal tips. He could be seen parading on the streets mounted on a snow-white horse and followed by a pack of hound dogs.

Tumblety's practice—whether it was based in fraud or actual experience—was surprisingly modern in its philosophy. He condemned surgeons with a "horror of cutting," criticized the popular use of metals in medicine, such as arsenic and mercury, and condemned the long-standing practice of bleeding patients. Instead, he insisted that herbal remedies offered the only necessary cures. A promotional poem explained:

Our Father—whom all goodness fills,
Provides the means to cure all ills;
The simple herbs beneath our feet
Well used, relieve our pains complete.

He expanded his business to a number of cities and developed an herbal cure that supposedly eliminated pimples, one of many dubious patent medicines that were then in fashion. Tumblety must have made a small fortune, for he lived lavishly and seldom exhibited a need for money. He might have been thought of as a silly, greedy, and antisocial dandy, a pompous self-promoter, or a harmless buffoon—many of his acquaintances summarized him this way—but there were also dangerous aspects to his personality and he was surrounded by a series of unrelenting lawsuits and threats.

In Saint John, his inept medical treatments led to the death of a well-liked locomotive engineer, and an inquest was convened. By the time Tumblety was proved guilty of manslaughter, he had already left the country and settled in Boston. In Washington during the Civil War, his ostentatious use of army regalia and boasts about his connection to General McClellan's staff, earned him criticism from actual military men. He sued a music hall for ridiculing him and may well have engineered the episode for the sake of publicity. He manufactured testimonials from well-known people and was caught doing it. He was arrested and briefly jailed for wearing a military uniform.

Shortly after Lincoln's assassination, Tumblety was arrested as a possible collaborator and jailed for two days. When he later wrote about the incident, in a self-serving, self-published booklet called "Kidnapping of Dr. Tumblety, by Order of the Secretary of War of the U.S.," it seems that the confusion was caused by the name J. W. Blackburn, an alias used by Tumblety that was also the name of a Confederate spy who had been plotting to spread yellow fever through the northern states.

Tumblety moved his operations to Europe, favoring London, and boasted of his friendship with important American and British celebrities. His genuine fame, combined with his ability to exaggerate, make it impossible to evaluate these claims. Was he really a regular guest of President Lincoln? Was he a personal friend of Charles Dickens? Certainly, he had been able to charm a young, impressionable writer in Liverpool named Hall Caine.

Tumblety's acquaintances recorded the herb doctor's intense hatred of women. One colonel, who had been treated to an elaborate dinner at Tumblety's hotel room in Washington, D.C., noticed that no women had been invited and asked why. "His face instantly became as black as a thunder cloud." The doctor snarled that he would "sooner give you a dose of quick poison than take you into such danger." He proceeded with a lecture on the dangers of women, and fallen women in particular.

He invited the party of gentlemen into his office and opened the wooden cases, displaying a grotesque museum of glass jars filled with anatomical specimens. He seemed to specialize in the wombs "of every class of woman."

Other associates noticed that he considered women responsible for all the ills of society and felt they could not be trusted. He once explained to a visitor that he had married early to a beautiful woman who was a number of years older than he was. Just after the wedding he noticed her tendency to flirt with other men and he grew suspicious. Passing through the worst part of town one day, Tumblety noticed his wife entering a house of ill repute with another man, and he left her.

Tumblety's story of his marriage sounds as exaggerated and carefully crafted as his advertising claims, but associates recalled him habitually mumbling, "No women for me." He was uncomfortable around women throughout his life and was believed to be homosexual. He sometimes hired young men as employees who were well paid to accompany the quiet, moody boss; Tumblety was reportedly illiterate and he required a bright amanuensis. At other times, he hovered around the post office, seeking the company of the clerks, or gravitated to groups of young soldiers.

Letters from Tumblety show that Caine was clearly courted and, simultaneously, squeezed for any available money. When Tumblety left for London, he wrote to Caine, explaining that he planned to manufacture his pills in England, and encouraging him to invest in the project: "There is no place in the world like

England for good pills. The English people all indulge in eating late suppers which produces costiveness and they must have cathartic pills." On another occasion, he boldly demanded money from his young friend: "Don't trifle with my patience any longer. Send me two pounds to the above address, no more, nor no less, a paltry amount than two pounds and our friendly correspondence shall go on. . . ."

Challenged, Caine sent the two pounds, but avoided investing in the doctor's business ventures. As Tumblety seemed to never want for money, his admonishment must have been a test of loyalty. Caine was also finagled into writing a booklet for Tumblety, and he accepted invitations to visit him in London. These visits only encouraged more desperate letters or pleading telegrams in response: "Come here tomorrow evening. I must see you," or "Dear boy wire at once. . . . Wire, wire, wire, wire, wire, wire." In another letter after Caine's visit, Tumblety wrote: "You have proved yourself feminine and I feel under a great obligation and hope some time to be able to make some recompense." Caine told a friend that he found his visit to Tumblety "arduous."

Francis Tumblety left London for New York in August 1876, encouraging Caine to join him there. He followed, months later, with a pleading letter from San Francisco: "It gives me infinite pleasure to hear from you and I should dearly love to see your sweet face and spend an entire night in your company. I feel such melancholy when I read your amiable letter. . . . It only stimulates the affection I have for you."

Caine must have been relieved when the letters dissolved away shortly after that. There's no record that they corresponded after this brief, intense friendship. Tumblety returned to England just over ten years later, settling in London, and it's possible that he contacted his old friend. Hall Caine's fame as a novelist would have proved irresistible to him.

———•—•———

Tumblety became a sort of tourist attraction in cities throughout Europe and across America. A Chicago lawyer recalled his jaw-dropping appearance on a city street:

> I never saw anything quite equal to it. He had an enormous Es-
> pian shako [a tall military hat with a plume] on his head, an
> overcoat, the front of which was covered with decorations, ear-
> rings in his ears and by his side a very black negro, fantastically
> got up in a parti-colored dress that appeared to be a blending of
> the flags of all nations. A great crowd followed him but he didn't
> appear to notice them. . . .

In 1880 in New York, Tumblety brought a lawsuit, claiming that one of his bright young men had been given power of attorney and had then disappeared with some of the doctor's funds. When he was called to court and asked from what institution he had gradu-ated, Tumblety steadfastly refused to answer. The case collapsed. The employee then brought a suit against the doctor, "charging atrocious assault, and the evidence collected in this case was of the most disgusting sort."

In 1888 he traveled back to Liverpool and then on to London. He was now in his fifties and had stopped wearing military outfits, favoring sharp British-style clothing instead. Authors Stewart Evans and Paul Gainey, who researched Tumblety in their book

The Lodger, claim that he took up lodgings at 22 Batty Street in the East End (perhaps in addition to other rooms in the city). His presence in the dirty squalor of Whitechapel was a marked contrast to his usual lavish hotels and may have signaled an especially sinister change in his lifestyle or tastes.

Batty Street placed Tumblety in the geographic center of the Jack the Ripper murders. His manner of dress and foreign accent brought him to the attention of the police: A number of witnesses thought that the man seen in conversation with the victims had spoken with an accent, and foreign doctors, not registered in England, were naturally under suspicion.

In October 1888, well into the crime spree, Scotland Yard contacted the San Francisco police and asked for a sample of Tumblety's handwriting—the letters from Jack were considered some of the best clues. The San Francisco police responded, offering a sample.

Just weeks later, the November 19 *New York Times* reported that Tumblety had been arrested in London on suspicion of complicity in the murders. The *Times* article suggested that he was "proven innocent of that charge." That was an error, but it suggests that the detectives did not have enough evidence to charge him, perhaps hoping that his arrest would inspire additional evidence or a confession. A New York *World* article on Sunday, December 2, explained: "The police being unable to procure the necessary evidence against him in connection [to the Whitechapel murders], decided to hold him for trial for another offense."

Tumblety was charged under the Criminal Law Amendment Act of 1885; this was a sexual offenses act. Most of the sections apply to procuring underage female prostitutes or to holding women against their will. Considering that Tumblety would have avoided women, it's more likely that he was accused under Section 11: "Any male person who, in public or private commits or is a part to the commission of, or procures, or attempts to procure the commission by any male person of any act of gross indecency with another male person. . . ."

Section 11 was the famous Labouchère Amendment, coincidentally the legislative work of Henry Irving's old friend and patron, and a frequent guest at the Lyceum.

———•—•———

Labby, Henry Labouchère, returned to Parliament in 1880 and continued publishing his muckraking journal, *Truth*. Labouchère's causes were often libertarian; he joined the Radical wing of the Liberal Party. In 1885, a series of articles by the reformer W. T. Stead in the *Pall Mall Gazette* had called attention to underage female prostitutes. The government, anxious to quell the controversy before an upcoming election, pushed through the Criminal Law Amendment Act. The night before the vote, Labouchère added his amendment, which prohibited any homosexual "indecency."

The courts already had a law banning sodomy, but Labouchère's Section 11 expanded the charges against homosexual acts. It was vaguely written, leaving "consent" and "procuring" to judicial interpretation, and the amendment was unrelated to the bill that carried it. It shouldn't have passed, and would not have, except for the hurried legislative push.

Even today, it's unclear why Labouchère felt compelled to propose this amendment. It didn't match his causes or agendas. His friend, the publisher Frank Harris, insisted that Labouchère's

amendment had intended to "make the law ridiculous." It seems
that Labouchère had objected to the discussion of the age of consent and had hoped to force debate on the entire bill by adding his
purposely vague addition.

Author F. B. Smith has come to agree with Harris's theory, after
studying Labouchère's legislative work and editorials. He believes
that Labouchère's amendment was proposed as an "extravagant
motion designed to overturn the bill—but one which got away."
Labouchère's own editorials in *Truth*, which appeared the very
same day he moved the amendment, indicate his impatience with
the bill: "The Act itself is . . . very badly drawn up. . . . It would have
been better had the bill been sent before a large and representative select committee." He also warned, "The greatest care ought
to be taken not to confound immorality with crime. . . . I somewhat question whether there has been sufficient care in regard to
the above essentials."

Purposeful or reckless: Whatever Labouchère's intentions had
been, after the bill passed it became an invitation for blackmailers.
Labby learned to live with the amendment, later justifying it in
vague terms and with a variety of excuses. He was, after all, a
politician.

The bill was a convenient charge for the police when they were
dealing with a fellow like Tumblety. But within a decade, it forced
a famous showdown in the courts.

————•◦•————

Once charged, Tumblety's bail was set at 1,500 pounds ($7,500),
which should have been a prohibitive amount for anyone lodging
in the East End. But his bail was quickly made by two unnamed

gentlemen. They later asserted to the police that "they had only known the doctor for a few days previous to his arrest."

Not surprisingly, Tumblety jumped his bail, sailing for Le Havre, France, on November 24, under the name Frank Townsend. From there, he left on a seven-day voyage to New York, on the steamship *La Bretagne*. He must have remained secluded in his room. Passengers didn't recall seeing him aboard.

When he arrived back in America, he had already made headlines. Newspapers reported that New York detectives were waiting, at the gangplank, to follow him home. Tumblety arrived at 79 East Tenth Street, next to his herbal business, staying in a room with his landlady, a Mrs. McNamara. Then, according to the New York *World*, a British detective arrived on the scene, nervously pacing outside the residence and watching for the mysterious doctor.

New York Police Inspector Byrnes admitted that he "simply wanted to put a tag on him so we can tell where he is," conceding that Tumblety couldn't be arrested or extradited. "The [morals] crime for which he was under bond in London [according to the Criminal Law Amendment Bill] is not extraditable." Tumblety left the residence several days later, disappearing to an apartment uptown.

The *Pall Mall Gazette* reported only that the search for Jack had moved from Whitechapel to New York City; British newspapers never mentioned Tumblety, and presumably Scotland Yard was embarrassed by his escape.

———————

The significance of Tumblety was made clear in 1993, when author Stewart Evans discovered a letter that had been written by John G.

Littlechild, a chief inspector of the Scotland Yard's Secret Department during the time of the Jack the Ripper murders. In 1913, Littlechild had responded to a journalist's inquiry about the case.

> Amongst the suspects, and to my mind a very likely one, was a Dr. T. . . . He was an American quack named Tumblety. [He] was at one time a frequent visitor to London and on these occasions constantly brought under the notice of police, there being a large dossier concerning him at Scotland Yard. Although a 'Sycopathia [sic] Sexualis' subject, he was not known as a 'Sadist' (which the murderer unquestionably was) but his feelings towards women were remarkable and bitter in the extreme, a fact on record.

Littlechild concluded his note by observing that, significantly, the murders ended after Tumblety left for France.

———

A New York *World* reporter finally caught up with Francis Tumblety, and the interview appeared on January 29, 1889. Tumblety avoided mention of the morals arrest, insisting that he was arrested simply because he had gone to Whitechapel for "the excitement and the crowds and the queer scenes and sights." He happened to be wearing a slouch hat and was unaware that English detectives had been looking for a suspect that matched his description. In Tumblety's telling, it was a simple, awkward case of mistaken identity and sloppy police work. He concluded the interview with the expected boasts: "If it were necessary, I could show you letters from many distinguished people who I have met abroad. I am a frequenter of some of the best London clubs, among others the Carlton Club and the Beefsteak Club."

The phrase "Beefsteak Club" offers a chill.

———•—•——

In 1888, there was a Beefsteak Club, an offshoot of the Sublime Society of Beefsteaks that had been founded at Covent Garden. They had headquarters near the Savoy Hotel in London. Three years later, Bram Stoker restored the original Beefsteak headquarters at the Lyceum Theatre and rechristened this the Beefsteak Room. This, too, was an offshoot of the Sublime Society of Beefsteaks—principally celebrating the theater association and serving as a social dining room for Henry Irving's guests.

Was Tumblety a guest of the Beefsteak Club or the Beefsteak Room? (Confusion over the terms was common, even for Londoners.) As a proper club, with a small group of members, the Beefsteak Club may not have been an option. But to gain access to the Beefsteak Room, upstairs at the Lyceum, he would only have had to finagle an invitation from his old friend, Hall Caine, a Beefsteak Room regular. Or, through Caine, he may have made entreaties directly to Bram Stoker, who was always accommodating to colorful Americans, and then attended a performance at the Lyceum, offering praise for Henry Irving.

Stoker's records from the Beefsteak Room are not complete, and there's no way to know if the proud, social-climbing Francis Tumblety ever shook Henry Irving's hand and offered toasts to Bram Stoker. Most intriguing, did they share advice about fallen women or crime on the street?

Two years after the Whitechapel crimes, Bram Stoker began

compiling his notes for *Dracula*. He was in a unique position to hear that Tumblety had been connected to the crime—as a friend of Hall Caine and a visitor to New York with Henry Irving's company, where the newspapers had buzzed over the odd American doctor who became a suspect.

———•·•———

Francis Tumblety lived the remainder of his life out of the headlines. He spent most of the year with an elderly niece, Alice Fitz-Simons, in Rochester, New York, where he kept a small office. He wintered in St. Louis, and he was there when heart disease struck. He checked himself into St. John's Hospital, and died on May 28, 1903, at age seventy.

Ten

THE ACTOR, "ABJECT TERROR, GRIM HUMOR"

F or nearly a century, the primary suspect for inspiring Dracula has been Henry Irving. It's a delicious story: The dutiful, abused worker gets his quiet revenge; the arrogant boss gets his comeuppance. Was literature's greatest monster inspired by thirty years of high-handed, monstrous behavior? Was Dracula modeled after Henry Irving? Author and *Dracula* expert David Skal neatly explains the appeal of this theory:

> Virtually all of Stoker's chroniclers find in *Dracula* an allegory of an unequal, draining relationship between the two men; Stoker locked up in the Lyceum castle, as it were, serving a master's wishes while having his own attempts at written expression inhibited. Harker's letters are confiscated; Stoker's direct dramatic collaboration with Irving is never realized.

The recent Norton critical edition of *Dracula*, edited by Skal, uses a cover portrait of Irving as Mephistopheles—it makes an effective and convincing picture of the infamous vampire. Stoker's biographer Barbara Belford also endorsed Irving as the inspiration. "Dracula became a sinister character of Irving as mesmerist and depleter, an artist draining those about him to feed his ego. It was a stunning but avenging tribute."

The first edition of Belford's book is called *Bram Stoker: A Biography of the Author of Dracula*. The paperback edition includes a cover portrait of Henry Irving and was retitled *Bram Stoker and the Man Who Was Dracula*.

When the anecdote is told, "He wrote it about his boss," and the climactic phrase is inserted, "a blood-sucking vampire," every long-suffering employee smiles and pumps a fist. This is exactly the way we would like the story to end; this is the twist that turns Stoker into a folk hero. Orson Welles once chuckled to Daniel Farson, Stoker's great-nephew: "Stoker had his revenge. . . . If you read the description of the Count, you will find it identical to Irving!"

Welles had heard—or more precisely, read—the backstage scuttlebutt from the Lyceum. He was right in a theatrical sense but wrong in a personal sense. The Count was certainly not identical to Irving, and Stoker never gave evidence that he needed, or exacted, revenge.

───────·◆·───────

Henry Irving overcame a humble, provincial upbringing, as well as a lanky, ungainly body, an erratic gait, a homely face, a speaking voice that hissed and slurred, and a barrage of affectations that often left his onstage characters maddeningly opaque when they should have been perfectly clear.

Once, on a train journey during an American tour, Ellen Terry noticed Irving gazing out the window with an odd expression. She asked him what he was thinking about. "I was thinking how strange it is that I should have made the reputation I have as an actor," he told her softly. "With nothing to help me. With no equipment. My legs, my voice, everything has been against me. For an actor who can't walk, can't talk and has no face to speak of, I've done pretty well."

This was no self-effacing anecdote, the great man professing humility. Irving seemed genuinely puzzled and in a careless moment of honesty admitted it to his lover. She thought to herself, "And I looking at . . . the whole strange beauty of him, thought, 'Ah, you little know.'"

Irving was born John Henry Brodribb in 1838, at the Somerset village of Keinton Mandeville, in southwestern England. As a boy he was raised in Cornwall and adopted the short *a* and the hard *o* of this region. He also spoke with a stammer. When he became devoted to acting at a young age, his elocution teacher helped him overcome the stammer and soften the vowels, imparting a natural form of acting. When he auditioned for Samuel Phelps, a Devon-born actor who managed Sadler's Wells Theatre, Phelps listened to young Brodribb's speech from *Othello* and gave him some advice: "Have nothing to do with the theatre." This only stiffened Brodribb's resolve. Phelps, in turn, was inspired by his determination, and he offered the boy a salary.

John Henry changed his name to Henry Irving—taken from the American writer Washington Irving—and worked as a professional actor in Sunderland, Edinburgh, and Manchester, learning roles and earning praise from the critics. He was a natural mimic and had an early success in Manchester with a parody of the

American performers the Davenport Brothers. The Davenports held apparent séances on the stage, supposedly contacting ghosts. They were frauds, of course, and Irving made the most of their claims in his burlesque performance. His scientific introduction, offered with the twang of an American accent, began:

> I do not deem it necessary to offer any observations upon the extraordinary manifestations. I shall therefore at once commence a long rigamarole—for the purpose of distracting your attention, and filling your intelligent heads with perplexity. Many really sensible and intelligent individuals seem to think that the requirement of darkness seems to infer trickery. So it does. But I will strive to convince you that it does not. . . .

He was slowly becoming known for his Shakespearean roles and supported Edwin Booth when the famous American actor played in Manchester in 1861. Irving played Hamlet for the first time in that city in 1864, and critics applauded his effort as they criticized his shortcomings, "physique . . . and voice unequal to the demands which Hamlet makes upon [them]." Of course, his Hamlet became more refined and sophisticated (in Manchester he played it in a blond wig, which was then the fashion for the role), but those physical and vocal tics continued to frustrate the critics throughout his career.

Irving's peculiar, bent-legged gait suited later roles such as Richard III and Mephistopheles (whom he played with a sort of skipping limp). His crablike way of skittering around the stage became a target for caricature artists and music hall comics, who later lampooned Irving, the same way he had imitated the Davenport Brothers. Edward Gordon Craig, Ellen Terry's son, insisted that Irving's gait offstage was perfectly normal, but as he approached the stage, "Something was added to the walk—a consciousness, a springing motion, sometimes it wasn't really walking, but dancing. He was essentially an artificial in distinction to being merely natural."

Even more distinctive was Irving's voice and inflection. An American journalist gave a cruel interpretation of Irving's role of Shylock:

Wa, thane, et no eperes Ah! Um! Yo ned m'elp.
Ough! Ough! Gaw too, thane! Ha! Um! Yo com'n say
Ah! Shilock! Um! Ouch! We wode hev mounies!

(Well, then, it now appears you need my help;
Go to, then, you come to me and you say
Shylock, we would have moneys.)

Irving used his sibilant *s* and broad vowels, adding a strange power to ordinary lines. Many spectators who saw him perform *The Bells* recalled his haunting performance, especially the last line as he staggered across the stage in a death throe: "Tak . . . the rup . . . from . . . mey . . . nek!" (Take the rope from my neck.) His biographer, Laurence Irving, wrote: "Rightly or wrongly, he strove to make words convey not only an idea but an emotion. Those who criticized his methods were those to whom a visit to the theatre was an intellectual exercise rather than an emotional experience."

Critic William Archer thought that Irving's strengths were attuned to villainy: "Hatred, malignity, and cunning dwell familiarly in his eye, his jaw can express at will indomitable resolve or grotesque and abject terror. Grim humor lurks in his eyebrows, and cruel contempt in the corners of his mouth. No actor has ever full command of the expression which has been happily called a 'lurid glance.'"

It was at the Lyceum, working with Stoker, that Irving gradually developed the repertory plays that showed off his abilities and thrilled audiences. He was a magnificent Hamlet, praised by critic Clement Scott as "a Hamlet who thinks aloud." He was a scheming Iago but a weak Othello—"I could not bear to see him in the part. It was painful to me," wrote Ellen Terry, his Desdemona. His Richard III should have been wonderful but was disappointing, even to Irving—for some reason the play ended up being bad luck for him. *Macbeth* was spectacularly staged, but it was Terry, as Lady Macbeth, who won the public's favor. Terry thought that Irving played it as a "great famished wolf." His Lear was played as too old; his Romeo could not be played as young enough.

But in a melodramatic part—haunted or supernatural—he was perfectly cast. "He had an incomparable power for eeriness, for stirring a dim sense of mystery . . . a sharp sense of horror," according to Irving's friend, the English essayist and caricaturist Max Beerbohm. He also played comedy with a sardonic, grotesque sense of humor. He was serenely magisterial in roles like Richelieu and Becket.

Terry considered him "an egotist of the great type, never a

mean egotist. . . . All his faults sprang from egotism which is, in one sense, after all, only another name for greatness. So much absorbed was he in his own achievements that he was unable or unwilling to appreciate the achievements of others. . . . It would be easy to attribute this to jealousy, but the easy explanation is not the true one. He simply would not give himself up to appreciation."

Of course, Terry never became an egotist; indeed, she remained so fair-minded that she was able to make excuses for egotists. Ellen Terry found her success alongside, and sometimes in spite of, Irving. To a critic like George Bernard Shaw, she was more than a supporting player—she seemed to hold Irving aloft, providing the grace notes in any performance and preventing him from drowning in his indulgent, overwrought puddles of Shakespeare. "Ellen Terry is the most beautiful name in the world; it rings like a chime through the last quarter of the nineteenth century," Shaw once wrote in praise of the actress.

Shaw was a fellow Dubliner, but he really knew Wilde and Stoker only when the three all converged in London. He was irascible and sometimes devastating in his criticisms of Irving. In 1896, he wrote that Irving did not interpret roles but used them to adorn himself, "compelled to use other men's plays as the framework for his own creations." When the actor's own understandings came into conflict with Shakespeare's, for example, "He simply played in flat contradiction of the lines, and positively acted Shakespeare off the stage. [In *Hamlet*] he achieved the celebrated feat of performing Hamlet with the part of Hamlet omitted and all other parts as well, substituting for it and for them the fascinating figure of Henry Irving."

Irving tried to dismiss him and insisted that he didn't read Shaw's reviews, but Shaw was becoming impossible to ignore. Shaw's work as a playwright was interesting and daring, and Stoker tried on several occasions to bring him into the Lyceum fold, writing for Irving. Stoker played diplomat between Irving and the Irish playwright.

Shaw began a long correspondence with Ellen Terry, offering her advice on roles and criticizing the choices that had been made for her. His influence might be romanticized as Svengali to Trilby (as in the fashionable London play) or Higgins to Doolittle (as in Shaw's later *Pygmalion*). But Terry was smarter and more self-conscious than either Trilby or Doolittle—she had better instincts than Shaw when it came to the theater. Ellen was flattered by Shaw's attention and evaluated his advice wisely.

———

On May 24, 1895, Stoker received a telegram at his office from Irving, who was at his rooms in Grafton Street. "Could you look in at a quarter to six. Something important."

Stoker was often summoned to the dark, smoky rooms in Grafton Street, sometimes several times a day. Irving liked to work from home and his Acting Manager would be asked to bring drawings, scripts, or letters. But Irving's summons on that day had been especially mysterious. Bram Stoker suspected that Irving wanted to talk about the latest news—for the last week, the newsboys had been announcing the twists and turns of Oscar Wilde's court case, and the theater profession had been following the details with a sense of dread.

When Stoker arrived on that spring day, he bounded up the stairs, anticipating the worst. He started the conversation, "Have you heard the latest news from court?"

But Irving quickly dismissed the question with a wave of his hand, suggesting that Stoker was concerning himself with trivialities. Irving looked priest-like in his serenity. He remained deliberately silent, gesturing for Stoker to take a seat. Stoker was uneasy. He searched Irving's face for a clue, but the actor offered only a sly smile; this was one of his greatest performances.

He handed over two pieces of paper and fell back into his chair. As Stoker opened the letters, Irving watched his expression.

The first letter was from the prime minister, the Earl of Rosebery, with the pleasurable news that Queen Victoria had conferred the honor of knighthood on the actor. The second letter was from the Prince of Wales, offering his personal congratulations.

Stoker inhaled reflexively. It was wonderful news, an antidote to the oppressive gloom of the Oscar Wilde court case. He then looked up at his employer with wide eyes. Irving erupted in a long, uncharacteristic laugh. He had, indeed, been laughing most of the afternoon. Stoker joined him, offering loud congratulations and sharing a toast of good Irish whiskey—with memories of their meeting in Dublin. They took the letters to Ellen Terry's home in Longridge Road, Stoker later reported, to share the news with her.

When the honors list was officially announced, the following day on the Queen's birthday, Irving's office at the Lyceum was quickly piled with tied bundles of congratulatory letters and telegrams—from celebrities, his many guests over the years,

admirers, critics, coworkers, and actors from all over the world—
especially from actors. This would be a spectacular honor for the
profession—Henry Irving would be the first actor knighted by
British royalty. Irving dismissed the bundles of notes, telling
Stoker, "I really can't read any more of these at present. I must leave
them to you, old chap. They make my head swim."

Normally, Stoker would have been ready to step in and handle the paperwork, but he realized that Irving was exaggerating. The actor would, indeed, read each letter, poring over
the contents with satisfaction. A group of three men were put
in place in the office, copying out answers and thanks. Stoker
advised, knowingly, that it was unnecessary to send distinct
answers—a generally worded note, handwritten, would be perfectly proper.

That night, Irving performed in *Don Quixote*, the current
Lyceum production. By coincidence, there was a line in the play
that Quixote delivered, "Knighthood sits like a halo 'round my
head." A cheer went up from the pit. Irving held his composure—
the perfect picture of the befuddled adventurer—but the audience
insisted on an impromptu ovation for their star. A roar of laughter
and applause stopped the show.

Bram Stoker later admitted that the subject of knighthood had
been broached twelve years earlier, when Gladstone was prime
minister. Stoker had been privately asked if Irving would be comfortable with such an honor. Stoker, of course, immediately relayed
the conversation to Irving, who considered the offer and then dismissed the idea. Irving thought it would be a strain for one actor

to be singled out that way. The Lyceum was always proud that casts were listed with the same size type on the programs, and actors were always credited democratically on posters.

Could Irving have really been so modest in 1883? It's possible. This was before his first American tour, during his early years at the Lyceum, and the notion of an actor so honored would have been surprising, and even embarrassing. Perhaps he thought it would have seemed suspicious as well; Gladstone was a fan and a frequent visitor to the theater.

In the subsequent twelve years, a number of artists and designers had been knighted, and Irving's modesty had been tempered. During a lecture at the Royal Institution, Irving claimed that acting should officially be classified among the fine arts. George Bernard Shaw, who took a poke at Irving every chance he could, reported on the lecture knowingly: "What Mr. Irving means us to answer is this question: The artist who composed the music for *King Arthur* is Sir Arthur Sullivan; the artist who composed the poem . . . died Lord Tennyson; the artist who designed the suit of armor worn by King Arthur is Sir Edward Burne-Jones; why would the artist who plays King Arthur be only Mister Henry Irving?"

Stoker scoffed at the accusation that Irving had selfishly demanded the honor. Nonetheless, when knighthood was considered again in 1895, "no judicious opinion was asked," Stoker wrote. Irving's speech at the Royal Institution had signaled that he was ready and waiting.

On the Queen's birthday, Bram Stoker heard that his brother Thornley was also being honored with a knighthood for his important medical work. Thornley had been serving as an unofficial consultant on Bram's book about vampires, explaining details of the head injuries that were responsible for Renfield's death.

On July 18, 1895, Henry Irving was knighted. Max Beerbohm happened to see Irving in his carriage as he traveled to Paddington Station, en route to Windsor Castle. "Irving in his most prelatical mood always had a touch, here and there, of the old bohemian," he wrote. "But as I caught sight of him on this occasion . . . he was the old bohemian and nothing else. His hat was tilted at more than his usual angle and his long cigar seemed longer than ever; and on his face was such a look of ruminant sly fun as I have never seen equaled."

He was ushered into Windsor Castle with the other recipients and watched the simple ceremony repeated for each man—the sword, the medal, the nod of congratulations. It was customary for the Queen to remain silent as she performed her part, tapping a sword on the shoulders and bestowing the rank of knight, but on that day, those standing nearby noticed her say quietly to Irving, "I am very, very pleased." She was a fan.

Irving always showed restraint and never used the title "Sir." After his knighthood, the Lyceum officially honored him with the merest wink of proud recognition: Lyceum programs replaced the usual credit "Mr. Irving" with "Henry Irving." His knighthood proved to be an important step for the profession, the first of many such awards for actors. Ellen Terry was made a Dame Grand Cross of the Order of the British Empire, the second actress so honored, in 1922.

Henry Irving as Mephistopheles in his famous production of *Faust*; here Bram Stoker found inspiration for his vampire. *(All photos are from the author's collection unless noted otherwise.)*

Henry Irving's *Faust* featured the Brocken scene, in which the demon summoned an army of supernatural creatures.

TOP LEFT: Bram Stoker of the Lyceum Theatre, the author of *Dracula*.

TOP RIGHT: Florence Balcombe, in a sketch by Edward Burne-Jones; she was a classical beauty, and almost Mrs. Oscar Wilde before becoming Mrs. Bram Stoker.

BOTTOM LEFT: Henry Irving; this was the portrait signed to Bram Stoker in Dublin in 1876.

BOTTOM RIGHT: Ellen Terry, Henry Irving's leading lady, was a devoted friend of Stoker.

Stoker's page of notes displays his prideful decision on the new title, *Dracula. (Courtesy Rosenbach Museum and Library)*

Vlad Tepes, the historical Dracula, provided the name for Stoker's character. *(Courtesy Rosenbach Museum and Library)*

The Lyceum Theatre was the site of Irving's success and Stoker's *Dracula* dramatization.

TOP LEFT: Bram Stoker's play was given only one performance, to register the copyright.

TOP RIGHT: The American actor Richard Mansfield as Jekyll and Hyde.

BOTTOM LEFT: *Dracula* was dedicated to Stoker's friend Thomas Hall Caine, the Victorian novelist. (© *Corbis*)

BOTTOM RIGHT: An engraving of suspect Francis Tumblety's arrest in St. Louis, from a booklet published by Tumblety. He was later suspected of the Jack the Ripper murders.

LEFT: Henry Irving was respected as England's leading actor, famous for his spectacular and melodramatic productions.

CENTER: Ellen Terry as Portia in *The Merchant of Venice* at the Lyceum Theatre.

RIGHT: Walt Whitman, a model for Dracula, and an important influence on Bram Stoker's artistic career. (© *Corbis*)

Oscar Wilde early in his career, at the time of his North American tour. (© *Corbis*)

LEFT: Clyde Fitch was an early paramour of Wilde, and Mansfield's collaborator.

BELOW: Richard Mansfield starring in *Beau Brummell*, Clyde Fitch's play.

Oscar Wilde, the successful playwright, at the height of his fame. (© *Corbis*)

TOP LEFT: Herbert Beerbohm Tree as Svengali; his production of *A Woman of No Importance* was at the center of Wilde's trials.

TOP RIGHT: The Marquess of Queensberry (John Sholto Douglas) accused Wilde of "posing as a sodomite." (© *Corbis*)

BOTTOM LEFT: Ellen Terry with her terrier Drummie and, right, Irving's terrier Fussie.

BOTTOM RIGHT: Henry Irving's career ended with a series of missed opportunities and failures.

Bram Stoker, at the time of Henry Irving's death.

Bela Lugosi as Dracula in 1927; he popularized the vampire for the twentieth century, first on Broadway and then in Hollywood. *(Florence Vandamm Photo © Corbis)*

There was a curse to the vampire: Henry Irving's fortunes began changing around 1897, just as *Dracula* was being prepared for publication.

Fussie, Irving's terrier, died in an accident onstage. The dog had shared dinner each night with Irving; he was free to wander backstage at every theater. One day on a stage in Manchester, as the company rehearsed the show, Fussie was drawn to a workman's coat that had been tossed on the floor—he smelled the ham sandwich in the pocket. The dog greedily nudged and tugged at the garment, failing to notice the open trapdoor alongside it.

Fussie's lifeless body was discovered in the basement just before the show. The company was too miserable to tell the Governor. Only after the performance did they break the sad news, each man removing his hat and bowing his head as poor Fussie was handed over to Irving.

The actor was distraught. For years he had managed to lavish all of the attention that he could not summon for his fellow men onto Fussie. Just days later, when Irving returned to the Lyceum, one of the theater cats seemed to sense his loss and for the first time strutted into his dressing room, promptly curling up on Fussie's cushion. From then on Irving and the cat were inseparable.

Then, his relationship with Ellen Terry began to cool— personally and professionally. Irving was flattered and courted by a fashion writer and gossip columnist, Mrs. Aria (Eliza Davis Aria). Ellen Terry was now being professionally courted, in correspondence, by George Bernard Shaw. He was writing plays that,

he felt, provided ideal roles for Terry. "Your career has been sacrificed to the egotism of a fool," he wrote her.

When Irving produced *Richard III* on December 19, 1896, the
opening performance was bumpy. Irving went to the Garrick Club
for dinner, then slinked back to his rooms in Grafton Street. As he
was climbing the stairs, he slipped and banged his knee on a chest,
tearing the ligaments. After one miserable performance, *Richard III* was withdrawn and the theater closed for three weeks.

Shaw couldn't resist piling on. He contributed his review of
Richard III to the *Saturday Review*, listing Irving's fidgets and
mumbles in the role and implying that the actor had been drunk
on opening night. Shaw, of course, knew better. Irving would never
have set foot onstage if he had been intoxicated.

Terry grew tired of the feud, turned down Shaw's roles, and
accepted an offer to play in *The Merry Wives of Windsor* opposite
Herbert Beerbohm Tree, the successful star and producer at Her
Majesty's Theatre—Irving's friend and competitor. No one was
happy.

———— • ————

The next tragedy struck in the early morning of February 18, 1898.
Stoker was awakened by a pounding on his door in Chelsea. The
police were trying to locate him. The Lyceum's storage, in Bear
Lane, Southwark, was on fire.

The Acting Manager jumped in a cab and raced to the storage
facility, beneath the arches of a railway. The street was already
filled with fire pumps and hoses. Stoker pushed his way through
the crowd. All his life he'd been attracted by the sound of fire bells,
running to watch the brave firemen at work. But as he stumbled

into Bear Lane, trying to find someone in charge, he felt sick to his stomach. The hot orange blaze filled the railway arches and spit sparks into the road.

When he identified himself, the firemen told him that they were there only to keep the fire from spreading to other buildings; there was nothing that could be done to save the scenery. The painted canvas and wood would burn, and burn, until it burned itself out completely.

The store consisted of many of the finest hand-painted drops, the most artistic castle interiors, cityscapes, and gardens, props, armor, platforms, and walls. It was the work of the finest scenic painters in the world, the designs of the finest technicians, the pictures that had formed the frame for Henry Irving's artistry. Stoker watched as over 2,000 pieces of scenery, 260 scenes, and 44 complete plays were turned to ash, including the scenery from *Hamlet, The Merchant of Venice, Macbeth, The Corsican Brothers, Faust, Becket,* and *The Bells.*

Stoker estimated the loss at over 30,000 pounds ($150,000). The storage had been insured for a third that amount but, earlier that year, in an effort to economize, Irving had urged Stoker to reduce the insurance to 6,000 pounds. It didn't really matter. No amount of effort could reassemble the artists and replace the scenery.

"It was checkmate to the repertoire side of his management," Stoker wrote. Irving's business had depended on his ability to assemble a tour of his most popular plays, or quickly swap one play for another—reinstating an old favorite that was sure to draw a crowd. If the new *Peter the Great* proved a flop, a quick production of *The Bells* was in order to keep the box office humming. This was possible only because of the store of scenery. Now the process of putting on a favorite play—even for a short run—would involve a massive investment of capital.

Only a few shows were rebuilt—obvious moneymakers like *The Bells*. In fact, there was little taste for the spectacle shows of a decade earlier. The new fashion was for modern, tight dramas like the works of Ibsen and Shaw.

———•◦•———

Herbert Beerbohm Tree's *Trilby*—taken from George du Maurier's novel *Trilby*—premiered in 1895. The play was a roaring success for Tree, who played Svengali, a dark foreign hypnotist who exerts an unhealthy influence over a young singer. The success of *Trilby* inspired Irving's *The Medicine Man*. This play was written especially for Irving by H. D. Traill and Robert Hichens, following the actor's suggestions. "I want a modern play," Irving told his authors. "The character for me must be something strange. Occult perhaps. I could play the part of a doctor—couldn't I?" *The Medicine Man* premiered in 1898. It told the story of a mysterious doctor who dabbles in hypnosis, then abuses his powers.

It was a flop. Ellen Terry's presence in it was a mere formality. As a society maiden, she was little more than a hollow reminder of Ophelia's mad scenes. Terry was crushed that Irving had neglected her part. *The Medicine Man* earned only twenty-two performances before it was withdrawn. The play's silliness meant that Shaw's review virtually wrote itself: "When, after some transcendently idiotic speech that not even her art could give any sort of plausibility to, [Terry] looked desperately at all us with an expression that meant, 'Don't blame me, I didn't write it.'"

Irving found it difficult to adapt, even when given the opportunity. Arthur Conan Doyle approached Herbert Beerbohm Tree and Henry Irving in 1897, offering the dramatization of his popular character, Sherlock Holmes. Both actors turned him down. Tree would have been unsuitable, but Irving would have made a remarkable Holmes: the tall, thin, loping detective who approached each problem with icy logic.

The role went to the American actor William Gillette two years later, who made Holmes the role of his career. Stoker was present at the play's premiere in New York City, and he later recommended it for the Lyceum, where Gillette reprised his role; both Stoker and Irving experienced the mixed emotions of *Sherlock Holmes*'s triumph at their own theater.

It was easy to imagine Henry Irving as the detective and imagine his success. This was a missed opportunity.

Dracula was probably his second missed opportunity.

———

In 1929, a Chicago newspaper offered a review of the play that had arrived from Broadway, *Dracula*. The longtime critic Frederick Donaghey recalled his conversation with Bram Stoker from February 1900, when Stoker's *Dracula* was a topic of conversation and the Lyceum company was playing in Chicago. "He knew he had written, in *Dracula*, a shilling shocker [otherwise, a 'Penny Dreadful'], however a successful one, and was frank about it."

Bram Stoker told me that he had put endless hours in trying to persuade Henry Irving to have a play made from *Dracula* and to act in it[;] he had nothing in mind save the box office. "If," he explained, "I am able to afford to have my name on the book the

Governor certainly can afford, with business bad, to have his name on the play. But he laughs at me whenever I talk about it, and then we have to go out and raise money to put on something in which the public has no interest."

The Acting Manager had imagined Dracula as the perfect part for Irving, "a composite of so many of the parts in which he has been liked." Stoker saw Dracula as a combination of Matthias in *The Bells*, Shylock, Mephistopheles, Peter the Great, Dubosc in *The Lyons Mail*, Louis XI, and Iachimo in *Cymbeline*.

If Donaghey's recollection was correct, this had been Stoker's plan for *Dracula*. It seemed ridiculous that Henry Irving was commissioning *The Medicine Man* when the novel *Dracula* had been sitting, unopened, on his desk. Unfortunately, his decisions were now conspiring against him. Irving had always been stubborn and dismissive of Stoker's talents. The Lyceum was desperate for cash, but its star was unadventurous.

In this way, Henry Irving certainly inspired *Dracula*—the story was constructed and fitted to best complement his tastes and abilities. But Irving was not Dracula. Rather, Irving was supposed to play Dracula.

One of Stoker's early notes for the novel divides it into four "books" of seven chapters each. Researchers have noticed that this corresponds to the format of a play, with four acts of seven scenes. The play construction may have been familiar to Stoker, but none of his later notes indicate that he was intending to write a play. By

1890, Stoker had written novels, and it's clear from the chapter designations that Stoker designed *Dracula* as his next novel.

Donaghey's recollection that Stoker wanted Irving "to have a play made from *Dracula*" is probably accurate. Stoker was unable to turn the novel into a play, and he realized that Irving had often found authors to carry out his idea and adapt works. Stoker had depended on convincing Irving of the story's merit, then working with Irving and other writers and designers to carry out the plan—to sculpt Dracula into a villain worthy of Henry Irving.

Stoker may have been insistent, but the idea probably came ten years too late, and his dramatized production, the copyright performance, proved only that the show could be a bore and the Count could be a dull, insignificant villain. If Stoker saw it all in his imagination, Henry Irving did not.

When Henry Irving wandered through the Lyceum, listened to the Count's scattered bits of monologue, mumbled "dreadful," and ambled to his office, it was the final tragedy of his career. As in any great theatrical tragedy, "Pride goeth before the fall."

Eleven

THE POET,
"PERENNIAL SWEET DEATH"

Master" is a word that appears throughout the novel. Dracula describes himself as a master of his people; he assumes, with old-world propriety, that Harker's employer in Exeter is his master; Van Helsing is introduced with particular honor as Seward's "friend and master." But the word is most memorable from the lips of Seward's patient, Renfield. As Dracula approaches London, a mysterious energy seems to overtake Renfield, "that shifty look . . . when a madman has seized an idea." Renfield tells his warders, "I don't want to talk to you; you don't count now; the Master is at hand."

Later that night, when Renfield dashes from the asylum and runs to the next property, Carfax Abbey, he calls out to the man to whom he's pledged his life. Stoker gives him a speech that highlights his desperation—the master has been only a dream, only an ideal, an act of faith imagined "long and afar off." Even Stoker's capitalization suggests Renfield's religious fervor:

> I am here to do Your bidding, Master. I am Your slave, and You
> will reward me, for I shall be faithful. I have worshipped You

long and afar off. Now that You are near, I await Your com-
mands, and You will not pass me by, will You, dear Master, in
Your distribution of good things?

———•—————

While he was still a student at Trinity, young Abraham Stoker became obsessed with the poetry of Walt Whitman. Whitman was a
cause célèbre for a young man at university. The American poet
was unexpected, iconoclastic, and dangerously elemental. He required fans, but even more, he required defenders, as Whitman's
subject matter could be coarsely erotic, earning sniggers from less
sophisticated readers.

> *I am he that walks with the tender and growing night,*
> *I call to the earth and sea half-held by the night.*
>
> *Press close bare-bosom'd night—press close magnetic*
>   *nourishing night!*
> *Night of south winds—night of the large few stars!*
> *Still nodding night—mad naked summer night.*
>
> *Smile O voluptuous cool-breath'd earth!*
> *Earth of the slumbering and liquid trees!*
> *Earth of departed sunset—earth of the mountains*
>   *misty-topt!*
> *Earth of the vitreous pour of the full moon just tinged*
>   *with blue!*
> *Earth of shine and dark mottling the tide of the river!*

Earth of the limpid gray of clouds brighter and clearer
   for my sake!
Far-swooping elbow'd earth—rich apple-blossom'd earth!
Smile, for your lover comes.

Prodigal, you have given me love—therefore I to you give love!
O unspeakable passionate love.

In 1872, overwhelmed by Whitman's imagery and convinced that he had found a kindred soul, Stoker composed his long confessional letter to Whitman. This was the letter that he reconsidered, and then hid in his desk. Four years later, having left Trinity, he found himself in another debate about the merits of the poet. He returned to his rooms and wrote an introduction.

Dublin, February 14, 1876

I hope you will not consider this letter from an utter stranger a liberty. Indeed, I hardly feel a stranger to you, nor is this the first letter I have written to you. . . . Four years ago I wrote the enclosed draft of a letter which I intended to copy out and send you. . . . It speaks for itself and needs no comment. . . . You know what hostile criticism your work sometimes evokes here, and I wage a perpetual war with many friends on your behalf.

In the note, Stoker insisted that he was being open and honest with Whitman, as "I feel that with you one must be open." The

1872 letter, which he enclosed, provided an amazing vision of
Bram Stoker as a young man: his insecurities, his passions, and his
talent for unabashed hero worship.

Dublin, February 18, 1872

*I know that I would not long be ashamed to be natural
before you. You are a true man, and I would like to be one
myself, and so I would be towards you as a brother and as a
pupil to his master. In this age, no man becomes worthy of
the name without an effort.*

Stoker's choice of the title "master" is significant, for it exhibits
the same faithful pledge, to a far-away ideal and a dreamy aspira-
tion, that he later wrote for the madman Renfield. "If I were before
your face, I would like to shake hands with you, for I feel that I
would like you," Stoker wrote to Whitman. More important, he is
convinced that Whitman would like him. As the letter continues,
he attempts to naively seduce his master in any way necessary to
win his approval—intellectually, artistically, and erotically. He
seems confident that Whitman would appreciate all three.

*I am twenty-four years old. Have been a champion at
our athletic sports and have won about a dozen cups. I have
also been President of the College Philosophical Society and
an art and theatrical critic of a daily paper. I am six feet
two inches high and twelve stone weight naked and used
to be forty-one or forty-two inches round the chest. . . . I*

*have a heavy jaw and a big mouth and thick lips—sensitive
nostrils—a snub nose and straight hair. . . . I think you
would like to know of the personal appearance of your
correspondents.*

*Be assured of this, Walt Whitman—that a man of less
than half your own age, reared a conservative in a conservative country, and who has always heard your name cried
down by the great mass of people who mention it, here felt
his heart leap towards you across the Atlantic and his soul
swelling at the words, or rather the thoughts.*

*. . . You see, I have called you by your name. I have been
more candid with you—have said more about myself to you
than I have ever said to anyone before. . . . You will not laugh
at me for writing this. . . . How sweet a thing it is for a strong
healthy man with a woman's eyes and a child's wishes to feel
that he can speak so to a man who can be, if he wishes, father, and brother, and wife to his soul.*

Whitman was pleased by the letters, if taken aback by Stoker's
exuberance. "All of it from the inside, almost painfully so," Whitman told his friend Horace Traubel years later when they reread
the letters together. "He is youthfully self-conscious; sees things in
their exaggerations!" When he responded to Stoker, the poet
shared the wish to meet.

*Your letters have been most welcome to me—welcome to
me as a person and then as author. I don't know which most.
You did well to write me so unconventional, so fresh, so*

manly, and so affectionately, too. I too hope (though it is not
probable) that we shall one day personally meet each other.

———•◦•———

Whitman scholar Dennis R. Perry has pointed out that "Whitman
has been called one of the two greatest influences on Bram Stoker's
life," along with Henry Irving. The relationship with Irving has
been memorialized in many books, including Stoker's own book
in tribute to his boss. Whitman's influence—from Stoker's early
years—has often been ignored. It seems to have left an indelible,
suggestive mark on *Dracula*.

Walter Whitman Jr. was a first-generation resident of the United
States of America, born in 1819 on Long Island, just thirty years
after George Washington had been inaugurated as president in
New York. The family moved to Brooklyn—Walt spent the rest of
his life devoted to the wilds of Long Island and the urban bustle
of Brooklyn and Manhattan. As a young man he learned the
trade of a printer and worked as a journalist for local newspapers.

He became a fan of books, theater, and lectures, and also worked
as a teacher in various towns on Long Island before returning to
journalism. Through the 1840s he kept notebooks of poetry and
quickly developed a novel, free-form style—abandoning the usual
rhyme and meter and focusing on unexpected, common images
combined in beautiful ways.

Leaves of Grass, his great book of poetry, was first published in
1855. As a former printer, he oversaw the text, cover, and binding.
The earliest edition was confined to 795 copies and consisted of
just twelve poems. The author's name did not appear in the book,
although his portrait appeared opposite the title page—Whitman

was wearing workman's clothing, with a hat pushed back on his head and a hand on his hip. He didn't look like a poet. The poems didn't sound like normal poetry.

Emerson thought that Whitman's poetry was "a remarkable mixture of the Bhagvat Ghita and *The New York Herald.*" Later additions gradually swelled the number of poems; Whitman titled them, rearranged them, and relegated new poems to appendixes. The 1860 edition of the book included the "Calamus" poems, which celebrated homosexuality in warmly innocent terms, and the "Children of Adam" poems, which were heterosexual in content and more explicit in imagery.

Leaves of Grass and its author were met with instant condemnation—many thought the poetry abominable and the suggestiveness immoral. The *Saturday Press* advised the author to commit suicide. The *Criterion* labeled it "a mass of stupid filth" and accused its author of "that horrible sin not to be mentioned among Christians" (this critique was written in Latin to further disguise the indecency). Booksellers and publishers protested, and the city of Boston rejected a later edition, demanding the removal of specific poems, but Whitman was always steadfast, refusing to censor the book and gradually adjusting editions to add poems. The poet later believed that his only mistake had been not introducing the poems through lectures—directly to the public. "If I had gone directly to the people, read my poems, faced the crowds, got into immediate touch with Tom, Dick and Harry instead of waiting to be interpreted, I'd have had my audience at once."

The Civil War changed him. He had been an opponent of

slavery and was drawn to camps and army hospitals, nursing the injured troops, offering friendship and support to tens of thousands of soldiers—Union and Confederate prisoners as well. After the war he published *Drum-Taps*, a series of poems inspired by the war; his *Sequel to Drum-Taps* also included his famous elegies to Abraham Lincoln, "When Lilacs Last in the Dooryard Bloom'd" and "O Captain! My Captain!"

D. H. Lawrence wrote critically, "Walt's great poems are really huge fat tomb-plants, great rank graveyard growths." Some of his work—particularly the poetry of immortality after his experiences in the Civil War—sound like the romantic poetry of the undead. This is particularly true of his famous obsessions with the tomb and the twinning of death and love. In Whitman's earthy, honest images we can imagine Dracula—his pungent breath, coarse hands, strong arms fit for physical labor. He is never far from the tomb—smudged with the dirt of his last resting place, smeared with the blood of his last meal. Dracula is not a scrubbed, perfumed aristocrat but a proud creature of the earth that might be found in Whitman's verses. From "Pensive on Her Dead Gazing":

> *Absorb them well O my earth, she cried, I charge you lose*
> *   not my sons, lose not an atom,*
> *And you streams absorb them well, taking their dear*
> *   blood,*
> *And you local spots, and you airs that swim above lightly*
> *   impalpable,*

And all you essences of soil and growth, and you my rivers'
   depths,
And you mountain sides, and the woods where my dear
   children's blood trickling redden'd . . .

Exhale me them centuries hence, breathe me their breath, let
   not an atom be lost;
O years and graves! O air and soil! O my dead, an aroma
   sweet!
Exhale them perennial sweet death, years, centuries hence.

From Whitman's "Trickle Drops":

Trickle drops! my blue veins leaving!
O drops of me! trickle, slow drops,
Candid from me falling, drip, bleeding drops,
From wounds made to free you whence you were prison'd,
From my face, from my forehead and lips,
From my breast, from within where I was conceal'd, press
   forth red drops, confession drops,
Stain every page, stain every song I sing, every word I say,
   bloody drops. . . .

Or from "Scented Herbage of My Breast":

Tomb-leaves, body-leaves growing up above me above death . . .
Death is beautiful from you, (what indeed is finally beautiful
   except death and love?)

O I think it is not for life I am chanting here my chant of lovers,
  I think it must be for death,
For how calm, how solemn it grows to ascend to the atmosphere
  of lovers,
Death or life I am then indifferent, my soul declines to prefer,
(I am not sure but the high soul of lovers welcomes death
  most) . . .

If Stoker recalled Whitman's imagery when he was constructing *Dracula*'s prose, Dennis R. Perry has found a wonderful example— a striking parallel that demonstrates Whitman's influence. "Song of Myself" is a poem that must have left a deep impression on young Bram Stoker. It was one of the author's most notorious examples of erotic (and homosexual) imagery. "Song of Myself" would have been precisely the poem that made the Trinity students giggle and made Stoker defend his master:

I mind how once we lay, such a transparent summer morning;
How you settled your head athwart my hips, and gently turn'd
  over upon me,
And parted the shirt from my bosom-bone, and plunged your
  tongue to my bare-stript heart,
And reach'd till you felt my beard, and reach'd till you held
  my feet.

In the vampire novel, the image has been perfectly inverted. It is no longer a sunny, impetuous moment of love, but a nightmarish moment of rape:

With that he pulled open his shirt, and with his long sharp nails opened a vein in his breast. When the blood began to spurt out, he took my hands in one of his, holding them tight, and with the other seized my neck and pressed my mouth to the wound, so that I must either suffocate or swallow some of the [blood].

———

The comparison is even more convincing in the other direction. Perry writes, "Dracula is the only character [in the novel] who speaks with a sense of rhythm, parallelism, and balance that is characteristic of Whitman." In fact, Stoker's clunky dialogue in dialect works against most of his characters, particularly Van Helsing. But somehow, Dracula's careful, clipped English is imbued with a lovely and unexpected poetry.

A house cannot be made habitable in a day; and after all, how few days go to make up a century. I rejoice also that there is a chapel of old times. We Transylvanian nobles love not to think that our bones may be amongst the common dead. I seek not gaiety nor mirth, not the bright voluptuousness of much sunshine and the sparkling waters which please the young and gay. I am no longer young; and my heart, through weary years of mourning over the dead, is not attuned to mirth. . . . I love the shade and the shadow, and would be alone with my thoughts when I may.

Even the Count's snarling speech to the vampire hunters sounds like verse.

You think to baffle me, you, with your pale faces all in a row, like sheep in a butcher's. You shall be sorry yet, each one of you. You think you have left me without a place to rest, but I have more. My revenge is just begun! I spread it over centuries, and time is on my side. Your girls that you all love are mine already; and through them you and others shall yet be mine—my creatures to do my bidding and to be my jackals when I want to feed. Bah!

———•+•———

Bram Stoker finally met Walt Whitman in 1884, when he and Henry Irving brought the Lyceum company to Philadelphia, and he found himself instantly enchanted with the poet. This was the meeting when Whitman surprised him by recognizing the name Abraham Stoker. Whitman was instantly open, friendly, and curious in an ingratiating way. He was especially receptive to Stoker's opinions and impressions of friends from Ireland. The poet spoke with a rich voice—his own rich, baritone Long Island accent was a treat for Stoker, who had become fascinated with the various American twangs that he encountered from city to city.

———•+•———

Stoker had first seen a portrait of Whitman in *Leaves of Grass*, but as he entered the room in Philadelphia, he took note of the old poet's distinctive appearance. Whitman resembled a sort of mythological creature, a powerful beast who exhibited only sensitive traits. He was over six feet tall and thickly built, but only gentle, inviting, and habitually kind. During one of Stoker's visits, he noticed the poet sitting in a special rocking chair that had been constructed for his large, heavy frame. Whitman's clothing, similarly, had been hand-stitched to perfectly fit his body and his tastes: it was coarsely woven and simply cut, in simple shades of gray. The old woman who cared for him had adorned his collar and cuffs with lace or fabric decorations. These bits of lace were "clumsily sewn on and . . . pathetic to see," according to Stoker, but signs of the woman's devotion and Whitman's honored status. Whitman had become a sort of Christmas tree, to be celebrated and decorated. He seemed oblivious to this attention. His jacket cuffs bristled with straight pins, which he habitually pulled out to use to attach manuscript pages in his work.

Bram Stoker recalled the poet as

> an old man of leonine appearance. He was burly, with a large head and high forehead slightly bald. Great shaggy masses of grey-white hair fell over his collar. His moustache was large and thick and fell over his mouth so as to mingle with the top of the mass of the bushy flowing beard.

When Stoker visited him years later, he found Whitman's appearance only slightly altered.

> He looked like King Lear in Ford Madox Brown's picture. . . . His hair seemed longer and wilder and shaggier and whiter than when I had seen him two years before.

The tall, powerful, animal-like Whitman forms a nearly perfect parallel to Count Dracula, as Jonathan Harker first encounters him.

Clean-shaven save for a long white mustache, and clad in black from head to foot, without a single speck of color about him anywhere. . . . His face was a strong—a very strong—aquiline, with high bridge of the thin nose and peculiarly arched nostrils; with lofty domed forehead, and hair growing scantily round the temples, but profusely everywhere. His eyebrows were very massive, almost meeting over the nose, and with busy hair that seemed to curl in its own profusion. The mouth, so far as I could see it under the heavy mustache, was fixed and rather cruel looking. . . .

The 1902 Doubleday edition of the novel included a portrait of the vampire on the cover. The illustration shows Dracula alongside a wolf; he has dark hair instead of white, but his wild, natural appearance bears a striking resemblance to Walt Whitman.

A number of Stoker's acquaintances may have suggested the physical traits of Dracula. Henry Irving was tall and angular; Henry Stanley had a dark, haunted look; Jacques Damala (actress Sarah Bernhardt's husband) gave the appearance of a dead man. Sir Richard Burton's canine teeth and Franz Liszt's white hair have also been cited for their inspirations. But of all Stoker's friends, or the Lyceum's visiting celebrities, Whitman presents the best match. Although he had a full beard and was more solidly built than the Count, his natural height, strength, wild white hair, and mustache suggest the vampire's physical appearance. Dracula's tomb-like obsessions, dark poetry, and ambiguous sexuality further suggest that Bram Stoker used the famous American poet, his self-proclaimed "master," as a model for literature's most famous vampire.

Stoker began writing his notes for *Dracula* in 1890, less than three years after he last saw Whitman, and the poet died in 1892, before Stoker's next visit to America. Walt Whitman never read *Dracula.*

————•—•——

One of the most fascinating chapters in *Personal Reminiscences of Henry Irving,* Bram Stoker's book about his associate, is the chapter devoted to Walt Whitman. It is one of the few autobiographical sections of the book, for the Whitman story is Stoker's story. He recounted his discovery of Whitman's poems at Trinity and his having written letters to the author—without quoting them (perhaps he didn't have copies, or perhaps he understood how desperate they sounded so many years later). He reproduced Whitman's response to him and recorded his later visits to Whitman in America.

Stoker was honest enough to address Whitman's reputation for indecent prose.

In 1868 [the British edition, *Selected Poems of Walt Whitman*] raised a regular storm in British literary circles. . . . Those who did not or could not understand the broad spirit of the group of poems took samples of details which were at least deterrent. . . . From these excerpts it would seem that the book was as offensive to morals as to taste. They did not scruple to give the *ipsissima verba* [that is, the very words] of the most repugnant passages.

Stoker believed that Whitman's words were being taken out of context.

In my own University the book was received with Homeric laughter, and more than a few of the students sent over to Trubner's [the U.S. publisher] for copies of the complete *Leaves of Grass.* . . . Needless to say that amongst young men the objectionable passages were searched for and more noxious ones expected. For days we all talked of Walt Whitman and the new poetry with scorn—especially those of us who had not seen the book.

Stoker, however, was given a copy by a student who was tired of it.

I took the book with me into the park and in the shade of an elm tree began to read it. Very shortly my own opinion began to form; it was diametrically opposed to that which I had been hearing. From that hour I became a lover of Walt Whitman.

On Stoker's third visit to Whitman, in 1887, he brought up a conversation he'd had with Talcott Williams, an editor at the *Philadelphia Press.* Stoker found Whitman looking "hale and well" at his Mickle Street house. When there was a pause in their conversation, Stoker leaned over, looking into Whitman's clear blue eyes, and offered his plan.

I ventured to speak to him what was in my mind as to certain excisions in his work. "If you will only allow your friends to do this—they will only want to cut about a hundred lines in all— your books will go into every house in America. Is not that worth the sacrifice?" He answered at once, as though his mind had long ago been made up and he did not want any special thinking.

Neither Stoker nor Williams really knew Whitman, and neither suspected that Whitman had already had this conversation hundreds of times—with Ralph Waldo Emerson and the Boston district attorney. Whitman told him:

"It would not be any sacrifice. So far as I am concerned they might cut a thousand. It is not that—it is quite another matter." Here both his face and voice grew rather solemn. "When I wrote as I did I thought I was doing right and right makes for good. I think so still. I think that all that God made is for good—that the work of His hands is clean in all ways if used as He intended! If I was wrong I have done harm. And for that I deserve to be punished by being forgotten! It has been and cannot not-be. No, I shall never cut a line as long as I live!"

This account attests to Stoker's skills as a reporter, for it sounds exactly like Whitman. In his book, Stoker concluded, "One had to respect a decision thus made and on such grounds. I said no more."

Could Bram Stoker have failed to recognize the indecent elements in his own book?

When he sent a copy of *Dracula* to Prime Minister Gladstone, he added a note: "The book is necessarily full of horrors and terrors but I trust that these are calculated to 'cleanse the mind by pity and terror.' At any rate there is nothing base in the book and though superstition is brought in, with the weapons superstition, I hope it is not irrelevant."

The notion of cleansing the mind through "pity and fear" is from Aristotle's *Poetics*. The implication is that Stoker recognized the value of thrills—providing a new perspective or morality through the experience. By "base," Stoker refers to the crudities of superstition and folklore. Presumably, like many of his reviewers, he overlooked any sexual content.

In 1908, two years after the publication of *Personal Reminiscences of Henry Irving*, Stoker contributed a long essay on "The Censorship of Fiction" to *The Nineteenth Century and After*, a monthly publication. Stoker was in a unique position to address this issue—as a writer recognized for his sensational horror, as a man of the theater who had consistently dealt with the Lord Chamberlain's office, and as a solicitor. He seems to have turned his back on Whitman's lesson and, indeed, on Dracula's appeal.

Not surprisingly, Stoker first championed simple restraint in the creation of artistic works. "The measure of the ethics of the artist is expressed in the reticence shown in his work; and where such self-restraint exists there is no need for external compelling force."

Censorship was necessary as a result of a gradual winnowing-away of values: an audience that thrills to increasing "weaknesses" and a writer or producer who profits through increasing "avarice."

This goes on till a comparison between what was and what is shows to any eye, even an unskilled one, a startling fact of decadence. Then, as is too often observable in public matters, official guardianship of ethical values wakes up and acts—when it is too late for any practical effect. To prevent this, censorship must be continuous and rigid. There must be no beginnings of evil, no flaws in the mason work of the dam. . . . It is not sufficient to make a stand, however great, here and there; the whole frontier must be protected.

This is, of course, a remarkably harsh theory and is only muddled by the vagaries. Stoker must have been mindful of Walt Whitman, for he quoted him in the essay. Whitman had popularized the term "en masse," meaning a sort of public mentality. Stoker pointed out that imagination doesn't apply to Whitman's "en masse" but is the result of an individual. The author cautioned against the worst "evils of imagination."

It is through the corruption of individuals that the harm is done. A close analysis will show that the only emotions which in the long run harm are those arising from sex impulses, and when we have realized this we have put a finger on the actual point of danger.

To a modern reader, Stoker's essay borders on dumbfounding. Could the author really overlook the sex impulses that provided the magical frisson in *Dracula*'s pages? Could he have written those scenes and not understood the literary high-wire act he had just negotiated? Or did he consider himself too clever for his own values?

There is a hint that Stoker was drawing a line between suggestive literature and obscene literature. He pointedly distinguished between "natural misdoing based on human weakness, frailty, or passions of the senses," and books with "vices so flagitious . . . that the poignancy of moral disgust is lost in horror." As he refused to name the books of his examples "and give the writers the advertisements which they crave," we can only guess at his targets.

Presumably *Dracula*'s issues of "human weakness" and Whitman's "passions of the senses" fell outside of his criticism. Unfortunately, the essay ended with the heavy thud of a legislator, not the feathery distinctions of an artist.

> This article is no mere protest against academic faults or breaches of good taste. It is a deliberate indictment of a class of literature so vile that it is actually corrupting a nation.

Stoker must have been aware of Whitman's sensuality and, by extension, the eroticism that could be encoded in literature. He addressed exactly this issue with Whitman. But when Stoker wrote about censorship, he refused to take into account the sensuality he had encountered in his American master's poems. He made no effort to include Whitman's rule that "right makes for good" or the "broad spirit" of the poems that had caused him to once swoon over verses as a young man—the spirit that had allowed him to overlook crudities and appreciate the genius of the poet.

Bram Stoker's conversation with Whitman took a place of pride in his book and provides an especially honest and noble tribute to the American poet.

By contrast, the indecencies of Oscar Wilde, Stoker's child-hood friend—Wilde was convicted and sentenced to jail for immorality—earned him no such respect, nor any consideration. Stoker completely omitted his name from *Personal Reminiscences of Henry Irving.* It is a remarkable effort, in itself, spectacularly single-minded. Wilde was a good friend of Stoker, Irving, and Ellen Terry. He was often in the audience at the Lyceum, a guest at special dinners, reciting poetry, or in the Beefsteak Room leading bright conversation. Wilde deserved a place on Stoker's list of visiting celebrities.

Of course, once Wilde was convicted in the English court, a number of late Victorian authors expunged his name from their biographies or histories, befuddled by his status in society and choosing the path of least resistance. But for Stoker to omit any reference to Wilde demonstrates either the author's embarrassment or a coarse, careless attempt at revenge.

When it came to Oscar Wilde, Stoker had reasons for both embarrassment and revenge. Wilde's story was intertwined with Stoker's and, indeed, with *Dracula's.*

Twelve

THE PLAYWRIGHT, "THE MYSTERY OF HIS SIN"

In his book *Personal Reminiscences of Henry Irving,* Bram Stoker worked hard to include every famous person and surround Irving with fame. The book is often dismissed as hagiography.

But it is much more complicated than that. Like many of Henry Irving's most popular spectacles, the audience—the reader—becomes fascinated with the sheer stage management of this two-volume *Reminiscences.* This is Bram Stoker's show, told from his own "personal" perspective. Why have some events, people, and recollections been pushed into the spotlight and others hidden backstage?

It becomes apparent that a significant part of the story is who, or what, has been locked in the dressing room.

As the story favors Irving, the author has sometimes ignored his personal life, so Stoker barely mentions his own wife. She only factors into the story—"the wife"—when he discusses moving to London or meeting with Hall Caine. He never mentions his son,

Noel. He omits mention of any of his novels or short stories, including *Dracula*.

Louis Austin and Austin Brereton, two employees who openly competed with Stoker for Irving's attention, aren't credited with any work at the Lyceum but have been relegated to Stoker's long list of guests at the Beefsteak Room. In *Personal Reminiscences*, this list of small type is just one step from complete exile.

Information about the play *The Medicine Man* has been expunged. In the index, the name of the play appears, but without a single page number next to it; that's a hint that information has been edited out. The only reference to the play is in a list of Irving's productions. At another place in the text, Stoker mentions the names of the authors preparing a work—it is simply "the play," and never named.

Did he eliminate *The Medicine Man* because it was a failure? That's too simple an explanation. Stoker is surprisingly honest about Irving's financial mistakes and failed productions. He mentions other works that were "costly and unsuccessful" and demonstrates that he can be a gentleman, offering the famous actor a fig leaf for his decency when other failures are discussed: "Irving made himself a personal success; it was the play in each case that was not successful." So *The Medicine Man* seems to present a case of exceptional embarrassment. This was the play produced in the shadow of *Trilby* and *Dracula*. Instead of taking Stoker's advice, Irving had chosen to commission *The Medicine Man*, a story wreathed in hypnosis, murder, and the occult.

More embarrassment has been omitted from *Personal Reminiscences*: George Bernard Shaw's name never appears. By rights, Stoker should have included him as a famous visitor to the Lyceum and an almost collaborator with Irving and Terry. But he found it difficult to deal with Shaw's nagging criticisms of Irving.

In the book, Stoker defended Irving against Shaw's charge that he had sought knighthood without mentioning Shaw's name; Stoker simply writes, "A statement was made. . . ."

Even worse, shortly after Irving's death, Shaw became infamous for his obituary of the actor. Shaw had been asked by a Viennese newspaper to write the obituary. One of his sentences returned to his usual criticism, with a dose of Shavian honesty: "Irving took no interest in anything except himself . . . and was not interested even in himself except as an imaginary figure in an imaginary setting."

This phrase was badly translated into German for *Neue Freie Presse* and then badly translated back into English for the British press, where the sentence was published as, "He was a narrow-minded egoist, devoid of culture, and living on the dream of his own greatness."

It was a misunderstanding that Irving's friends never quite understood nor forgave.

———

But the most astonishing omission in *Personal Reminiscences* was Oscar Wilde. Here, the exile was complete. His name was removed, the hints of his presence were erased, and the list of famous, glittering guests was scrubbed clean of Wilde. It is as if he had never existed in the London theater world.

Of course, as Wilde was one of the late Victorian theater's greatest figures—today we might conclude, the greatest figure— a childhood friend of Stoker, a suitor to his wife, Florence, a great admirer and associate of Irving, a frequent visitor to the theater and the Beefsteak Room, a famous wit who offered poems to Irving's guests, a loving friend and admirer of Terry—scrubbing the record of Wilde was a Herculean task. He was omitted for the same reason that many Victorians quietly red-penciled his name from memoirs or reviews. He had humiliated society with his homosexuality, his court case, and his jail sentence. Many of Wilde's friends regretted his time in the spotlight. When Stoker wrote his *Personal Reminiscences*, he did something about it. He simply pretended that Wilde had never played a part.

———•◦•———

For decades, it was popular to suppose that *Dracula* had been inspired by events in Stoker's life. Jonathan Harker's cruel imprisonment in Dracula's castle was easily seen as a sad tribute to his friend Oscar Wilde, who was convicted of gross indecency and sentenced to two years behind bars in 1895. But when Bram Stoker's notes for the novel were rediscovered in the 1970s in Philadelphia, researchers were amazed to find that Stoker had devised that part of the novel in 1890—"a prisoner for a time"—and almost certainly outlined Harker's confinement by the time he assigned all of the events to a calendar, in 1893. That was two years before Wilde's conviction.

Oscar Wilde arrived in London in 1880, two years behind his friend from Dublin, Bram Stoker. Through his association with Henry Irving, Stoker had started work at the top of his profession, quickly welcomed into society as a man that society had to know. But this instant prestige came with a cost. Stoker had sacrificed his literary aspirations—his experiments with poetry, theatrical criticisms, and short stories. His early novels were produced hurriedly and generated little interest.

Wilde arrived in London perfectly poised for a literary career—as the winner of the Newdigate Prize at Oxford for his poem "Ravenna," as an essayist and critic. Those early achievements were gained at the rate of a gallop, in which every step seemed effortless and artistic. During the first decade of his career, some of Wilde's ambitious work had paralleled Stoker's.

For example, Wilde toured America in 1881 with a series of lectures and visited Whitman as a devoted fan of his poetry. He returned to England and offered a popular lecture, "Personal Impressions of America."

Stoker met Whitman two years later, in 1884, and lectured on "A Glimpse of America" the following year.

Similarly, Stoker's first book of fiction was *Under the Sunset*, a book of fairy-tale stories inspired by his Irish upbringing. Wilde's first book was *The Happy Prince and Other Tales*, his own fairy tales, in 1888.

Like Stoker, Wilde also worked as a drama critic (Wilde wrote for the *Dramatic Review*) and an editor (Wilde edited *Woman's World* magazine).

If Stoker treated Wilde as an equal when they first met in London—two ambitious young men from Dublin—it became obvious that Wilde had surpassed him in achievements. Wilde was a guest at Lyceum dinners, having befriended Henry Irving and Ellen Terry. He was turning his attention to playwriting and submitted his first play, *Vera, or, The Nihilists*, to Irving and Terry in September 1880. At the Lyceum, Oscar Wilde walked through the front door, instead of entering through the stage door.

Oscar Wilde was often criticized in the press for his bold clothing tastes, his long hair, and his feminine traits—for wearing
lavender gloves, carrying lilies, languidly drawling his vowels, or
walking with a rhythmic, loose-limbed saunter. These were all
codes for an artistic homosexual, the traits that earned Wilde
parody in Gilbert and Sullivan's 1881 operetta *Patience* as the fop-
pish aesthete, Bunthorne. It wasn't a secret among his friends
that Wilde was homosexual. It could not have been a secret in the
theatrical world, which had always depended upon talented homosexual artists, actors, writers, and designers and drew many
homosexual fans. There was a tacit acceptance within this sub-
culture.

In 1897, Havelock Ellis and John Addington Symonds published the English edition of their book *Sexual Inversion*—their
term for homosexuality. Through their case studies, the authors
categorized it as neither immoral nor criminal. Wilde's biographer Richard Ellmann pointed out the hypocrisy associated with
the charge in Victorian England; it was "common in the public
schools which most of the legal personages . . . had attended."

To the Victorians, who tried to be prudish, homosexuality
could be dismissed as a youthful or adolescent fixation. It was the
secret obsession of lovelorn young boys in public school, a simple
phase of their development. This was basically the classical Greek
model, as understood by the Victorians: a sometimes embarrassing, but accepted, rite of passage. This sweet, "innocent" boy-love
might be ignored if it was part of an especially artistic tempera-
ment. Artists or actors were tolerated for their imaginative and

childish tendencies. As in *Patience*, these people were sometimes perceived as merely funny—not a subject of morality, but a subject of comedy. In other words, homosexuality was quietly tolerated when it was associated with innocence and scorned when it was combined with experience.

Ellen Terry may have been more innocent than many in her profession. She once heard her friend Oscar Wilde blurt out to the actress Aimee Lowther, "Oh, Aimee, if you were only a boy, I could adore you." Later, when Wilde, Terry, and Irving were sitting with a group of friends, she repeated the remark and impulsively asked, "Oscar, you didn't really mean it . . . !" An uncomfortable silence fell over the group. Someone quickly changed the subject. In the carriage home, Henry Irving explained the remark to Ellen Terry, who was reportedly "too innocent to take it in."

Stoker, an older and closer friend of Oscar Wilde, and a man who monitored theatrical gossip as part of his job every day, could not have been so deceived.

The crime of sodomy had been illegal, but for many years other homosexual practices—including solicitation—were not. In 1885, Henry Labouchère's unexpected amendment suddenly outlawed "Gross Indecency," any sexual activity between men.

The amendment did not apply to lesbians; a long-held myth—and only a myth—suggested that Queen Victoria dismissed this need for such a law, noting, "Women do not do such things."

The Labouchère Amendment seems confusing because Labouchère had never expressed the issue as a cause and may have crafted the amendment as a plan to scuttle a bill. Labouchère had been a supporter of Wilde's, endorsing his tour of America, but Labby later was offended by Wilde as a ridiculous, artistic homosexual. In his magazine *Truth*, he reviewed Wilde's lecture on America and pointed out his "epicene" appearance and "effeminate" phrases. Listening to Wilde's discussion of America, Labouchère obsessively counted the word "lovely" forty-three times, "beautiful" twenty-six times, and "charming" seventeen times. In an article titled "Exit Oscar," he predicted the imminent failure of Wilde's career.

Ironically, it was Labouchère who had guaranteed that failure. The Labouchère Amendment did very little to increase morality in society. It failed to snare Scotland Yard's Jack the Ripper suspect. But it inspired a cottage industry in blackmail, and it provided the trap that would demolish Wilde's career.

In 1878, Oscar Wilde had been engaged to Florence Balcombe in Dublin. This was when he presented her with a golden cross on a chain. When he devoted his time to Oxford University and their plans dissolved, Florence went on to marry Bram Stoker. Wilde received the cross as a memento of "the sweetest years of my youth."

But in 1884, in London, Oscar proposed to Constance Lloyd. She was a quiet, modest beauty who came from a wealthy London family. Constance attempted to be a model modern woman but also pledged herself to Oscar's work and was humbled by his literary talents. She shared his tastes in art and fashion. The Wildes made their Tite Street home a showplace for their aesthetic tastes and a fashionable salon for London society. His marriage officially signaled to his society friends that he'd grown up and become a responsible man. The couple had two sons, Cyril and Vyvyan.

Oscar's marriage also signaled that there was no longer any rivalry over Florence. The Wildes and Stokers socialized together. Oscar accepted tickets to the Lyceum, dined with Irving and Stoker, and proffered tickets for the opening night of his 1892 play, *Lady Windermere's Fan*. He also sent inscribed copies of several of his books to Florence.

In July 1889, the Metropolitan Police arrested a fifteen-year-old telegram delivery boy named Charles Swinscow on suspicion of some petty thefts. The boy was found with eighteen shillings, a suspicious amount for a telegraph boy, but Swinscow insisted on his innocence. Finally, in an effort to clear his name, he explained how he'd earned the cash. "I got the money by going to bed with a gentleman at his house."

He explained that a male brothel at 19 Cleveland Street, near Oxford Street, had been the source of cash for a number of willing telegram boys. When the police made their arrests, Chief Inspector Abberline (who later became famous during the Jack the Ripper case) questioned the boy who had been recruiting others, a telegraph employee with the unfortunate name of Henry Newlove. Newlove admitted his part but shrugged off his responsibility. "I think it is hard that I should get into trouble while men in high positions are allowed to walk free." He then named a group of prominent men: Lord Arthur Somerset, the Earl of Euston, and Colonel Jones. A group of policemen kept watch on the house and were dumbfounded to see the widening range of the scandal. In the subsequent months, there were strong hints that Prince Eddy, Albert Victor, would be implicated. Eddy was the eldest son of the Prince of Wales, a grandson of Queen Victoria.

The Prince of Wales maneuvered behind the scenes to keep his son's name out of the case. Lord Somerset was warned of his imminent arrest and he fled the country. Henry Labouchère stood in the House of Commons and accused the prince's associates of tipping him off and urging him to flee.

Prince Eddy was never actually implicated in the case. For several months the sordid newspaper stories—and then the sudden newspaper silence—focused attention on the notorious London "rent boys," the young male prostitutes who made money by accommodating their older customers and, thanks to the Labouchère Amendment, made even more money by blackmailing those customers.

The Cleveland Street scandal might have served as a mad, immoral postscript to Victorian history but instead seems to be the first domino to tip over, clattering against a row of precarious dominoes.

———————

In the July 1889 issue of *Blackwood's Magazine*, Oscar Wilde published his imaginative work of fiction, "The Portrait of Mr. W.H." Wilde's work was often unexpected and impetuous, but here his timing was especially unfortunate. "The Portrait of Mr. W.H." sat on the same smoking-room ottomans and was read at the same breakfast tables as the Cleveland Street newspaper headlines.

"The Portrait of Mr. W.H." is a dazzling high-wire fantasy inspired by a real literary mystery. Shakespeare's sonnets were dedicated to a mysterious "Mr. W.H." That much is fact. In the eighteenth century, a writer named Thomas Tyrwhitt theorized that W.H. may have been a boy actor who appeared in Shakespeare's plays, Willie Hughes. Tyrwhitt believed he found the name "Hughes" punned within the sonnets. Otherwise the theory was complete conjecture.

Wilde wove the theory into a plot, together with Robbie Ross, a young friend who may have provided Wilde's first homosexual affair several years earlier. Wilde's finished tale ended up as a scandalous romance—not fact, but the sort of convincing storytelling at which he was adept. By conflating W.H. with the "fair youth" of the sonnets, Wilde constructed a wonderful homosexual fantasy of the Bard's love for a seventeen-year-old boy: "The master-mistress of Shakespeare's passion, the lord of his love to whom he was bound in vassalage, the delicate minion of pleasure, the rose of the whole world . . . the lovely boy whom it was sweet music to hear, and whose beauty was the very raiment of Shakespeare's heart, as it was the keynote of his dramatic power."

In the story, Wilde's narrator professed not to "pry into the mystery of his sin [Willie's sin, that is], or the sin, if such it was, of the great poet who had so dearly loved him." But the plot was ingeniously constructed in nested frames: The unnamed narrator tells the story of the modern (fictional) researcher Cyril and his friend Erskine; they have stumbled on the evidence of Shakespeare and Willie Hughes. Wilde is ingenious and relentless. As storytellers pledge themselves to Willie Hughes, each of these frames resolves with another revelation of homosexual desire—even from the narrator who has been telling us the story.

Oscar Wilde knew that it would shock. That was his intention. He predicted, "Our English homes will totter to their base when [Mr. W.H.] appears." The story is literate and ingenious, but at its root Wilde had managed to cast England's great bard as a hopeless pederast—or, to be topical, the sort of man who might have visited Cleveland Street. "The Portrait of Mr. W.H." presented Wilde with "incalculable injury," according to his friend, the author and editor Frank Harris. "It gave his enemies for the first time the very weapon they wanted, and they used it unscrupulously and untiringly with the fierce delight of hatred. Oscar seemed to revel in the storm of conflicting opinions which the paper called forth."

Harris was the editor of the *Fortnightly Review*, and a friend of both Wilde and Labouchère. But Harris's publication had rejected the manuscript. Similarly, Wilde's friends, the politicians Arthur Balfour and H. H. Asquith (who both later served as prime minister) had listened to the story and discouraged his effort, pointing out the potential harm to his reputation. Wilde ignored them and submitted the article to *Blackwood's*, where it was finally published.

Of course, Wilde's novel theory on Shakespeare must have caused a great deal of consternation within the walls of the Lyceum, where Shakespeare had been enshrined as a god: Henry Irving was the high priest, and Bram Stoker had been preoccupied with stoking the altar flames. If they were surprised by Wilde's recklessness, they were about to realize that there was nothing surprising about it.

Clyde Fitch was a twenty-three-year-old American playwright and poet. He had first met Oscar and Constance Wilde in 1888, during a vacation to England. He returned in the summer of 1889—at the time of Cleveland Street and "Mr. W. H." Fitch was in London when Oscar was alone and Constance was away from Tite Street, spending that summer in the country with a friend.

Fitch was a small, handsome young man with a sweep of black hair and a waxed mustache. He was described by a good friend as "whimsical as a child, loving, loveable," with "many of the more charming qualities that we used to call feminine, without being effeminate." He bubbled with excitable energy, giggles, and nervous, impulsive gestures. He dressed in fussy, sartorially perfect clothing of distinctive bright colors. He was remarkably honest to his friends and schoolmates about his passions. He was certainly homosexual and almost certainly had a relationship with Oscar Wilde that summer.

Part of Oscar's seduction was now "The Portrait of Mr. W.H." When Fitch arrived, Wilde presented him with the issue of *Blackwood's*. Fitch found himself transfixed by the story. He wrote to Wilde: "'I will just look at it,' I thought. But I could not leave it. I read, unconscious of the uncomfortability of my position and of the fact that one arm and two legs were asleep, fast. Oh, Oscar! The story is *great*—and—fine! *I* believe in Willie Hughes. I don't care if the whole thing is out of your amazing, beautiful brain. I don't care for the laughter, I only know I am convinced and I *will*, I *will* believe in Willie H."

Fitch's letters to Wilde are pleading, flirtatious, desperate: "*Nobody* loves you as *I* do. When you are here I dream. I and the chiming clocks we have our secrets." In another letter, he wrote, "Your love is the fragrance of a rose—the sky of a summer—the wing of an angel. The cymbal of a cherubim [*sic*]. You are always with me. . . . I have not seen you since time—it stopped when you left."

Wilde was made uncomfortable by the heat of Fitch's attention. He seems to have deliberately avoided some of their scheduled assignations, which only generated more simmering correspondence from Fitch: "It is 3. And you are not coming. I've looked out of the window many, many times. . . . I have not slept. I have only dreamt, and thought. I don't know where I stand, nor why. . . . I will only wonder and love. Passionately yours, am I, Clyde."

Fitch's enthusiasm was also manifested in his theater career. Fitch had been promoting himself as a playwright, and the previous year had brought selections from his new manuscript, *Frederick Lemaitre*, attempting to interest London producers. He sold himself by exaggerating his efforts and then stringing together associations, using names carelessly to get through the door—the typical salesman's trick. Fitch visited the acting couple William H. and Madge Kendal and began an association with Herbert Beerbohm Tree and Henry Irving. He was later invited to dinner with Irving. The problem for Wilde was Fitch's presence at parties or the offices of London producers. There, his enthusiastic, giddy discussion of Wilde would have raised eyebrows. Within the insular world of the theater, it was impossible to keep Oscar Wilde's latest infatuation a secret.

An example of Fitch's galumphing enthusiasm—his carelessness when he tried to impress—became a controversy just months later.

Clyde Fitch had been approached to serve as a playwright for Richard Mansfield. Mansfield, of course, was the impatient, argumentative American actor who had premiered *Dr. Jekyll and Mr. Hyde* at the Lyceum in 1888 and generated suspicion in the Jack the Ripper case. Mansfield's friend, the newspaper critic William Winter, had suggested that Mansfield develop a play based on Beau Brummell. It was a clever idea, capitalizing on Mansfield's vanity and his ability to play pathos. Winter sketched out an outline, noting the settings and key scenes that should be included by Mansfield, but he was unable to devote time to writing the play.

Richard Mansfield didn't want to take on the task himself; many of his plays were produced with cowriters. Clyde Fitch was recommended to him, and Mansfield was impressed by the young, enthusiastic playwright. He gave Fitch Winter's outline and talked through his ideas for each scene. He generously promised Fitch a salary and royalties, as well as credit as playwright—this would be Fitch's first credit, an important step in his career.

Fitch wrote the show in the autumn of 1889, just after leaving Oscar Wilde and returning to New York. Correspondence shows that Mansfield was depending on Fitch's creativity, and he hurried him through the process, anxious for the new play.

When *Beau Brummell* was a hit in 1890, Fitch naturally claimed it as his own and began to exaggerate his part in its planning. Mansfield noted that Fitch "convinced himself that he was creator of *Beau Brummell*." Mansfield, characteristically, took offense. Much like Fitch, he seemed to exaggerate the process to his own advantage, deciding (despite their contract) that he'd dictated almost all of the play and that Fitch had been little more than a stenographer.

Fitch's worst mistake was the indiscreet way he used the play to promote himself, reading it to Herbert Beerbohm Tree before it had been produced and even boasting that the project was something he'd developed for Henry Irving. This tight little knot of names—Fitch, Wilde, Mansfield, Irving, and Tree—demonstrated how gossip and controversy would spread through the theatrical community.

Today the dispute over *Beau Brummell* is impossible to settle. William Winter and Richard Mansfield decided that Fitch had not authored the play "except with his pen," but this seems a ridiculous exaggeration. It was, no doubt, a collaboration. Fitch went on to prove himself as a talented playwright. He originated a number of successful American plays before his untimely death in 1909.

———————

With the publication of "The Portrait of Mr. W.H.," and then his affair with this flamboyant American playwright, it was obvious to Oscar Wilde's associates that he had abandoned any pretense about his sexuality. Wilde was incapable of the "reticence" that, Stoker would later write, was required of self-censorship. He'd dragged the scandalous behavior of Cleveland Street into the London theatrical world.

To a number of Oscar Wilde's supporters, like the Stokers, his offense was a personal insult: They had been lied to and their friendship misused. Bram Stoker's theatrical connections allowed him to realize the situation years before the rest of London society—five years before Wilde's indiscretions erupted into the famous court case.

Bram Stoker was probably feeling embarrassed by Wilde's indiscretions, and the reason was Florence. It would have been humiliating to see Wilde being dishonest with Constance, his wife—the whispers of his immorality behind her back. But it was a personal humiliation when the Stokers realized that Wilde had once wooed and promised, tempted and then pledged his soul to Florence during their engagement. He had almost betrayed Florence Balcombe.

———————

The pestilence of Cleveland Street seemed to be tied to Oscar Wilde's behavior. It was the corrupting influence that polite society would not discuss: the perversion that was carelessly, lustfully passed from an old man to a young man.

And perhaps this was the inspiration behind one of Bram Stoker's most original inventions. In *Dracula*, he created the convention that a vampire's bloody, sexual bite begins the gradual process by which the victim will be forever corrupted, turning into another vampire. As Van Helsing explains, "It is out of the lore and experience of the ancients and of all those who have studied the powers of the Un-dead. . . . All that die from the preying of the Un-dead become themselves Un-dead, and prey on their kind. And so the circle goes on ever widening, like the ripples from a stone thrown into the water."

When Van Helsing first applies the rule to Lucy, the analogy is even clearer. "In a trance [Dracula could] best come to take more blood. In a trance she died, and in a trance she is Un-dead, too." In other words, the vampire's victim dies while under a trance, which allows them to participate in immoral crimes.

This is not only the vampire as temptation but the vampire as a spreading moral pestilence. It's the danger of initiation, the intrigue, the seduction, and the trap: a widening threat of immoral sex.

It deepens the story and provides a lurking danger around every turn. The vampire's infection is what transforms *Dracula* from a supernatural murder mystery into a supernatural morality play. It threatens the good with things far worse than death; it inspires the hunters to find more than a solution. They must find redemption.

When Jonathan Harker sees Dracula in his coffin in Transylvania, he simultaneously sees the danger to society: "This was the being I was helping to transfer to London where . . . he might, amongst its teeming millions, satiate his lust for blood and create a new and ever–widening circle of semi-demons to batten on the helpless. The very thought drove me mad."

Seven months after Cleveland Street, "The Portrait of Mr. W.H.," and Oscar Wilde's careless affair with Clyde Fitch, Bram Stoker began taking notes for his new novel, *Dracula*. In those earliest notes, the pestilence was already identified and may have been haunting his nightmares: "This man belongs to me. I want him."

Thirteen

THE ACCUSED, "MONSTROUS AND UNLAWFUL"

O scar Wilde wasn't finished.

His next literary fillip was his astonishing short novel published in *Lippincott's Monthly Magazine* in July 1890, *The Picture of Dorian Gray*. This was the work that set London buzzing and critics stammering, just at the time that Bram Stoker was constructing his plot for *Dracula*—in the summer of 1890.

"The Portrait of Mr. W.H." and *The Picture of Dorian Gray* form nearly perfect counterpoints in Wilde's gallery of revelations. Shakespeare's Elizabethan boy-love for Willie Hughes seemed remote and idealized—the sort of thing capable of inspiring the sonnets. But now Wilde told a contemporary story. Lord Wotton's leering fascination with the pretty Dorian Gray was played out in Turkish-tobacco-smoke-wreathed club rooms and thickly carpeted, crystal- and porcelain-adorned salons. It produced an increasing fascination with the lewd and sensual, suggesting mysterious unnamed crimes.

Dorian Gray is a striking young man who has been immortalized in a painting by the artist Basil Hallward. Hallward's friend, Lord Henry Wotton, arranges to meet Gray. Wotton has a powerful reaction to the pretty boy: "When our eyes met, I felt that I was growing pale. A curious sensation of terror came over me. I knew that I had come face to face with some one whose mere personality was so fascinating that, if I allowed it to do so, it would absorb my whole nature, my whole soul, my very art itself."

Wotton seduces him with his witty, carefree, hedonistic philosophy; this has a powerful effect on the young man: "The only way to get rid of a temptation is to yield to it. Resist it, and your soul grows sick with longing for the things it has forbidden to itself, with desire for what its monstrous laws have made monstrous and unlawful."

Dorian understands that he is at a crossroad, and he chooses to neglect his innocence in search of a life of sensual pleasure. "How sad it is! I shall grow old, and horrible, and dreadful. But this picture will remain always young. . . . If it were only the other way! If it were I who was to be always young . . . I would give my soul for that!"

During the course of the novel, Dorian pledges his love to a pretty actress, then casually abandons her, causing her to commit suicide. He inspires rumors of notorious behavior and leaves friends' reputations ruined through his association. Like Jekyll and Hyde, Dorian's crimes become more horrible for being unspecified.

Young Dorian Gray remains blemish-free and as beautiful as ever, but these crimes have been secretly registering themselves upon his portrait—the cruel expressions, wrinkles, and hard lines of a wicked life. He conceals the painting in a room of his house.

Dorian shows the horrifying painting to Hallward, the artist, and then murders him, blackmailing another friend to dispose of the body.

The young man has selfishly dismissed his crimes, but he is horrified to be watching the catalog of sins register on the painting—chronicling the state of his soul. When he slashes at the painting with the knife he used to murder Hallward, his servants hear a blood-piercing scream. They arrive to investigate. The painting is now beautiful again, but a decrepit, hideous corpse is on the floor, with a knife in its heart. Examining the jewelry on the body, they identify it as Dorian Gray.

———————

Critics condemned *Dorian Gray*. The *Athenaeum* thought it was "unmanly, sickening, vicious," and the *Daily Chronicle* thought it was "dullness and dirt . . . a gloating study of the mental and physical corruption of a fresh, fair and golden youth." The *Scots Observer* suggested that "Mr. Wilde has brains, and art, and style," but could only manage to write "for none but outlawed noblemen and perverted telegraph-boys."

Wilde visited the offices of the *St. James Gazette* and spoke to the journalist Samuel Henry Jeyes, who had offered a particularly scathing review. Oscar insisted that Jeyes was wrong to make personal assumptions based on a work of art. Jeyes was incredulous. "What is the use of writing . . . hinting at, things that you do not mean?" Wilde parried, "I mean every word I have said, and everything at which I have hinted in 'Dorian Gray.'" The journalist shook his head. "Then, all I can say is that if you do mean them you are very likely to find yourself at Bow Street [standing in a courtroom] one of these days."

Lord Henry Wotton became, to most readers, Oscar Wilde—the amusing, diverting bons mots, the wave of the cigarette, the witty, rapid-fire chatter that offers sparkles with laughter, wisdom, or immorality, and the disarming endorsements of rich, sensual pleasures. The novel paints a vivid portrait of the author, which, like Dorian's own, is first beautiful and then frightening. The name Dorian Gray was inspired by a famously pretty young poet, John Gray, who won Oscar Wilde's affections after Clyde Fitch left for America.

The Picture of Dorian Gray was published as a book in 1891. Wilde made slight adjustments and deleted a few—only a few—of the suggestive lines. Bookseller W. H. Smith refused to sell it, calling it "filthy." Constance Wilde, Oscar's wife, was haunted by the slender novel, but naively overlooked its significance. "Since Oscar wrote 'Dorian Gray,'" she said, "no one will talk to us." It was his only novel.

In 1891, Wilde was proposed for membership in a literary association, the Crabbet Club. There, George Curzon, the politician and an old acquaintance from Oxford, stood to address his qualifications. He ended up frankly detailing Wilde's taste for sodomy at Oxford and then moving on to the hints of this activity in *Dorian Gray*. "Poor Oscar," a friend observed, "sat helplessly smiling, a fat mass, in his chair." Wilde gathered his composure and offered a typically witty and insightful defense. But he never went back to the Crabbet Club.

Just as "The Portrait of Mr. W.H." had once seduced Clyde

Fitch, Wilde had inspired a particularly adoring fan with *The Picture of Dorian Gray*. Lord Alfred Douglas, a student at Oxford, an aspiring poet with blond hair and bright blue eyes, had read the book fourteen times. He eagerly arranged a meeting with the author to tell him so.

———— · · ————

Stoker must have noticed the story, too. Some of his earliest pages of notes on his vampire story show the influence. He considered the inclusion of a character who was a painter, Francis Aytown, and noted characteristics of the vampire that would make him the anti–Dorian Gray:

> Painters cannot paint him [Dracula]—their likenesses always like someone else.
> Could not photograph—come out like a corpse or black.
> Insensitivity to music.
> Power of creating evil thoughts—& destroying will.

Neither the painter nor the failed portrait made it into Stoker's novel, but he was clearly experimenting with supernatural themes that would adorn his vampire. The influence from Wilde's story is seen in more subtle ways.

Like Dorian Gray's, Dracula's crimes are sometimes left to the imagination—or suicide signals that a noble man has chosen death rather than disgrace. This is true when the vampire crosses on the *Demeter*; the crew disappears during the voyage, without further explanation. In *Dracula*, the first mate commits suicide, throwing himself overboard. The captain is found dead, lashed to the wheel. The actual threats and the actual crimes are left unstated. Presumably Dracula's very presence creates the danger.

———•·•———

Wilde went on to conquer the London theater, not with the lavish spectacles he'd so admired at the Lyceum, or even his poetic *Salome*, which was published but had a difficult time finding its way onto the stage. Instead, he produced a succession of witty, satirical, drawing-room comedies. Florence Stoker accepted a ticket for the premiere of *Lady Windermere's Fan* at the St. James Theatre on February 22, 1892. (Bram was busy that night with *Henry VIII*, starring Irving as Cardinal Wolsey.) *Lady Windermere* was the famous premiere where Wilde arrived wearing a dyed bright green carnation, surrounded by a group of admiring young men who were similarly adorned with green carnations. This was Wilde's little trick to stir gossip, suggesting a special club from which the rest of society had been excluded. After the curtain fell, a loud ovation drew the author to the stage. Wilde appeared, wearing his surreal green flower, indolently holding a half-smoked cigarette in his fingers, and carelessly congratulating the audience on their good taste— "which persuades me that you think almost as highly of the play as I do myself!"—the sort of performance that made him famous.

Surprisingly, it was those green carnations that proved to be the problem.

———•·•———

The Green Carnation was published anonymously in 1894, but it soon became known that it was the work of Robert Hichens, a young journalist and novelist who had befriended Alfred Douglas during a recent trip in Egypt. Just several years after *The Green Carnation*, Robert Hichens entered Bram Stoker's circle of associates when he was hired by Henry Irving to write *The Medicine Man*—the particularly ineffective supernatural play.

The anonymous novel was a parody of Oscar Wilde and Lord Alfred Douglas—a completely transparent parody, from the famous green carnations to the names of the characters, Esme Amarinth and Lord Reginald Hastings. Wilde and Douglas were first amused by it, but in offering a privileged view of their relationship, it surrounded them with scandal. In the book, Amarinth—Wilde—was portrayed as the corrupting influence, like Henry Wotton in *Dorian Gray*. Hastings—Douglas—slavishly imitates his conversation and his morality. Hastings explains the symbol of the green carnation "to have the courage of one's desires, instead of only the cowardice of other people's. . . . Do you love this carnation . . . as I love it? It is like some exquisite painted creature with dyed hair and brilliant eyes It has the supreme merit of being perfectly unnatural. To be unnatural is often to be great. To be natural is generally to be stupid."

The book was probably not representative of Wilde and Douglas; it seems that Douglas was far more manipulative than Wilde, actively seeking out "rent boys" for their entertainment, arguing, pouting, or cajoling to keep the relationship going.

The Green Carnation inflamed Lord Alfred Douglas's father, the Marquess of Queensberry. The marquess was a mean-spirited, bowlegged little man with pugilistic sensibility—quite literally, as he had devised the Marquess of Queensberry rules for boxing. His wife had divorced him—a highly unusual and difficult procedure in Victorian England, attesting to his abusive treatment of his family. His four sons hated him to various degrees; they had spent their childhood abused or neglected. In 1893, when the marquess first realized that his youngest son was keeping company with Oscar Wilde, he first warned him and then threatened him. When none of that worked, he threatened Wilde.

Alfred Douglas—his friends called him Bosie—encouraged the feud and relished the thought of a definitive showdown with his father. Ironically, it did not have to happen. Wilde's tendency was to make peace. One day when he was lunching with Bosie, the marquess came into the restaurant and saw them together; Wilde invited him to the table and then succeeded in charming the older man completely. "I don't wonder you are so fond of him," the marquess confessed to his son. "He is a wonderful man."

But after the marquess left the lunch meeting, the glow of Wilde's charm was forgotten.

The marquess was a crude man of crude threats and simple thoughts; that much is demonstrated by his correspondence. But the urgency of his concern was borne out by a real tragedy. In October 1894, just a month after *The Green Carnation* was published, Queensberry's eldest son, Lord Drumlanrig, the heir to the title and Alfred Douglas's brother, was killed in a hunting accident.

At least, newspapers politely reported that it was an accident. It was almost certainly a suicide; he had shot himself in the mouth. Drumlanrig had been the secretary to the Earl of Rosebery when Rosebery was foreign secretary, and then a junior minister in the House of Lords when Rosebery became prime minister. The two had been suspected of a homosexual relationship. These rumors had been rattling the windows of the government and there was fear that it would ruin Rosebery's career—rumors that may have been made worse by the marquess's writing threatening letters to Rosebery.

Rosebery was the prime minister who would, within the year, be writing to Henry Irving, informing him of his knighthood.

With Drumlanrig's suicide, and the obsession that his sons were being preyed upon by secret, highly placed homosexuals, Queensberry turned up the pressure on Oscar Wilde.

Wilde's private life had been intruding into his career. In 1893, for his second play, *A Woman of No Importance*, Fred Terry, Ellen Terry's brother, was engaged to portray Gerald Arbuthnot. He hated the part and the ridiculous, unrealistic dialogue that Wilde used. He recalled one particular line in which Gerald, a young man, said to his father: "I suppose society is wonderfully delightful." Fred Terry associated the dialogue with the "unhealthy, unnatural" manner of Oscar Wilde, the artificiality of the green carnation. Offstage, Terry and his friends ridiculed Wilde for his obvious homosexuality.

The play was probably Wilde's least successful, but it gave the producer and star Herbert Beerbohm Tree an opportunity to play a larger-than-life, Oscar Wilde–inspired character, Lord Illingworth. The comedy centers around the lord's discovery that his new private secretary, Gerald, happens to be his illegitimate son, which leads to other revelations about his past relationship with Gerald's mother, Mrs. Arbuthnot.

During the preparation of the play, a seventeen-year-old boy named Alfred Wood made a dangerous threat. He had spent time with Oscar and Bosie, and accidentally acquired a letter between the two of them. In the letter, Wilde noted how Douglas's lips were made "for madness of kisses" and pledged his "undying love." Wood sent a copy of the letter to Herbert Beerbohm Tree, who quietly alerted Wilde to the threat. Tree, of course, was Irving's chief competition in London, the man who finally lured Ellen Terry from the Lyceum to star in *The Merry Wives of Windsor*.

Wilde's following play, *An Ideal Husband*, in January 1895, led to even more difficulty. Charles Brookfield was an actor and playwright who had developed an intense hatred for Wilde— supposedly it stemmed from Wilde's criticism of Brookfield for not removing his gloves at a tea party. The remark, and Brookfield's disproportionate reaction, suggests a plot from a Wilde comedy, but the actor simmered for years. He wrote a parody of *Lady Windermere's Fan* in 1892 and then was cast as the butler in *An Ideal Husband*, which gave him special access to observe Oscar Wilde, his mannerisms, and his friends. "There came a time when he could not keep Wilde out of his talk," a friend observed.

———————

The Marquess of Queensberry planned to ruin the opening of Wilde's fourth comedy, *The Importance of Being Earnest*, on February 14, 1895. He would wait until Wilde was called to the stage at the conclusion, then stand in the audience and denounce him as a dangerous, immoral man, hurling a bouquet of rotting vegetables. Bosie heard about the plan, and Wilde alerted the police. The marquess, and his bouquet, were denied entrance.

Wilde arrived at the St. James Theatre, proudly wearing a green carnation, and listened to the rolling laughter of the audience and the loud bursts of applause. *The Importance of Being Earnest* was his most successful play—that was instantly apparent, from the response of that first crowd. The *New York Times* reported that the play had, "by a single stroke of the pen, put [Wilde's] enemies under his feet." But the spell it cast lasted for exactly two weeks.

On February 28, Wilde called at the Albemarle Club, where he was a member, and was handed a calling card that had been left for him by the Marquess of Queensberry ten days earlier. Wilde turned the card over and found the message: "To Oscar Wilde, ponce and Somdomite."

At least that's what it appeared to read. The handwriting was sloppy and there was an obvious misspelling. The marquess later insisted that he'd written "To Oscar Wilde, posing as a Sodomite." This became important, as it was a much easier charge to defend.

Wilde was devastated by this accusation, but Bosie convinced him to see a lawyer and press charges. Queensberry was arrested and accused of libel; the trial was set for April 1895. Wilde's friends could see that he was doomed. Frank Harris told him, "You are sure to lose," as Queensberry would present himself as a father defending his son and the jury would find this irresistible. At a lunch, Harris and George Bernard Shaw urged Wilde to immediately leave London for Paris and then begin asking for forgiveness in the press. Wilde was shocked by their certainty, but by now he was in Bosie's thrall—he had to trust him—and he had to convince himself that he would win.

Charles Brookfield, the actor who became Wilde's enemy, was

happy to share the results of his observations. Queensberry also hired several investigators to scour London for additional evidence against Wilde. One of these investigators was John G. Littlechild, who had become convinced of Francis Tumblety's guilt during the Jack the Ripper case and had now retired from the Metropolitan Police. Littlechild found the incriminating letter between Wilde and Douglas—once a subject of blackmail—and a handful of "rent boys" who would testify about their assignations, as well as hotel employees who had witnessed Wilde's sleeping arrangements with his guests.

———•◦•———

Wilde arrived at the Old Bailey in Bow Street on April 3 in a stylish carriage with liveried attendants. He was neatly dressed and carefully composed. He wanted to present the picture of self-assurance for the court, for the legal wrangles had become excruciating and were taking a toll on his health. During the trial he was questioned by Edward Carson, engaged as Queensberry's barrister. Carson had been a boyhood friend of Wilde's from Trinity, but if Wilde expected any favors extended, he was wrong. Carson was persistent. Wilde's usual flippancy and charm wilted under the pressure. Oscar was quickly caught lying about his age. When he was asked about the unnamed sins of Dorian Gray, Oscar was first elusive: "What Dorian Gray's sins are, no one knows. He who finds them has brought them." But as Carson pushed, Wilde was forced to admit that he had revised the text for the book, omitting a phrase because "it would convey the impression that the sin of Dorian Gray was sodomy."

Then Carson switched to another subject, Wilde's relationships with a long list of boys—some mere "rent boys." Wilde was exasperated by the sordid tone of the questions and Carson's excruciating attempt to detail these visits. To the jury, it seemed incredible that England's great writer could have spent so much time at dinners, or on walks, or in conversations in his hotel rooms, with such common young men.

On the second day, Wilde was visibly exhausted when he was questioned about one particular boy. "Did you kiss him?" Oscar was asked. He drawled, "Oh no, never in my life; he was a peculiarly plain boy—" Carson stopped him. "He was what?" Wilde stammered, attempting to complete his thought. ". . . His appearance was so very unfortunately—very ugly—I mean, I pitied him for it."

Wilde knew he'd made a terrible mistake and tried to shrug off the remark. Carson let it sink in for the jury. "Didn't you give me as the reason that you never kissed him that he was too ugly?"

That evening, Wilde's legal council, Sir Edward Clarke, encouraged his client to leave the country, but Wilde was now tired, disgusted, and determined to stay. The next morning, Clarke explained Wilde's offer to withdraw the case, admitting that he had been "posing as a sodomite" only in terms of his writing. But the justice would not allow him to restrict the verdict that way: Queensberry would have to be judged guilty or not guilty of libel. The jury was excused and, within minutes, returned with a verdict: The Marquess of Queensberry was not guilty of libel and was justified in his accusation that Wilde was a sodomite.

The courtroom burst into applause for the marquess.

The muck that had been sloshed about during the libel trial—
Carson's list of young men and the details of their meetings—
would now, certainly, result in a charge against Wilde and his
arrest. Carson had won the case; he'd done what he'd had to. But
he also realized the cost. That night Edward Carson told his wife,
"I have ruined the most brilliant man in London."

Wilde was arrested that same evening and put into a cell at the
Bow Street police station. Sodomy would have been too difficult a
charge to prove. Wilde was charged with indecency, under the
Labouchère Amendment.

———————

A woman in a heavy veil arrived at Wilde's Tite Street house, leaving a horseshoe, for luck, and a bunch of violets. Laurence Irving,
the grandson and biographer of Henry Irving, was later convinced
that the veiled lady was Ellen Terry. The clue was the violets, the
favorite flowers of Terry and Henry Irving, a code that the couple
was offering support. Around this time, Terry also wrote to Constance Wilde. "Be of good cheer & when you can give me please a
wee sign of you[.] I suppose I could be of no use to you or you wd
have written? . . . I hope yr little boys are ever so well. I send my
dear love to you—if it can not serve you, it at least can do no harm."

Terry's vague good wishes indicated that it was now difficult
to offer support to both husband and wife. Oscar Wilde had gathered a small group of supporters, and, out of self-defense, Constance had found her own. She now accepted the evidence that
she'd politely ignored for years and sought legal advice about the
best way to protect her children from their father's publicity as
well as his debt. Creditors moved in. The Wildes lost their Tite

Street house and most of their possessions, including Oscar's library, his letters to Constance, and the children's toys.

Constance informed Lady Wilde, Oscar's ailing mother, that she had decided to change the boys' last name in an effort to insulate them from scandal. They became Constance, Vyvyan, and Cyril Holland, and later she sued for divorce.

Wilde's trial started on April 26, 1895, and lasted for five days. It was even more sordid, even more desperate, than the Queensberry trial. Wilde's biographer Richard Ellmann wrote, "Never in the nineties was so much unsavory evidence given so much publicity." Wilde was now disheveled, gaunt, and careworn. But during his cross-examination, Sir Charles Gill sought to trap him by asking, "What is the love that dare not speak its name?" Wilde drew himself up and answered in measured tones:

> It is that deep, spiritual affection that is as pure as it is perfect. . . . It is in this century misunderstood that it may be described as the love that dare not speak its name, and on account of it I am placed where I am now. It is beautiful, it is fine, it is the noblest form of affections. There is nothing unnatural about it. It is intellectual and it repeatedly exists between an elder and a younger man, when the elder man has intellect, and the younger man has all the joy, hope and glamour of life before him. . . .

It was one of the finest, most remarkable moments of a brilliant career—even more so because it was apparent that the career was ending. His speech earned applause, but the jury failed to reach a verdict.

———•———

The final trial began May 22. Now it was being tried by Sir Frank Lockwood, the solicitor general himself. The evidence offered the same testimony, the same sordid sensations. Throughout the trials, newspaper headlines had been screaming of Wilde's scandals. Like Mr. Hyde or Dorian Gray, they could never report details of the crimes, which were too awful for publication and had to be imagined, perhaps even exaggerated, by the readers.

On May 24, 1895, as the trial wound to a conclusion, Bram Stoker was summoned to Henry Irving's flat to hear the news that he'd been offered a knighthood. When they rode to Ellen Terry's home to tell her the news, it is certain that the three friends not only celebrated Irving's honor but sadly discussed the Wilde trial, which had occupied the week's headlines.

On Saturday, May 25, the day that Irving's knighthood was officially announced to the public, Oscar Wilde's trial concluded. He was found guilty.

The judge turned to Wilde, who was standing in the dock.

The jury have arrived at a correct verdict in this case. . . . People who can do these things must be dead to all sense of shame, and one cannot hope to produce any effect upon them. It is the worst case I have ever tried. . . . That you, Wilde, have been in the center of a circle of extensive corruption of the most hideous kind among young men [is] impossible to doubt. I shall, under such circumstances, be expected to pass the severest sentence that the law allows ... [that] you be imprisoned and kept to hard labor for two years.

"My god, my god!" Wilde muttered. "And I? May I say nothing, my lord?" His remarks could barely be heard above the gasps and the hissed cries of "Shame!" He seemed to buckle at the knees, and then struggle to remain standing. He was allowed to say nothing. The warders took him by the arms and pulled him from the court. It was finished.

May 25, 1895, offered the proudest honor that the theatrical profession had ever received; and then, just hours later, the day ended with the greatest humiliation the theatrical profession had ever endured. In recalling that day, Bram Stoker refused to mention Oscar Wilde.

Shortly after Oscar Wilde's conviction, his brother, Willie, wrote to Bram Stoker. The two had been boyhood friends in Dublin. "Bram, my friend, poor Oscar was *not* as bad as people thought him. He was led astray by his vanity & conceit & he was so 'got at' that he was weak enough to be guilty of indiscretions and follies—that is *all.* I believe this thing will help to purify him body and soul. Am sure you and Florence must have felt the disgrace of one who cared for you both sincerely."

During Wilde's trial, Stoker was still assembling notes on the novel and was probably in the process of writing his first draft. Just two years later, on May 26, 1897, *Dracula* would be published.

––––––––

Author Talia Schaffer's analysis of *Dracula* is titled "'A Wilde Desire Took Me.'" In it she identifies a number of images and references woven into Stoker's novel, conscious or subconscious ties to Oscar Wilde. For example, when Jonathan Harker finds Dracula in his coffin, sated from a meal of blood, he describes a face that seems transformed from the pale, thin Count who welcomed him at the castle. Now Dracula reminds us of Wilde.

> There lay the Count . . . the cheeks were fuller, and the white skin seemed ruby-red underneath; the mouth was redder than ever. . . . Even the deep, burning eyes seemed set amongst swollen flesh, for the lids and pouches underneath were bloated. It seemed as if the whole awful creature were simply gorged with blood; he lay like a filthy leech, exhausted with his repletion.

A newspaper described Wilde at his trial as "ponderous and fleshy, his face dusky red." Frank Harris remembered Wilde critically as "oily and fat . . . his jowel was already fat and pouchy. His appearance filled me with distaste. . . . The carven mouth, too, with its heavy, chiseled, purple tinged lips . . ."

Schaffer likewise found similarities between the dark dens of Wilde's "rent boys," where sunlight was excluded, and the dank crypts that formed Dracula's bedroom—the vampire literally slept in dirt. When the vampire hunters destroy Dracula's coffins, they note that the act is "purification," the virtual word applied by Willie Wilde to Oscar's punishment.

Of course, Oscar Wilde was precisely the sort of author who would be expected to encode messages or key words into his texts. Bram Stoker was not. The literary references in *Dracula* are apparent, often clumsy, or applied like a paper-thin veneer. It becomes difficult to imagine Stoker plotting his adventure and simultaneously planting concealed references to Wilde. We're reminded of Samuel Goldwyn's famous advice to his film writers, "If you want to send a message, use Western Union."

But it is equally easy to imagine how elements of Wilde's friendship, Wilde's fame and fall from grace, left subconscious evidence as Stoker was constructing his story. The evidence is tempting.

Stoker's 1890 notes did not originally include the little crucifix that Jonathan Harker receives from a peasant woman as he leaves for Dracula's castle—"For your mother's sake." This scene was integrated into the story as Stoker was writing it, presumably around 1895, after Wilde's trial.

Harker's crucifix is the talisman that saves his life when he cuts himself shaving. It repels Dracula's reflexive attack. A similar crucifix in the hand of Van Helsing, "a little gold crucifix," drives away the vampire after he defiles Mina.

When he added the crucifix to his story, wouldn't Bram Stoker have remembered his wife's little gold crucifix? This had once been a gift from Oscar Wilde, a pledge of his love for Florence, and was returned to Wilde after she chose to marry Bram.

That little cross, passing between them, was the talisman of Florence's near-tragic romance. It was the object that had once united three friends and rivals during their carefree days in Dublin. Stoker was certainly mindful of the great man, suddenly powerless to help himself; he had made a wreck of his own existence and then corrupted so many others with a dangerous kiss.

Fourteen

THE STRANGER, "HERE I AM NOBLE"

After Oscar Wilde's conviction, the theater critic Clement Scott wrote in the *Daily Telegraph*, "Open the windows! Let in the fresh air."

Henry Labouchère sniffed that he was sorry that Wilde had been sentenced to only two years in jail; his amendment, he claimed, had originally suggested seven years. But by 1895, Labouchère had made a specialty of misremembering the details behind his amendment; he was anxious to portray himself as a hero. Now he was on the public's side by excoriating the playwright. Wilde's imprisonment was a fine thing, Labby declared in his magazine, *Truth*. "Far from his being any the worse for the imprisonment, there seems to be every reason to anticipate that he will benefit by it physically, if not morally."

The Marquess of Queensberry sent a letter to the editor of the *Star*, dismissing the idea of sympathy. "I would treat [Wilde] with all possible consideration as a sexual pervert of an utterly diseased mind, and not as a sane criminal. If this is sympathy, Mr. Wilde has it from me to this extent."

Actor Fred Terry recalled a joke that circulated through the

profession. "Which was Wilde's favorite play?" "Obviously, 'A
Woman's of No Importance!'"

When Oscar Wilde's trial had begun, two of his successful
comedies were playing in the West End, *An Ideal Husband* and
The Importance of Being Earnest. With the scandal, Wilde's name
was removed from the signboards and programs at the theaters.
For a short time, the plays continued, drawing laughs and an occasional catcall. Then the plays were withdrawn. Julia Neilson, an
actress in *An Ideal Husband*, remembered, "Public feeling ran so
high against Wilde that our audience vanished."

Wilde was taken to Pentonville, where he worked on the tread-
mill and was given general labor, making postbags, or picking
oakum—pulling apart the fibers of old ropes so that they could be
used for insulation. He was transferred to Wandsworth and, later,
Reading, where he worked in the gardens and in the library.

Oscar Wilde was released on May 18, 1897, and headed immediately to France. He was reconciled with Alfred Douglas but
never with his wife and children. "The Ballad of Reading Gaol," a
poem written after his release, was published in 1898. Wilde spent
his last years in self-imposed exile, living meagerly, supported by
his friends. He died in Paris on November 30, 1900. His long, confessionary letter to Alfred Douglas, his understanding of their relationship, was published as the essay, "De Profundis." This was
composed at Reading and published five years after Oscar Wilde's
death.

———◦◦◦———

Stoker's perfect silence about Wilde is now impossible to interpret,
except that he intended to give no interpretation. If we look at the

reactions of his friends, Stoker's silence might suggest his genuine discomfort.

An associate of Hall Caine recalled Caine's deep shock just after Wilde's conviction: "To think of it! That man, that genius as he is, whom you and I have seen feted and flattered. . . . It haunts me. It is like some foul and horrible stain on our craft and on us all, which nothing can wash out. It is the most awful tragedy in the whole history of literature."

It's easy to imagine Bram Stoker struck with the same impression—hurt and deep embarrassment for the profession. Irving and Terry were two of the few actors who refused to criticize Wilde, even after his conviction. They sent their best wishes—through Wilde's friend Charles Ricketts—just before Oscar's release from prison. Ellen Terry explained her own reactions in her autobiography. As expected, she was deeply honest and compassionate. "When Oscar was found guilty of that unnameable sin . . . I was revolted by his very name," she wrote. "Then he wrote 'De Profundis' . . . it purified Oscar and I loved him again." Once again, it's easy to imagine Stoker sharing this view; certainly Ellen Terry's magnanimity would have had a strong influence on him.

Terry told how, after Wilde's release, she visited Paris with her friend Aimee Lowther when they saw "a man gazing wolfishly into a pastrycook's windows, biting his fingers." They recognized Oscar and went to speak with him. "We induced him to come and eat with us in a quiet hotel and for a while he sparkled, just as of old."

This recollection is especially interesting, as a Stoker family rumor held that Bram Stoker later visited Paris, quietly taking money to Wilde. Perhaps this kindness was Stoker's own idea or

Florence's suggestion; she later referred to her old Dublin beau as "poor Oscar." Or maybe Stoker was reprising his usual role as the emissary for Irving and Terry. There's no evidence of this mission to Paris, but—true or not—the significance of the story is that Stoker's support seemed possible, and even logical, within his family.

Although the book was published just after he left Reading, there's no evidence that Wilde ever read *Dracula*.

———

One of the continuing puzzles of *Dracula* is the author's view of his inspirations. For many years, there was a necessary corollary to the theory, "Henry Irving is Count Dracula." That was, "Bram Stoker hated his boss." Could Stoker have imagined Henry Irving as an ancient villain, an unholy creature? Was he intending to wreak his revenge, after a long career, within the pages of his novel? Similarly, could Stoker have imagined Walt Whitman as the devil? Could he have been so incensed at his failure to self-censure that he attempted to pass judgment on the wise old poet? Did Oscar Wilde's imprisonment signal something much deeper than embarrassment and confusion? Could Stoker have truly come to loathe him and then portray him as a dangerous, unholy beast?

There are hints within the book. Dracula, considered one of literature's greatest villains, may not have been a villain in the novel that bears his name. He almost perfectly matches the description of a Byronic hero.

Lord Byron introduced the convention in *Childe Harold's Pilgrimage*, written in 1812, a poem that was thought to be partly autobiographical. The character type returned in other works of his, such as *Manfred* and *The Corsair*. Unlike most protagonists, Byron's heroes were dark, haunted characters—combinations of charm and cruelty and unapologetic about their situations. They were nobles who might find themselves cast as rebels, in exile or seeking revenge. His inspiration is often thought to be Milton's Lucifer, a powerful but flawed character.

Byron's Conrad, in the poem *The Corsair*, epitomizes the Byronic hero:

He knew himself a villain—but he deem'd
The rest no better than the thing he seem'd; . . .
He knew himself detested, but he knew
The hearts that loath'd him, crouch'd and dreaded too.
Lone, wild, and strange, he stood alike exempt
From all affection and from all contempt.

The connection to Lord Byron is tempting, in terms of literary history. Byron was the guest at Lake Geneva in 1816 who suggested that everyone write a ghost story. This was the impetus for *Frankenstein*, and Byron's physician and traveling companion, John Polidori, wrote *The Vampyre*, which became the model of the aristocratic vampire. Polidori may have used his employer, Byron, as a model for the vampire, just as Stoker later used his employer, Irving.

Varney the Vampire, the vampire novel that preceded *Dracula*, first suggested the idea of a sympathetic vampire, frustrated by his own dilemma. But Stoker's Dracula is something more and exhibits the pride and the blindness that would have earned him a place in tragedy.

Dracula is a mysterious nobleman with a tragic past. He triumphed in war and endured through centuries due to his peculiar curse. In Transylvania, Dracula functions very efficiently. He is surrounded by a group of "brides" who depend upon him and who, in the past, must have shared a relationship with him. His necessary crimes seem easy in that setting, and perhaps even expected. (The novel portrays only one mother whose child has been stolen.) The local residents fear him but obediently work for him.

His mistake is in aspiring to something more. He confesses to Jonathan Harker:

> I long to go through the crowded streets of your mighty London, to be in the midst of the whirl and rush of humanity, to share its life, its change, its death, and all that makes it what it is. . . . Here I am a noble; I am boyar; the common people know me, and here I am master. But a stranger in a strange land, he is no one; men know him not—and to know not is to care not for. . . . I have been so long master that I would be master still— or at least that none other should be master of me.

Why does he wish to go to London? There is that awful pun that the vampire wishes to "share its life," but Dracula presumably can find all the blood he needs in Transylvania. Jonathan Harker imagines infesting the city with a new circle of demons, but Dracula himself neither proselytizes nor recruits. He goes to London because he "longs." He aspires to the city because it offers "the whirl and rush of humanity."

Immediately, he has difficulty when he confronts contemporary society. Jonathan Harker does not obey. In London, Dracula's early crimes draw reprisal. His victims refuse to be complacent. He is hunted down and driven from the city. When he finally admits defeat and races back to Transylvania, he is not allowed a retreat. The vampire hunters anticipate his route by analyzing his experience in battle. They chase him back to his castle and punish him.

In this case, Dracula's great crime is overreaching, the same way the Greeks would have portrayed his hubris. He cannot properly evaluate the new world, its moral men and intelligent women, just as he is surprised by the touches of innovation that surround him: shorthand, the typewriter, the phonograph. Had Dracula remained in Transylvania, the tragedy would not have taken place as, presumably, he had found a way to exist peacefully in Transylvania for centuries.

This perspective changes the story. Stoker similarly saw that Whitman's poetry was perfect in its artistry until it was included in certain books and distributed to certain readers (like the sarcastic young men at Trinity).

Wilde was free to exercise his personal choices within the cloistered worlds of literature and the theater, but by overreaching, by boldly expressing those views to the general society, he had to be driven back.

Similarly, Henry Irving's career could be seen as a West Country actor, a man of little education, who made an assault on the London theater. There he found an uncomfortable fit with society. He was criticized by highbrows for his lowbrow tastes and he fought for acceptance from critics and intellectuals because he had aspired to be a part of the "whirl and rush" of the great capital city, organizing its greatest theater.

Irving was an instinctive actor but not an intellect. He received only limited education and never gave speeches extemporaneously; he memorized the words and then acted as if it were extemporaneous. He could make plays sensational; he could make parts dramatic. But when the taste for spectacle changed, he had no instinct for a new direction, nor would he trust the intellect of others. Shaw, Conan Doyle, and Stoker tried to tempt him into modern productions, without success. Eventually, he was pushed out of the Lyceum.

If Dracula is a Byronic hero, we see the tragedy of his place in modern society and anticipate the inevitable punishment for his aspirations. Dracula withdraws into the story—becoming less of a character and more of a dilemma, a pestilence—but his "humanity" comes to be recognized by Mina, who forms a psychic connection with him and generates sympathy for him. She insists that the pursuit of the hunters should not be "a work of hate." She believes, "That poor soul who has wrought all this misery is the saddest case of all. Just think what will be his joy when he, too, is destroyed in his worser part that his better part may have spiritual immortality. You must be pitiful to him, too, though it may not hold your hands from his destruction."

When Mina watches Dracula die, she notices a surprising "look of peace" in his face, "such as I never could have imagined might have rested there before."

In creating the character of Dracula, Bram Stoker may have been inspired by the great men of his life, their flaws, and their limitations. But the puzzling, tragic elements of Dracula's character suggest that Stoker could always have sympathy—not hatred—for these inspirations.

Readers have identified little bits of Bram Stoker within the novel; the author used his own traits and preferences in conjunction with other characters'. As the protagonist at the start of the story, Jonathan Harker shares Stoker's profession, solicitor. He probably experiences Stoker's dream, the attack of the vampire brides and the appearance of Dracula. When locked in Castle Dracula, he becomes a mixture of clerk and adventurer, a perfect blend of Stoker's fastidious job of Acting Manager and his taste for athleticism.

With the introduction of Abraham Van Helsing, we see traces of Stoker again. The most obvious clue is the character's name. Abraham is the author's name, as well as his father's name. Van Helsing is an insightful researcher and a thorough investigator. He is gallant with women and fatherly in his advice. To all the people around him, he is the man with the answers, the man who is able to solve the problems and describe a course of action.

Paul Murray, Bram Stoker's biographer, suggested that Dracula also exhibits Stoker-like qualities. "Like Dracula . . . Stoker is a man of many parts, willing to turn his hand to more or less anything. Just as Stoker tackled a multiplicity of roles for Irving, so the Count has made himself generally useful, acting as a coachman, cook and domestic servant. He also arranges travel and transport (his boxes of earth resembling the theatrical baggage which Stoker looked after), reading reference works and dabbling in the law. Like Stoker, too, he is immensely strong physically."

Stoker also saves the very best lines for Dracula, and, as previously noted, gives him the only literate or poetic voice in the novel.

Bram Stoker as Dracula? It's an interesting picture. He was a boy from Dublin who toiled away as a civil servant, set his sights on a literary or theatrical career, and aspired to life in London. Once there, he had success and acceptance in some areas—primarily as the Lyceum's Acting Manager. In London, he also discovered disappointing limitations: personally, as an Irish immigrant, and professionally, as a writer. In fact, this was apparent when he visited America, where he seemed more interesting to the press than he was in England.

If Stoker could imagine himself as a Byronic hero, it was a sign of the successes of the men around him, Wilde and Irving. Stoker's own career left him feeling unappreciated and out of place. The best clue about his building resentment is his confession to Frederick Donaghey, the Chicago newspaperman: "If I am able to afford to have my name on [*Dracula*] the Governor certainly can afford, with business bad, to have his name on the play. But he laughs at me whenever I talk about it." Beyond that, Stoker's view of himself in the novel must be left to speculation. The careful, stoic author never explained.

During his long, protracted process of writing *Dracula*, Stoker had published another book, *The Shoulder of Shasta*, in 1895. The book was a return to Stoker's typical adventure stories, here set in the California west; Stoker had visited San Francisco with the Lyceum tour. The story concerns Esse Elstree, a young English heiress, who falls in love with Grizzly Dick, a rough-around-the-edges trapper and guide. The *Athenaeum* didn't like it: "The want of maturity and sense of humor may be due to haste, for the book bears the stamp of being roughly and carelessly put together. Mr. Stoker can probably do much better work than this."

Of course, he did better work two years later, with his famous vampire. But his next novel, *Miss Betty*, provided another sharp contrast. *Miss Betty* was written in 1890, when he began his notes for *Dracula*, but it wasn't published until March 1898. The book was dedicated to Florence and was an eighteenth-century romance about a pretty heiress and a highwayman. Critics found it charming and sweet and, of course, they couldn't resist the contrast with *Dracula*. "We had a most unpleasant recollection of a *nuit blanche* which followed the reading of *Dracula*," the *Bookman* reviewer wrote. "But Mr. Bram Stoker had prepared a delightful surprise. . . . It is almost impossible to believe that both novels came from the same pen." *Miss Betty* was given a copyright performance at the Lyceum in January 1898 but must have been another disappointment for Stoker; it never resurfaced as a play.

Henry Irving's famous Lyceum found itself in an unfortunate downhill slide—the scenery fire, the failed productions, and chronic overspending conspired against the actor. In 1898, Irving was struck with pleurisy and pneumonia in Glasgow during a tour. Stoker realized how sick he'd been; he claimed that Irving went through hundreds of pocket handkerchiefs each week, coughing into them and then deftly tucking the handkerchiefs into his pocket or in a corner of his dressing table before reaching for another. The theater was temporarily closed and Irving went to Bournemouth to recover.

Ellen Terry saw him there, "twiddling his poor thumbs and thinking out the best way to get to work again. He is ruined in pocket, heavily in debt." During his convalescence, he was visited by representatives of the Lyceum company. They outlined a proposition to purchase his interest in the theater. Irving saw the cash offer as a quick solution to his financial straits, and he desperately agreed to the terms. He was to stay on as actor-manager and transfer his interests to the company; in exchange, he would commit to performances at the Lyceum and tours of England and America.

The agreement was made without consulting Stoker, who was then on a ship for America to arrange the next tour. When Irving told him the details of the arrangement, Stoker was horrified. "I protested to Irving against the scheme." In working through the figures, Stoker saw that Irving would turn over everything, then relinquish a percentage of his salary and share the costs of future productions. "The contract which Irving made," Stoker later reported, "was not in any way a beneficial one for him, but an excellent one for them."

The arrangement may have been a sign of Irving's gradual withdrawal from his associates and perhaps a growing mistrust of Stoker. When he became especially secretive, he made foolish decisions. "Quiet, patient, tolerant, impersonal, gentle," Ellen Terry noted his traits at this time, "close, crafty. Crafty sounds unkind, but it is H.I."

Much of Stoker's work had been done quietly, behind Irving's back—a continual scramble to accede to the boss's elaborate wishes and still balance the books without him noticing the effort. When the theater was successful, Stoker's delicate dance went unnoticed. When the business failed, his dancing looked futile, especially to Henry Irving.

Years later, Laurence Irving, the actor's grandson and biographer, criticized Stoker for his business failings. "Stoker, inflated with literary and athletic pretensions, worshipped Irving, reveling . . . in the opportunities to rub shoulders with the great." Stoker's inclination to please the boss and flatter him left Stoker "handicapped . . . in dealing with Irving's business affairs in a forthright and sensible manner. . . . Irving got the service he deserved, but at a cost which was no less fatal because it was not immediately apparent."

The record demonstrates that Stoker was more right than he was wrong. Those who had known Irving and Stoker realized Stoker's importance to the Lyceum. "Had it not been for his old friend Bram Stoker," Henry Labouchère said, "Irving would have been eaten out of home and theatre very speedily."

In 1903, when the Lyceum company completely collapsed, the board debated turning it into a music hall. Stoker attended the meeting, expecting that he would be assigned the blame, with Irving, for the poor receipts.

Instead, Stoker prepared a careful report, filled with facts and figures, demonstrating how Irving had precisely fulfilled his obligations. When called upon, he stood and surprised everyone with a methodical list of facts, the profits, losses, and the receipts from Henry Irving's tours. Actually, Stoker told the board, Irving's contracted performances had swelled the company's bank account. Irving had done his part perfectly. It was the company's own mismanagement that had ruined the business.

To the shareholders, of course, this was all bad news. But they couldn't resist Stoker's rousing speech and his revelation that the great actor, suspected of being the villain, suddenly emerged as the hero. That shareholder's meeting was the perfect counterpoint to Irving's performance for Bram Stoker, "The Dream of Eugene Aram," which had inspired their relationship almost thirty years before. Now Bram Stoker's recitation paid tribute to the great, noble Henry Irving.

The shareholders stopped the meeting with loud, continuous cheers for Irving's efforts. They were, Stoker reported, "the only cheers I ever heard at a meeting of the Company."

The Lyceum was reorganized as a music hall.

———•—•———

Bram Stoker was engaged to manage Henry Irving's 1903 tour—now it was simply Henry Irving and a supporting cast, not the Lyceum company. Ellen Terry, his popular leading lady, remained in London.

On one of Ellen Terry's visits with Irving, at the end of his career, she found her old lover frail, majestic, and unexpectedly reflective. "What a wonderful life you've had, haven't you?" she found herself saying. He looked up and mumbled a response. "Oh, yes, a wonderful life . . . of work."

"What have we got out of it all?" she asked. "You and I are getting on, as they say. Henry, do you ever think as I do sometimes, what you have got out of life?"

Irving was intrigued with the conversation, and he repeated her question in a whisper before answering. "Let me see. . . . A good cigar, a good glass of wine, good friends." He smiled and kissed her hand gently.

"That's not a bad summing up," she said. "And the end . . . How would you like that to come?"

Irving mumbled the question back at her, lost in thought. "How would I like that to come?" He was silent, staring into space, for a long time: thirty seconds, Terry later recalled. She was hypnotized by the image of the noble Irving, perfectly still and completely lost in thought. Then he found his answer. He quickly caught her eyes. He lifted his hand in a dramatic gesture and snapped his fingers.

"Like that!"

Fifteen

THE FRIENDS,
"INTO THY HANDS, O LORD"

Henry Irving decided he would retire after fifty years on the stage. This was announced in 1904, to give him another two years for a leisurely farewell tour of the United States, Canada, London, and the provinces.

But in 1905, during the tour, Irving's energy began to falter. Stoker rescheduled dates and postponed appearances to accommodate his health. In October, when Irving played Bradford, he seemed especially feeble offstage. Bram Stoker dreaded the night that he would play *The Bells*. "Every time [Irving] heard the sound of the bells, the throbbing of his heart must have nearly killed him," Ellen Terry later recalled of this role. "He used always to turn quite white—there was no trick about it. It was imagination acting physically on the body. His death as Mathias—the death of a strong, robust man—was different from all his other stage deaths. He did really almost die—he imagined death with such horrible intensity. His eyes would disappear upwards, his face grow gray, his limbs cold."

When he arrived at the theater in Bradford on October 12, 1905, Irving seemed especially tired. Stoker was shocked to see him sitting in his dressing room "in a listless way." Fortunately, as he put on his costume the old actor found his energy, and he played Mathias with the expected fire and pathos. The audience hadn't been aware of any problem. But Bram Stoker watched Irving leave the stage and shuffle to his dressing room. His shoulders drooped; he seemed to collapse, a sad old man once again.

Stoker went backstage to tell his master machinist to send the scenery for *The Bells* back to London the next morning. He knew that Irving should never play it again. When he went to Irving in his dressing room that night and told him his decision, Irving just nodded quietly. Stoker felt that Henry Irving had been testing himself in the role and now seemed relieved that someone had made the decision for him.

The next morning, October 13, Irving seemed to have recovered, but he told Stoker to abandon plans for the American tour. "We can see to it later," he said. "A kindly continent to me, but I will not leave my bones there if I can help it."

That night, Irving played *Becket*, an old favorite with his public. In the final scene, during Becket's murder, Irving's last lines were "Into thy hands, O Lord, into thy hands!" Then, according to the script, he collapsed onto the stage.

Stoker went backstage to find Irving in his dressing room and offered words of encouragement: "Now you have got into your stride again, and work will be easy." Irving thought for a moment, nodded, and said, "I really think that is so." Stoker was off with the advance man from Birmingham to discuss the schedule for the following week, so he said good-bye to Irving at the theater. "Muffle up your throat, old chap!" Irving told him with a wink. "It is bitterly cold tonight and you have a cold. Take care of yourself. Good night. God bless you!"

———•—•———

Minutes later a carriage drove up to Stoker's hotel, where he was settling down to a late dinner. The driver rushed inside and told Stoker that Sir Henry was ill. He had felt weak and then fainted just after he arrived at his hotel.

Stoker rushed into the Midland Hotel and found a cluster of men standing silently in the hall, near the lobby. As he pushed his way in, the men parted. Stretched out on the floor was Henry Irving. A doctor had been summoned, and he was crouched at the actor's side.

As the doctor stood up and caught Stoker's eye, the Acting Manager felt instinctively what had just happened. He drew in his breath. The doctor shook his head and offered his condolences. Henry Irving had died just two minutes before.

Bram Stoker bent down, placing his hand against the actor's chest. For some reason he felt an absolute need to check, to know for sure, for himself. There was no heartbeat. He reached up and closed Irving's eyelids.

———•—•———

Bram Stoker had spent the last twenty-nine years of his life in service to the vital force that personified the London theater. Lawrence Barrett, an American actor who had worked with Edwin Booth, once lamented, "An actor is a sculptor who carves in snow." Every Henry Irving performance became obsolete the moment

the curtain fell. There was only the promise of a next performance. With Irving's death, the memories of those magnificent
sculptures began melting away forever.

In the hotel room, where Henry Irving had been moved, Stoker
contemplated the actor's body, now slowly illuminated by the cold,
gray dawn. "It was all so desolate and lonely, as so much of his
life had been," Stoker later wrote. He turned his attention to the
imminent whirl of events. This is what he did best, and he owed
Irving one final tour back to London. Telegrams needed to be sent
to Irving's sons. Theaters needed to be informed. The press would
be notified. Undertakers arranged. Train schedules changed and
the company sent home. Associates informed, in widening waves,
according to the immediate business need or their personal relationship to the actor.

Stoker supervised the undertaker's duties and then arranged
a visitation service at the hotel for the members of the acting
company, who would now be free to return home. He planned a
carriage for the coffin, so Irving's remains would be carried to the
Market Street Station, where the Great Northern Railway would
return Stoker and Irving to London.

Stoker's small procession passed through streets packed with
people, "a sea of faces," he recalled, who stood, hats removed,
in complete silence: "street after street of silent humanity." Bram
Stoker was stunned with the mysterious, respectful attitude of
the Bradford crowd. Apparently the entire city had assembled to
pay tribute to the actor, and Stoker's view from the carriage was
"poignant, harrowing, overwhelming." At each intersection, the
crowd took their direction from the hearse and silently parted.
As the hearse passed, the crowd closed rank again and followed.

The tribute—perfect respect, perfect silence—was a heartbreaking contrast to the roars of applause that Irving had inspired through his lifetime. It was a magical, theatrical bit of choreography that was worthy of a Lyceum production.

A day of steady, necessary work had left Stoker no time to grieve. But during the sad carriage journey the dam broke, and he found himself unexpectedly shaking with emotion. He later wrote, "It moves me strangely to think of it yet."

Irving's ashes were buried in the Poets' Corner at Westminster Abbey, near Garrick's monument. England heralded him as a hero, but George Bernard Shaw would not relent. The playwright and critic refused to attend the funeral, noting, "Literature had no place at Irving's graveside." He summed up Irving's career with a typically frank assessment. "Irving had splendidly maintained the social status of the theatre, and greatly raised that of the actor; but he had done nothing for contemporary dramatic literature." Ellen Terry was disappointed by Shaw's lack of grace. Well aware of his publicized mania for healthy eating, she wrote to him, "I can't understand how one without gross food in him, who takes no wine to befuddle his wits, can have been so indelicate."

Bram Stoker's *Personal Reminiscences of Henry Irving* was published in 1906. With the memory of Irving still fresh, reviewers found much to praise: its insider's view of the great actor, his rehearsals and techniques, his painstaking detail and devotion to his craft. But the *Spectator* also thought that the book was the work of "a worshipper," under a sort of "hypnotic spell." The *Drama* sniffed that there was too much of Stoker and that he offered "little that is new or valuable." Similarly, the *Bookman* noticed that Stoker's story was tirelessly told as "we," or "Irving and I." Hence the only real revelations were those that Stoker shared, the finances or the management of the theater.

Blackwood's Magazine offered a long, insightful review that criticized the two friends simultaneously: Irving for his old-fashioned, stagy love of spectacle, and Stoker for his overwrought prose that attempted to make Irving's career seem artistic. In this, the reviewer implied that the rarefied air of the Lyceum made Stoker's biography curiously old-fashioned and uninformed, just like Irving's performances.

The review was brutally honest about the actor's legacy: "Irving did more than any man of his time to foster and indulge the depraved taste of the British public for 'realism' and spectacle. . . . He probably did more to expel the Shakespearean drama from the British stage by his gorgeous revivals than he did to prolong or renew it. . . . The appetite for a senseless show, once pampered, grows like others. . . . That [Irving] 'helped the audience to think,' may or may not be true. Certain is it that he would leave nothing to their imagination."

———— • ————

Shortly after the publication of his book on Irving, Bram Stoker suffered a stroke and was unconscious for a full day. When he recovered, his walking was uneven and his eyesight had been permanently affected—he needed a magnifying glass to write.

Bram Stoker's social contacts gradually waned. Failed investments in the 1890s, just when the Lyceum was collapsing, meant that Stoker's finances were uncertain. His royalties—even from

Dracula—amounted to very little. He depended on a steady output of writing to earn his living: magazine articles, short stories, and books.

The Mystery of the Sea, The Jewel of Seven Stars, and *The Man* were all written before Irving's death in 1905. Of these, *The Jewel of Seven Stars,* from 1903, is the most interesting, and one of Stoker's most successful books. It is the story of an Egyptologist, Abel Trelawney, who has fallen under the spell of Tera, an ancient Egyptian queen. Queen Tera has begun to possess the soul of Margaret, a modern woman. In an attempt to completely reincarnate the queen, Trelawney conducts a mysterious, Frankenstein-like experiment in a Cornish castle.

A fierce storm, "animated with the wrath of the quick," rages outside. "All at once the eager faces round the sarcophagus were bent forward. The look of speechless wonder in the eyes . . . had a more than mortal brilliance." But the sudden wind blasts through the shutters and destroys the experiment. The queen is resurrected but killed in the process. The other observers, including Margaret, have died "with fixed eyes of unspeakable horror." Only the narrator survives to tell the grisly tale.

In its review of the novel, the *New York Herald* marveled at Stoker's dual life. These wonderful horrors must have been a product of his theatrical work. "How does Mr. Stoker come by this quality?" the reviewer wondered. "His is the heartiest of material existences. To see him active in the role of theatrical manager is to be aware of a vital, virile personality. . . . It must be that the geist [spirit] of Sir Henry Irving enters into him, compounded of Hamlet, Mathias, Macbeth. . . ."

Stoker's story was evidently too spooky for its publisher,

Rider, who asked for a happier ending for the 1912 edition. Stoker rewrote it so that Margaret survives and offers solace for the queen: "Do not grieve for her. . . . She dreamed her dream, and that is all that any of us can ask!" *The Jewel of Seven Stars* was a clear inspiration for a long tradition of later Hollywood mummy films.

The Lady of the Shroud, from 1909, was a fascinating parallel to *Dracula*. Stoker returned to the Balkans, where the lady of the title, Teuta Vissarion, is a princess who pretends to be a vampire. The story included a distinctly modern touch, an airplane rescue.

Stoker's 1910 book *Famous Impostors* was an unexpected bit of journalism. In his chapters on historical impostors, he included the necromancer Cagliostro and the Victorian swindler, the Tichborne Claimant. But Stoker earned headlines with the elaborate, shaky theory that Queen Elizabeth had actually died when she was a young girl and was then impersonated by a boy. Stoker's chapter was a bit of racy historical speculation; perhaps he was reminded of Oscar Wilde's Elizabethan fantasy, "The Portrait of Mr. W.H."

The Lair of the White Worm, published in 1911, was Bram Stoker's last, and most contentious, work. Reviewers hated it from the moment it was published. The *Times Literary Supplement* felt Stoker was "attempting to exceed the supernatural horrors of Dracula" but had ended up with "something very like nonsense. . . . Coherence is a necessity . . . the book is disjointed and, in fact, very silly."

The novel tells the story of Lady Arabella March, a mysterious femme fatale who not only is serpentine in her appearance and vileness but reveals her natural form as a gigantic, foul white worm, two hundred feet long, that lives in a pit a thousand feet deep and drags victims down into this "noxious . . . poisonous" lair. An upright young man, Adam, and his learned adviser, Sir Nathaniel, decide to destroy the monster: "Being feminine, she will probably over-reach herself. . . . Our strong game will be to play our masculine against her feminine."

She is a daunting enemy, but Adam succeeds with multiple dynamite charges dropped into the deep, disgusting pit. The dynamite produces a lurid scene in which her "agonized shrieks" are heard, and the "seething contents of the hole . . . part of the thin form of Lady Arabella, [are] forced up to the top amid a mass of slime."

Stoker's great-nephew and biographer, Daniel Farson, found the book "so bizarre, almost ludicrous," that it could not be taken seriously. But he was fascinated by the blend of Gothic horror and surreal hallucinations: "Without a vestige of humor, it is immensely funny." Dracula expert Leonard Wolf suggested that such a story might be dismissed from a young man, as "whatever the author's misery, it would surely pass; but Stoker was sixty-four years old. . . . There is no way to ignore the signs of confusion and loneliness." Harry Ludlam, another biographer of Stoker, felt "some deep mystery between the lines—the mystery of the mind of the man who wrote it." The weird—and brutally apparent—sexual images seem especially odd just three years after Stoker's excoriating essays on censorship. Literary critics have fixated on *The Lair of the White Worm*'s sexuality and its streak of misogyny. The next step, of course, has been to send those judgments ricocheting back through *Dracula*—and those judgments are there, in decades of literary criticism.

This was the novel that made H. P. Lovecraft shake his head over Stoker more than a decade later, questioning if he could have written *Dracula*. "*The Lair of the White Worm* is absolutely the most amorphous and infantile mess I've ever seen between cloth covers," Lovecraft wrote. "Stoker was absolutely devoid of a sense of form, and could not write a coherent tale to save his life."

Daniel Farson concluded that the book might have been the result of medication. In the last years of his life, Bram Stoker was suffering from Bright's disease and gout, which may have required a treatment for the pain.

———·•·———

In his petition to the Royal Literary Fund, Stoker pointed out that he'd earned only 166 pounds ($830) from his writing in 1910 and that he'd been incapacitated since his later stroke, a difficult position for "one who has to depend on his brain and his hands." The fund awarded him 100 pounds. The Stokers economized, moving from their Chelsea house to a flat in Belgravia. Florence helped in collecting her husband's magazine short stories, in an effort to produce another book.

On April 20, 1912, just five days after the *Titanic* sank on its maiden voyage from England to New York, Bram Stoker died, with his wife and son at his bedside. The event was relegated to the inside pages of the newspapers, hidden in the swirl of *Titanic* headlines and accusations about the "unsinkable" ocean liner.

Bram Stoker's obituary in the London *Times* noted that he had been ill for the last six years. The newspaper paid tribute to his "lurid and creepy kind of fiction" that was found in *Dracula*. But, the *Times* was convinced, "his chief literary memorial will be his

Reminiscences of Irving, a book which with all its extravagances and shortcomings, cannot but remain a valuable record . . . [by] his devoted associate and admirer."

Of course, they got it wrong.

Bram Stoker's old friend Hall Caine put his life in perspective.

We who were very close to him realized . . . that with Irving's life poor Bram's had really ended. It was too late to begin afresh. The threads that had been broken thirty years before could not be pieced together. There could be no second flowing of the tide. . . . Though Bram made a brave fight for a new life, he knew well, and we knew well, that his chances were over.

He took no vain view of his efforts as an author. Frankly, he wrote his books to sell, and except in the case of one of them (his book on Irving), he had no higher aims. . . .

In one thing our poor Bram, who had many limitations, was truly great. He was indeed the genius of friendship. . . . I can think of nothing—absolutely nothing—that I could have asked Bram Stoker to do for me that he would not have done. It is only once in a man's life that such a friendship comes to him, and when the grave is closed on the big heart which we are to bury today, I shall feel that I have lost it.

Stoker's brilliant friendship, like Irving's acting, left no memorials behind, except the evanescent recollections of those who shared the experience. Unlike Irving, Stoker had forged a legacy that would not only survive him, but flourish.

Bram Stoker was cremated and interred at Golders Green Crematorium in London on April 24, 1912.

With the 1975 biography of his great-uncle, Daniel Farson offered a revelation. Bram Stoker's death certificate listed the causes as:

> Locomotor Ataxy, 6 months.
> Granular contracted Kidney.
> Exhaustion.

The kidney ailment was Bright's disease. But "Locomotor Ataxy" suggested, to Farson's doctor, General Paralysis of the Insane—these were the terms that signaled death caused by syphilis.

Farson was now able to interpret other significant symptoms, including Stoker's failing eyesight, instability, and mental deterioration. Then, counting backward (syphilis usually took ten to fifteen years before it became fatal), Farson saw how the medical condition began to inform his final years.

Irresistibly, this provided an explanation for *The Lair of the White Worm*—Stoker's last book was composed when he was delirious. It explained that his marriage to Florence had failed—her frigidity inspired the themes of his novels and his snarling censorship of sexual content. And it suggested another tie to Oscar Wilde—Stoker may have become infected from a French prostitute on the trip to Paris when he visited Wilde.

Such speculation isn't unexpected; everyone wanted to find some lurid, grinning skeleton in Bram Stoker's closet. Unfortunately, the death certificate was not conclusive. Author Leslie Shepard has pointed out that "Locomotor Ataxy" is not always associated with syphilis, especially if Stoker had been suffering for only six months. During the last years of his life, he was alert and busy with literary work until the time of his death. His family remembered him as a "rather dotty" old man, but this behavior wouldn't have been indicative of the illness. It seems unlikely that he suffered from the gradual paralysis or mental deterioration that would have been expected from syphilis.

Stoker's later biographer, Paul Murray, consulted with medical experts who were more decisive: Syphilis could have affected his reflexes or eyesight, but not his intellect. (In other words, there was no medical excuse for *The Lair of the White Worm*.) Murray's experts felt that the death certificate suggested a diagnosis of syphilis, although this may not have advanced to the point of a fatal disease. Bram Stoker probably died of kidney disease.

After all his concerns for money at the end of his life, Stoker left an estate worth over 4,600 pounds ($23,000), a respectable amount, to Florence. Thornley Stoker, his brother, died just weeks later, and an additional 1,000-pound bequest was also inherited by Florence. She earned additional money with the sale of Bram's library the following year.

In 1914, Florence Stoker published the collection of Stoker's short stories that he had been preparing before his death. In her preface, she explained that her husband had planned "three series of short stories." But with this collection of stories, she had added "a hitherto unpublished episode from *Dracula*. It was originally excised owing to the length of the book, and may prove of interest to the many readers." This anthology was titled *Dracula's Guest and Other Weird Stories.*

"Dracula's Guest" tells the story of an English traveler passing through Munich on Walpurgisnacht. When the carriage abandons him and he walks through a grove of trees, he encounters the tomb of Countess Dolingen; scrawled on the door are the words, "The dead travel fast." Taking refuge from a snowstorm, he watches as the inner tomb opens and he sees a beautiful woman, with round cheeks and red lips, apparently asleep on the bier.

Lightning strikes the tomb, destroying it and hurtling the traveler into the snow. He wakes to discover that an enormous wolf is lapping at his throat. A troop of horsemen approach and scare the wolf away. The mysterious wolf has been warming him and keeping him alive through the night. When the traveler arrives at his hotel in Munich, the innkeeper shows him a telegram that he received from Bistritz. The telegram warns the innkeeper to guard the English traveler from the "dangers of snow and wolves and night," as "his safety is most precious to me." The telegram is signed by Dracula.

Certain clues in the story—the English visitor in Munich, who we presume is Jonathan Harker, Walpurgisnacht, the vampire-like Countess, and the traveler's plan to visit Dracula—seemed to support Florence Stoker's introduction, that this was part of the first chapter of the novel.

Authors Elizabeth Miller and Clive Leatherdale have disagreed. Stoker's early notes for *Dracula* did include a line, "adventure snowstorm and wolf," that suggests that "Dracula's Guest" was derived from his earliest plot. But the short story is written in third person instead of first person. The unnamed character of the traveler is more aggressive and knows less German than the Jonathan Harker of the novel. Finally, the dates of this short story indicate that it could not have been simply pulled out of the novel. Leatherdale suggests that it might have been part of the earliest draft of the novel, and then removed and reworked as a separate story—sometime around 1890 or 1892. Or, perhaps, it was written as a short story, but "Stoker realized its potential and returned to construct a novel upon it."

The most illuminating phrase in Florence Stoker's introduction is the observation that *Dracula* was "my husband's most remarkable work." It was remarkable enough to market his posthumous book as *Dracula's Guest and Other Weird Stories.*

Like the mysterious wolf who appeared unexpectedly to offer warmth, *Dracula* would provide for Florence. In exchange, she would encourage Dracula's most startling metamorphosis—not into a bat or a wolf, but into a handsome leading man worthy of the twentieth century.

Sixteen

THE LEGEND,
"SPREAD OVER CENTURIES"

T he Little Theatre was just that, the West End's tiniest show-place: a simple, functional auditorium on John Street in the Strand, with a flat ceiling, a stage at one end, and some decorative paintings hung in the lobby. It accommodated just over three hundred people.

On Valentine's Day in 1927, Florence Stoker and her daughter-in-law arrived. They'd been offered prestigious seats, two on the aisle. The house manager had been alerted to watch for the tiny, pretty little lady, to escort her through the crowd, make conversation, then just smile and nod if she became difficult in any way. After all, the only reason everyone was there that night, the only reason there was a play, was Mrs. Stoker. Please be polite to her.

Bram Stoker had once been in charge of just such custodial duties at the Lyceum, escorting royalty to the smoking lounge, passing along invitations to the Beefsteak Room, engaging in small talk or providing refreshments to Henry Irving's guests. Florence was, by extension, an expert at just how such pleasantries were conducted and just how a grand theater should be operated.

The manager at the Little Theatre was clearly an amateur, she decided. Scuffed shoes, dirty fingernails. Bram wouldn't have had him for an usher.

She knew. She had attended most of the Lyceum's opening nights and been proudly introduced to the finest of London society. She had been at the opening of *Lady Windermere's Fan*, having been invited by the playwright himself. That was the night that she was complimented on her striking brocade wrap, and Oscar appeared onstage, holding a cigarette, his lapel adorned with the infamous green carnation.

At the Little Theatre there was none of that old grandeur. The theater's decor was ghastly and ordinary, just whitewashed walls and uncomfortable seats. Henry Irving would never have set foot in such a place. The audience shuffled in around her; they mumbled, rattled their programs, pulled at their coats, and sat down. This was not a Lyceum crowd. That night at the Little Theatre was a reminder of just how far she'd fallen.

Florence gazed at the program, which her cataracts prevented her from reading; her daughter-in-law whispered what was printed on the front: "Hamilton Deane and H. L. Warburton present The Vampire Play, *Dracula*, by Hamilton Deane. Adapted from Bram Stoker's famous novel." It was the opening night of *Dracula* in London. Florence sighed and shook her head. She'd hated the script from the first moment she read it, three years before. But she'd also been cashing checks, the seemingly endless royalties from the play's provincial tours. Once Count Dracula asserted his mysterious power over the box office, it was inevitable that he would invade London, just as he had in the novel.

Perhaps Florence had remembered the play as her husband's

onetime dream, but most likely Bram's plans had been long forgotten. She now analyzed *Dracula* as a simple, necessary source of income. It was the best thing she had.

The electric lights flashed and then were extinguished. A piano at the edge of the stage offered a quick overture, a Slovak melody that echoed in hard notes off the plaster walls. The curtain raised on a perfectly ordinary study—painted bookcases, overstuffed chairs, a chesterfield, a fireplace. An older man in a cutaway coat walked briskly onstage and stood at the fireplace. He looked at his watch. He drummed his fingers on the mantel. Florence Stoker leaned forward, into the wash of pale yellow light from the stage, waiting for something to happen. The seats around her creaked, like those in a schoolroom.

Onstage, a young man entered through a door, which slammed and wobbled with the telltale sign of cheap scenery. "Well, how is she?" the older man asked, pushing every word through his teeth without any special emphasis. "No change, pale and listless, but doing her best to keep up a show of brightness," the young man answered.

It was definitely poor acting.

"Well, this thing has beaten me. . . . In all of my experience as a medical man I've never seen anything like it. . . ."

The widow felt her heart sink. She had been there for Booth in *Othello,* and Ellen Terry in *Macbeth.* She'd heard the bubbling laughter generated by Wilde's unexpected bons mots. She'd acted in a play by Tennyson; what an opening night that had been! There was no doubt about it. She was now listening to some of the stupidest lines she'd ever heard in a professional theater. The amateurish enunciation made each word stab like a knife.

The young man paused a moment, then turned on his heel. "My God, if only your friend the scientist would come!"

What was it that Irving had said? Yes, *Dracula* was truly dreadful.

———————

Author and Dracula expert David Skal has chronicled the twists and turns by which Stoker's Victorian vampire entered the Jazz Age. According to Skal, "Dracula became Florence's guardian angel, of sorts, providing a steady, if meager sustenance. She was determined to make money from stage and motion picture rights, but interlopers vexed her."

After her husband's death, Florence Stoker lived comfortably but not extravagantly. She moved to Knightsbridge, was the center of a social circle, attended the theater and opera, and indulged in cruises and holidays with her son, Noel, and his family. She attracted a cult of Oscar Wilde fans; she referred to her onetime beau as "Poor O" and proudly showed off a small watercolor landscape that he had painted for her.

Always a head-turning beauty, she remained pretty and vain in old age. Her family called her Granny Moo and remembered her as "elegant, aloof," and "an ornament, not a woman of passion." Coincidentally, she was once visited by a young American student from the Courtauld Institute of Art, named Vincent Price. This was before he became interested in acting and, of course, years before he became famous for his horror roles. Price remembered Mrs. Stoker as "frail and small . . . holding court, surrounded by portraits from her youth."

She was also single-minded. In 1922 she sent 1 pound, 10 shillings to join the Society of Authors, which was her right as her husband's literary executor. When she was welcomed to the society, she instantly responded to G. Herbert Thring, its secretary, with a complaint. She'd been sent an advertisement for a screening of a new film in Berlin, titled *Nosferatu, a Symphony of Horror*, directed by F. W. Murnau.

It was the best pound and 10 shillings Florence Stoker ever spent. For the next fifteen years she bombarded Mr. Thring with a hectoring list of offenses and urged him forward in defense of her rights. *Nosferatu* was a special curse to her; she chased it from country to country, prevented it from being shown in Great Britain for many years, and pursued it to America, attempting to stop screenings. When she received a judgment in a German court, she almost managed to have prints of the film destroyed. Her legal maneuvers were especially complicated because the studio that produced it, Prana Film, quickly went bankrupt and Florence relentlessly pursued the receivers.

Mrs. Stoker never saw *Nosferatu*. She didn't want to see it. But fortunately this masterpiece has survived, one of the most famous examples of German Expressionist silent film. Of course, the plot is based heavily on *Dracula* (and in America, it was first billed as *Dracula*). In many ways, *Nosferatu* is more *Dracula* than *Dracula*. Producer and designer Albin Grau rejected the modern London setting—typewriters and phonographs—and set the story in Germany of 1838. It's creaky and foreign, the world of Mary Shelley's *Frankenstein*. Similarly, Count Orlok (the Dracula character) is tall and cadaver-like, a horrific monster with bat-like ears and rodent-like teeth. In *Nosferatu*, the analogy of pestilence is clear; when the ship with the vampire nears the harbor, a mysterious plague overtakes the city. Count Orlok reaching with his claws, or rising from his coffin aboard the ship, are some of the most nightmarish images in the history of the cinema.

In his novel, Bram Stoker's rule was that sunlight reduces the power of the vampire, but Grau and Murnau were the first to exaggerate this, suggesting that sunlight would prove deadly. It is a plot twist perfectly suited to special effects. At the end of *Nosferatu*, Count Orlok dissolves, becoming transparent and then disappearing completely. Hollywood later adopted this rule as a handy tool for the assortment of *Dracula* sequels that drew audiences through the 1930s and 1940s.

During her campaign against the German film, an Irish actor named Hamilton Deane approached Florence Stoker with a proposition. Deane had long obsessed over the idea of *Dracula* on the stage. His family had known the Stokers in Dublin, and when he had toured with Henry Irving's company in 1899, he had a chance to meet Bram Stoker—although he'd been too shy to discuss *Dracula* with its author.

For years he had attempted to interest playwrights in the idea, but they thought the novel couldn't be adapted. The diary style was impossible; the cast was enormous; the effects were prohibitive; the censor would never allow it. Finally, Deane's wife urged him to write it himself. In 1923 he was laid up with a cold and found himself instinctively composing the play he had been describing for almost twenty years.

Deane had his own repertory company that toured England,

so he wrote a play that was modest enough for his own needs. He stripped away the most thrilling opening chapters in Transylvania. He confined the action to three acts in a London parlor, Mina's bedroom, and a brief finale in a dark crypt. Quincy (not Quincey) Morris was now a pistol-packing American woman. Lucy was eliminated completely. And Dracula was a tall, continental gentleman in a satin opera cape, with white streaks of hair that suggested devilish horns. There was no chase back to Eastern Europe. Instead, the vampire hunters shuffled over to the house next door, found the coffin, and pounded in a stake.

The result was unexpectedly tame and cheap, a drawing-room thriller that would look more like *Lady Windermere's Fan* than a Lyceum production. He sought Mrs. Stoker's permission. She didn't like it. She could read that Deane had taken a simple way out. But she also realized that it would be a quick opportunity for income during her battle against *Nosferatu*. Deane's play was put in front of an audience—snuck in the middle of some repertory favorites—in June 1924, in Derby.

And from that first night, *Dracula* was an ironclad hit. Audiences weren't expecting a good play; they were willing to forgive the faults because it scared them. It made them scream; it made them giggle nervously. If the thrills were cheap—screams, bats, smoke, and exploding flash pots—there was a refreshing honesty about it.

More than likely, part of *Dracula*'s success was owed to the Grand Guignol productions just two years earlier. In 1920, the famous French theater of horrors had first premiered an English version of their peculiar plays at the Little Theatre in London—

the same whitewashed room that later hosted *Dracula*'s premiere. Grand Guignol attracted considerable comment for its bloody and psychological horrors. It was always an acquired taste, a foreign-feeling revue that was designed to leave audiences with the sensation of experiencing jolting extremes, "hot and cold showers." Once the public had been introduced to the fashion of Grand Guignol, *Dracula* appeared. The play was convincingly English, reassuringly clunky, and maddeningly familiar. But then it surprised with the latest thing: jolts of Grand Guignol stylishness.

Hamilton Deane chose to take the role of Van Helsing. His wife, Dora Mary Patrick, played Mina. Joining the cast later was a twenty-two-year-old actor, Raymond Huntley, who went on to portray the Count thousands of times. Hamilton Deane quickly excised the other twenty-two plays from his repertory. They weren't needed. The public wanted *Dracula*. He toured it for over two years in provincial theaters. "We never had a poor house with *Dracula*," he reported. "By that time I was simply coining money with play. I could not go wrong with it, anywhere."

When it premiered on Valentine's Day in 1927, Deane expected the worst from the London critics, and he got it.

The *Times* thought there was "very little of Bram Stoker," and although the surprises were crude, mostly loud noises, "most of us jumped out of our seats at least once in every act." The acting was amateurish. Deane's accent as Van Helsing was singled out, especially because it had disappeared during the interval. The *Morning Post* insisted that Mr. Deane simply could not write dialogue. Dora Mary Patrick, as Mina, was cited as one of the "life-long victims of elocutionists." The newspaper quoted her as complaining about the "Leth Are Gee" that affected her "Leems." (This was a nice twist on Henry Irving's sloppy pronunciation, which had long fascinated his audiences.) *Punch* ended its review with a weary conundrum, wondering "sadly why this sort of thing should be supposed to be adequate entertainment for adults."

Deane's pride was wounded, until he was shown the box office receipts. The audiences couldn't stay away. The play moved to a larger theater, the Duke of York's, to accommodate audiences, and Deane bolstered the play with publicity stunts. "A nurse will be in attendance at all performances," the advertising comforted. The nurse stood nervously at the edge of the stage, presumably watching for fainting spectators, and of course, some did faint. A similar gimmick had been used at the Grand Guignol shows at the Little Theatre, and then again in 1921, when music hall magician P. T. Selbit presented his new creation, "Sawing a Woman in Half."

At the first night in London, Mrs. Stoker didn't even come backstage to meet the cast. She was disappointed in the show and deeply resented sharing the profits with Deane. As the owner of the story, she promptly commissioned her own version of the script, by the playwright Charles Morrell. This *Dracula* was even stodgier and chattier, incorporating more incidents from the novel. It premiered in Warrington in September 1927 and quickly flopped.

Meanwhile, audiences continued to flock to London, where *Dracula* ran for over 250 performances before going back on the road. The demand was so high that Deane organized three separate touring companies. The play also boosted interest in the novel, which had been floundering but now sold twenty thousand copies a year.

Through it all, the checks kept arriving at Florence Stoker's flat.

———— · · ————

The publisher and Broadway producer Horace Liveright arrived in London in early 1927 and watched *Dracula* at the Little Theatre four times. He loved it. He hated it. He had to have it in New York.

He discussed a deal with Florence Stoker for the American rights, insisting that the Deane script would have to be rewritten for Broadway. Then he secured the services of American playwright John Balderston to do the rewriting and to handle the tricky negotiations with the impatient widow.

The American *Dracula*, which opened on Broadway in October 1927, was no more ambitious, but Liveright and Balderston had smoothed out some of the ridiculous dialogue. They also eliminated characters and added some of their own gimmicks. For example, an actress would sneak from backstage into the audience in the darkness and then groan loudly, on cue, as Dracula attacked his victim. It sounded as if a poor woman watching the show had been overcome with emotion. At the end of the play, Dr. Van Helsing now stepped forward to deliver a novel curtain speech: "Just a word before you go. We hope that the memories of Dracula and Renfield won't give you bad dreams, so just a word of reassurance. When you get home tonight and the lights have been turned out . . . and you dread to see a face appear at the window . . . why, just pull yourself together and remember that, after all, there *are* such things!"

Liveright had offered to bring Raymond Huntley, the Count, and Bernard Jukes, the lunatic Renfield, to America. Jukes accepted, but Huntley balked at the weekly salary of $125. Instead, the role went to a Romanian actor who was just starting his career on Broadway, Belá Ferenc Dezsõ Blaskó, who used the stage name Bela Lugosi.

Lugosi's English was spotty. He was uneven and strange in reciting his lines. As Liveright watched him rehearse, the producer wondered if he'd made the right choice. But when the actor finally had an audience, he summoned a weird, imperious snarl and a threatening, erotic energy. It was the role that made him famous and, indeed, he was the actor that made Dracula famous.

Dracula had been completely reinvented for this generation. Lugosi's patent leather hair and penetrating eyes were perfect reminders of Rudolph Valentino—the famously exotic silent film star who had created a mania among American women with his smoldering stare and cruel sexuality. In 1926, Valentino died unexpectedly. A year later, he had been resurrected as Dracula—part lover, part corpse. (Lugosi was given dark rings around his eyes and pale green makeup for Broadway.) Gone was Stoker's white-haired, snarling old nobleman. Dracula was now a 1920s heartthrob.

Another element of the play's success was its unexpected perspective. In the early 1920s, Broadway had been overrun with a series of supernatural thrillers like *The Cat and the Canary*, *The Bat*, and *The Spider*. These were basically detective stories in which a logical explanation was offered for the phenomena and a criminal was unmasked before the final curtain. *Dracula* thrilled by being unabashedly supernatural and never offering an excuse or a denouement.

Van Helsing's speech accentuated this element. To many in the audience, the thrill of the evening was the reminder that "there *are* such things."

———

The reviewers were cautious, as if they were in on the joke. *Vogue* magazine wrote, "The shoddiness of the production and the performances may add to the merriment, may, indeed, create it. If the piece were better done, it might not be so amusing." *Time* thought that "the material is morbidly magnificent. And, of course, it is all perfectly silly." The New York *Daily Mirror* compared it to a child wearing a bedsheet and shouting boo. The *New Yorker* thought it might be better without so much "arrant hokum." But Alexander Woollcott seemed to get into the spirit of the production when he pronounced, "Ye who have fits, prepare to throw them now."

And, of course, *Dracula* on Broadway was an enormous hit.

———

Hollywood called.

The success of the play meant that it was impossible to ignore the commercial possibilities of *Dracula*. After interest from a number of studios, Universal emerged victorious, even though the head of the studio, Carl Laemmle, thought the idea of producing horror films was "morbid." It was his son, Carl Laemmle Jr., the heir apparent, put in charge of the studio when he was twenty-one, who liked the idea.

Lon Chaney, the famous silent film star and "Man of a Thousand Faces," was reportedly slated for the role of Dracula before Chaney's unexpected death. The producers weren't interested in Bela Lugosi, who was considered strictly a stage star without any motion picture appeal. Lugosi actually contacted Mrs. Stoker to help negotiate the film rights and ingratiate himself to the studio.

Unfortunately, the rights were now hopelessly muddled between the original novel and three separate theater scripts, thanks to Mrs. Stoker's machinations. Just as *Dracula* seemed hopelessly doomed to a legal comedy of errors, slowly, mysteriously, the clouds parted on the vampire's full moon.

Lugosi was signed for the cut-rate price of $500 per week, for a total of $3,500. Florence Stoker accepted $60,000.

Universal Studio's *Dracula* may be one of the worst "great" films ever made. Tod Browning, the director of Lon Chaney's best films, was signed to direct. Edward Van Sloan reprised his Broadway role of Van Helsing. Dwight Frye, a Hollywood character actor, made the leering, laughing character of Renfield famous. But by the time the script had passed through the hands of various Hollywood writers, it was a messy pastiche of both the novel and the play. Now it is Renfield who goes to Transylvania to meet the Count—and is attacked there by Dracula, not the mysterious brides. This leaves the character of Jonathan Harker almost nothing to do. After the impressionistic scenes in Transylvania and at Dracula's castle, for which the film is fondly remembered, the action shifts to London and apes the drawing-room scenes of Hamilton Deane's script.

If the film *Dracula* charms, it is with its otherworldly qualities. It offers none of the self-conscious fun of the Broadway
show; rather, it is now dire and perfectly serious. Lugosi is fascinating and strange. The dialogue is sparse and odd. The action is
slow and trancelike. The film crackles and hisses in silence, without a note of background music. It ends with a whimper, the thud
of an offscreen stake. Van Helsing's famous curtain speech was
filmed, to leave the audience with a smile, but later omitted from
prints.

The movie opened in February 1931. Reviews were mixed. The
Los Angeles Times thought that it was "plainly a freak picture,"
a "curiosity devoid of the important element of sympathy that
causes the widest appeal." And, of course, it was a sensational hit.

The film doubled its investment in the first year and was revived, regularly, after that. Junior Laemmle, a film executive who
never gave the appearance of being very smart, ended up looking
like a genius when it came to *Dracula*. It began a trend for horror
that clawed Universal Studios out of the Depression; *Frankenstein*
followed that same year, then *The Mummy*, and a series of famous
monster sequels whenever ready cash was needed.

———•———

Dracula served Florence magnificently. "You think you have left
me without a place to rest, but I have more. My revenge is just
begun! I spread it over centuries, and time is on my side. Your girls
that you all love are mine already."

Hamilton Deane and Universal Studios allowed her to end her
life with some luxuries, including the addition of a second-story

gallery in her home. Florence Stoker died in 1937 and left an estate of almost 7,000 pounds ($35,000), considerably more than Bram Stoker had left at the time of his death.

———••—

And then, of course, it had to happen. Maybe it was poetic justice.

In March 1939, when Hamilton Deane's *Dracula* returned to London at the Winter Garden for another West End run, the producer used the American script. After years of playing Van Helsing opposite dozens of Draculas, Deane also took the plummier role of the vampire. When the show was extended and had to move, Deane searched at the last moment for available space—and found it at Henry Irving's old Lyceum.

The 1939 engagement seemed a spiderweb of haunted coincidences. Stoker's and Irving's ghosts, presumably, watched Dracula strut across their old stage. Hamilton Deane donned the opera cape to be the famous Count. And then, Bela Lugosi, in London for a movie, stepped onstage at the conclusion of one performance. That's where he met Deane for the first time. The two Draculas embraced and shared a bow. After *Dracula*, John Gielgud's *Hamlet* played at the Lyceum—Gielgud was Ellen Terry's nephew, and Hamlet was not only Irving's most famous role but the first part he played with Ellen Terry.

After *Hamlet*, the Lyceum was shuttered when the city announced plans to demolish it to widen the road. The theater sat empty for over a decade and then reopened as a ballroom. In 1996 it was fully restored, and it hosted Disney's *Lion King* in 1999.

Just months after he completed the film *Dracula*, Lugosi turned down the role of the monster in *Frankenstein*, feeling that the growling, snarling character would be limiting. *Frankenstein*, of course, made the unknown British character actor Boris Karloff a star. Lugosi's refusal to consider the role of Frankenstein was a special poetic justice; Raymond Huntley's refusal to take the role of *Dracula* on Broadway had once opened the door for Lugosi.

Lugosi was both blessed and doomed by the role of Dracula. He was hopelessly typecast but always able to draw an audience if he put on the famous cape. He played a series of horror roles and *Dracula*-inspired sequels, and in always-popular revivals of the play. In 1956, when Lugosi died, he'd suffered a series of decreasing, desperate movie roles and was emaciated by drug addiction. He was buried in his Dracula cape. It was, his son and former wife decided, the way he would have wanted it.

Hamilton Deane played Dracula until 1941, when he retired from the stage. He died in 1958.

Bram Stoker's monster appears on only sixty-two of 390 pages of the novel; he makes only a few speeches; he almost never shares his insights or motivation; his appearance is indistinct to the point of being confusing. Late in the novel, he becomes virtually lost in the torrent of diary entries, speculation, and itineraries generated by the vampire hunters. He turns into a vague disease, a pestilence that can be countered with scientific thinking and careful planning. He may be more of a tragic hero than a villain, but he is also more of a miasma than a human being.

"*Dracula* with so very little of Dracula" may have been Bram Stoker's greatest achievement. It meant that the Count has to be interpreted by the reader—characteristics need to be filled in; thoughts and motivations need to be inferred. This is what has made the search for Stoker's inspirations—like Irving, Wilde, Whitman, Jack the Ripper—not only a fascinating puzzle but a key to understanding the author.

The absence of Dracula has always offered another opportunity. The story could be reinvented, generation after generation, with new interpretations of the vampire. Dusted of its Victorianisms, the play could be easily planted in a 1920s London drawing room or a 1980s tract house. Removed from medieval Transylvania, Dracula could be re-created in the image of his latest audience—or even better, in the image of their nightmares.

Even if his skills as an author were limited, Stoker's personality left him open to the famous people that surrounded him, quietly observing their traits, synthesizing their weaknesses, and combining their tragedies. Stoker organized these into a new kind of nightmare: Whitman's bold carnality, Oscar Wilde's corrupting immorality, Henry Irving's haunted characters, and Jack the Ripper's mysterious horrors. These historical references elude us because those nightmares have passed from our memory and we don't need them anymore. We've replaced them with our own.

Even if Bram Stoker never fully realized it, if his views on censorship belied it, *Dracula* is about sex. The vampire story is a surrogate for sex. It's always a tempting adventure for readers who aren't otherwise allowed to think about sex.

Author Maurice Richardson, in attempting to psychoanalyze the novel, famously described it in 1959 as a "kind of incestuous, necrophilous, oral-anal-sadistic all-in wrestling match." A better way to express it is that *Dracula* can be almost anything we want, whenever we want it. Gabriel Ronay described the book as a "weathervane indicating the direction of the prevalent social winds." And the old vampire was right. Time is on his side.

———— • ————

Anne Rice's 1976 book *Interview with the Vampire* (and her subsequent series of books, *The Vampire Chronicles*) reinvented the genre by recognizing the fascinating, seemingly eternal life and passing relationships that must constitute a truly great vampire's life. Dracula seemed to be unaware of his centuries of victims— one meal after another. But Rice's Louis has all the insights of a great diarist, or, perhaps, a food critic who can recall the details of every delicious bite.

Interview with the Vampire preceded the onset of AIDS, but Rice's modern vampire story was quickly interpreted through the lens of this mysterious new plague. In the book, Louis explains how he was initiated into the society of vampires hundreds of years ago by Lestat. *Interview with the Vampire* had taken a step beyond Stoker, and Rice is unstinting in offering passions and unashamed of her bisexual vampires.

"The AIDS story was shaped as a stereotypical horror movie scenario," author David Skal has observed. "A wasting malady involving blood . . . each victim capable of creating more of his kind . . . the epidemic can only be controlled if traditional sex roles are observed . . . the monster is linked to sexual license."

In recent years, Dracula has been reincarnated as a teenager—as Edward Cullen, the new, dreamy, Byronic, hormone-fueled supernatural leading man. Stephenie Meyer's *Twilight*, from 2005, has been followed by a series of popular novels for young adults, with a cast of characters who sparkle rather than reek of the grave. Her mortal heroine, Bella Swan, appeals by allowing readers to imagine themselves in the middle of the vampire saga; Bella is the modern Mina Harker. "Bella is every girl," Meyer explained in an interview. "She's not a hero. She doesn't always have to be cool, or wear the coolest clothes ever. She's normal. Bella's a good girl, which is just how I imagine teenagers, because that's how my teenage years were.

"If I say to someone, you know, 'It's about vampires,' then immediately they have this mental image of what the book is like," she said. "And it's so not like the other vampire books out there. It isn't that kind of dark and dreary and blood thirsty world. Then when you say, 'It's set in high school,' a lot of people immediately put it in another [category]."

But as her *Twilight* books and films have proven, the combination is irresistible. Her vampires exhibit all of the deep tragedy and counterculture heroism that disenfranchised teenagers naturally see in themselves, plus a little more. And, of course, vampirism stands in for sex—a subject that teenagers aren't supposed to address. Vampires no longer need to be researched and categorized; they are part of the culture. Meyer mixed the traditional vampire clichés with her own mythology, but she didn't watch any vampire movies, nor had she even read Stoker's *Dracula*. "It's on the list," she said. "I should've read that one a long time ago. But I can't read other people's vampires."

———⋅•⋅———

Dracula has proven to be resilient, a wonderful money-spinner with almost every audience and in almost every medium. The last decades, however, have generated a number of interesting experiments—*Dracula* returned to opulent, Victorian London, *Dracula* as a musical, *Dracula* as an opera, *Dracula* dripping with special effects, *Dracula* applied to every specialized audience. A critic might take note that the Count's surreal charms are not limitless. Perhaps he has always been most comfortable in the dank, dirty confines of his coffin. *Dracula*'s cheap, nasty productions provide the right sorts of chills—the 1920s actors howling into a lamp chimney offstage to imitate the wolf. *Dracula*'s expensive, no-holds-barred indulgences leave audiences cold—a perfectly choreographed and computer-controlled vampire aerial ballet.

This may be why Henry Irving, a masterful showman and something of an old vampire himself, once laughed at Bram Stoker. Perhaps he realized that *Dracula* never needed the Lyceum. Just an old cape, a swirl of smoke, the hypnotic gaze of a woman in a nightgown—and he is there, stealthily sweeping into our dreams with the same determination with which he pushes against the French doors.

A truly great nightmare is once experienced, never forgotten. It is summoned again when we simply close our eyes. It needs nothing but imagination. It is never very far away.

ACKNOWLEDGMENTS
AND SOURCES

My agent, Jim Fitzgerald, was the very first to say to me, "Bram Stoker," quite unaware that I'd been following the twists and turns in Dracula histories for many years.

At Tarcher, the project arrived at the desk of my editor, Mitch Horowitz, and I am grateful for his enthusiasm and careful advice throughout the project.

Orson Welles, whom I'd worked with in the early 1980s, recounted his belief that Stoker had based his character on Henry Irving, but subsequent research has widened that net and added levels of complexity to the story. It was fascinating to assemble the pieces and draw from the decades of wonderful Dracula scholarship.

There is a great deal of fascinating material written on the subject of Dracula, and I benefited from the remarkable works of informative and insightful authors. I'd cite, in particular, David Skal, who first inspired me with his magnificent tale of the evolution of Dracula in popular culture, *Hollywood Gothic*. Mr. Skal has since gone on to publish a great deal of primary source material on Dracula, adding his own commentary.

Similarly, Elizabeth Miller has gathered together a great mass of important Dracula source material in her various books. This diligent research has been matched by her sensible, wonderful insights into the subject. I think that no one has provided a brighter light, and pointed it in precisely the right direction, than Elizabeth Miller.

At the Rosenbach Library, Farrar Fitzgerald and Elizabeth Fuller were most helpful.

Finally, thanks to my friends (and *Dracula* fans) Richard Kaufman and Marty Demarest, who looked at it all with a fresh eye and a critical eye. Thanks to David Regal and Ben Robinson for suggestions and encouragement. And to my wife, Frankie Glass, for her support, ideas, and advice throughout a long project.

CHAPTER ONE. THE DEMON, "IN A WAY YOU CANNOT DREAM OF"

I've based my description of Henry Irving's rehearsals, and the production of *Faust*, on various sources. Bram Stoker tells the story of the Brocken scene, and his doubt about its overall effect, in Bram Stoker, *Personal Reminiscences of Henry Irving* (New York: Macmillan, 1906). The production of *Faust* has been wonderfully described by Michael R. Booth, *Victorian Spectacular Theatre, 1850–1910* (London: Routledge & Kegan Paul, 1981), and George Rowell, *Theatre in the Age of Irving* (Totowa, NJ: Rowman and Littlefield, 1981).

Edwin Booth is quoted in Booth, *Victorian Spectacular Theatre*. This book also explains the special effects that were specially installed. There is speculation about Irving's personal lights, built within the hood of his garment. Michael R. Booth quotes several sources about this lighting effect, suggesting that Irving had three different colors of lights used throughout the play. Perhaps Irving experimented with this effect. It sounds far-fetched to me, and the subtlety required would have been difficult to achieve in 1885. Stoker, *Personal Reminiscences*, gives the details of the magical swordfight. Booth, *Victorian Spectacular Theatre*, explains the opening-night accident.

Faust gives a perfect impression of Irving's unique productions onstage, and a taste of his mixture of illusion and theatrics. I believe that this highly charged, melodramatic atmosphere was an important influence on Stoker, who saw his ideal stories in these same terms.

Irving's quotes to Stoker about the Brocken scene are from Stoker, *Personal Reminiscences*.

Ellen Terry's note about the light is quoted from Ellen Terry (with Edith Craig and Christopher St. John), *Ellen Terry's Memoirs* (New York: G. P.

Putnam's Sons, 1932). Booth's remarks, and Henry James's criticism, are from Booth, *Victorian Spectacular Theatre*. David Devant's observations are from David Devant's *Secrets of My Magic* (London: Hutchinson, 1936).

CHAPTER TWO. THE BOY,
"NATURALLY SECRETIVE TO THE WORLD"

Stoker's expressions of his relationship to Irving are from Stoker, *Personal Reminiscences*. For Bram Stoker's early life, I've used his own *Personal Reminiscences* (which contains a little autobiographical material about his childhood), and four biographies of Stoker: Harry Ludlam, *A Biography of Dracula: The Life Story of Bram Stoker* (London: Quality Book Club, 1962); Daniel Farson, *The Man Who Wrote Dracula: A Biography of Bram Stoker* (New York: St. Martin's Press, 1975); Barbara Belford, *Bram Stoker: A Biography of the Author of Dracula* (New York: Alfred A. Knopf, 1996); and Paul Murray, *From the Shadow of Dracula: A Life of Bram Stoker* (London: Pimlico, 2005). A number of these biographies are linked to Stoker's family members and associates. Ludlam wrote the book with the cooperation of Noel Stoker, Bram's son, and the recollections of Hamilton Deane, the actor and producer who adapted *Dracula* for the stage. Barbara Belford made extensive use of Stoker's papers from the Lyceum, including some personal papers. Daniel Farson, a great-nephew of Stoker, compiled his book after Noel had died. He had access to a cache of family letters as well as the assistance of Ann McCaw, Bram's granddaughter, and her son Noel Dobbs. The Stoker family papers are now housed at Trinity College.

Stoker's early accounts of Henry Irving are from Stoker, *Personal Reminiscences*.

Material from Oscar Wilde's childhood in Dublin is from Richard Ellmann, *Oscar Wilde* (New York: Alfred A. Knopf, 1988), and Eric Lambert, *Mad with Much Heart: A Life of the Parents of Oscar Wilde* (London: Fredrick Muller, 1967). Le Fanu is discussed in Murray, *From the Shadow of Dracula*, and Elizabeth Miller, ed., *Bram Stoker's Dracula* (New York: Pegasus, 2009). This is a fascinating collection of primary-source Dracula material.

Polidori's story is discussed in Miller, *Bram Stoker's Dracula*, and the vampire dramas are discussed in Roxana Stuart, *Stage Blood: Vampires of the 19th-Century Stage* (Bowling Green, OH: Bowling Green State University Popular

Press, 1994), and Richard Fawkes, *Dion Boucicault* (London: Quartet Books, 1979). The account of Stoker meeting Boucicault is from Murray, *From the Shadow of Dracula.*

Stoker's letters to Whitman are recounted (in vague terms) in Stoker, *Personal Reminiscences*, and quoted by Horace Traubel, *With Walt Whitman in Camden*, vol. 4: *January 21–April 7, 1889* (Philadelphia: University of Pennsylvania Press, 1953).

Stoker's account of Henry Irving and "The Dream of Eugene Aram" is from Stoker, *Personal Reminiscences.*

CHAPTER THREE. THE LEADING LADIES, "ONLY REAL FLOWERS"

Henry Irving's story is from Stoker, *Personal Reminiscences*; Belford, *Bram Stoker*; Laurence Irving, *Henry Irving, the Actor and His World* (New York: Macmillan, 1951); Austin Brereton, *The Life of Henry Irving* (Bronx, NY: Benjamin Blom, 1969); Frances Donaldson, *The Actor-Managers* (Chicago: Henry Regnery, 1970); and David Mayer, ed., *Henry Irving and The Bells*, with a memoir by Eric Jones-Evans (Manchester, England: Manchester University Press, 1980).

Florence Balcombe is from Ludlam, *A Biography of Dracula*; Farson, *The Man Who Wrote Dracula*; Belford, *Bram Stoker*; and Murray, *From the Shadow of Dracula*. Her relationship with Wilde is from Ellmann, *Oscar Wilde.*

Henry Labouchère's interest in Irving is from Irving, *Henry Irving.*

Ellen Terry's story is from Stoker, *Personal Reminiscences*; Belford, *Bram Stoker*; Irving, *Henry Irving*; and Terry, *Ellen Terry's Memoirs.*

Information on Noel and Florence Stoker is from Ludlam, *A Biography of Dracula*; Farson, *The Man Who Wrote Dracula*; Belford, *Bram Stoker*; and Murray, *From the Shadow of Dracula*. Wilde is from Ellmann, *Oscar Wilde*; Neil McKenna, *The Secret Life of Oscar Wilde* (New York: Basic Books, 2005); and Franny Moyle, *Constance: The Tragic and Scandalous Life of Mrs. Oscar Wilde* (London: John Murray, 2011).

Stoker's early books are described in Belford, *Bram Stoker*, and Murray, *From the Shadow of Dracula*. His short novels have been reprinted in *Complete Works of Bram Stoker* (London: Delphi Classics, Digital Edition, 2011).

Reviews are from Carol A. Senf, ed., *The Critical Response to Bram Stoker* (Westport, CT: Greenwood Press, 1993).

Both Terry's and Irving's voice recordings are available online. Max Beer-bohm is quoted in Belford, *Bram Stoker*. Irving's lines in Shakespeare, and Terry's objections, are from Stoker, *Personal Reminiscences*. Her remark about the steamroller is quoted in Donaldson, *The Actor-Managers*.

Irving's stage effects are from Stoker, *Personal Reminiscences*, and A. Nicholas Vardac, *Stage to Screen* (Cambridge, MA: Harvard University Press, 1949). Wilde's letter is quoted from Ellmann, *Oscar Wilde*.

Chapter Four. The Acting Manager, "Disagreeable Things"

Fussie is from Belford, *Bram Stoker*, and Murray, *From the Shadow of Dracula*. His appearance onstage is from Terry, *Ellen Terry's Memoirs*. Stoker's appearances onstage are from Stoker, *Personal Reminiscences*.

Irving's productions are from Brereton, *The Life of Henry Irving*; Irving, *Henry Irving*; Belford, *Bram Stoker*; and Ellmann, *Oscar Wilde*. The account of the performances before Victoria are from Stoker, *Personal Reminiscences*. Stoker's work at the Lyceum is from Ludlam, *A Biography of Dracula*; Farson, *The Man Who Wrote Dracula*; and Belford, *Bram Stoker*. Irving's speeches are described in Stoker, *Personal Reminiscences*.

Hall Caine is described in Miller, *Bram Stoker's Dracula*, and Vivien Allen, *Hall Caine: Portrait of a Victorian Romancer* (Sheffield, England: Sheffield Academic Press, 1997). Irving's dinners and the Beefsteak Room evenings are described in Stoker, *Personal Reminiscences*; Belford, *Bram Stoker*; and Murray, *From the Shadow of Dracula*.

Stoker's reviews are from Senf, *The Critical Response to Bram Stoker*, and his law training was described in Murray, *From the Shadow of Dracula*.

Irving's tours, and the visit to Whitman, are from Brereton, *The Life of Henry Irving*, and Stoker, *Personal Reminiscences*.

Caine is from Miller, *Bram Stoker's Dracula*. Descriptions of Stoker appear in Joseph Hatton, *Henry Irving's Impressions of America* (Boston: J. R. Osgood, 1884). Louis Austin is quoted in Farson, *The Man Who Wrote Dracula*.

The visits to Whitby are described in Belford, *Bram Stoker*; Murray, *From the Shadow of Dracula*; and Miller, *Bram Stoker's Dracula*. Stoker's notes are housed at the Rosenbach Library in Philadelphia, where I was able to see them. Librarian Elizabeth Fuller was most helpful and informative. The notes have been reproduced in Bram Stoker, *Bram Stoker's Notes for Dracula: A Facsimile Edition*, ed. Robert Eighteen-Bisang and Elizabeth Miller (Jefferson, NC: McFarland, 2008).

CHAPTER FIVE. THE VAMPIRE, "I AM DRACULA"

For the summary of Stoker's famous novel, I used two wonderful annotated editions, one older and one newer: Bram Stoker, *The Annotated Dracula*, annot. Leonard Wolf (New York: Ballantine Books, 1975), and Bram Stoker, *Dracula* (Norton Critical Edition), ed. Nina Auerbach and David J. Skal (New York: W. W. Norton, 1997).

Stoker's alternative ending is discussed in Miller, *Bram Stoker's Dracula*, and Stoker, *Bram Stoker's Notes for Dracula*.

CHAPTER SIX. THE VOIVODE, "RAGE AND FURY DIABOLICAL"

The story of the crab dinner first appeared in Ludlam, *A Biography of Dracula*.

The story of the Rosenbach notes, and quotations from those notes, are from Stoker, *Bram Stoker's Notes for Dracula*. I've also used information from Brereton, *The Life of Henry Irving*.

The meeting with Vambery and the description of Henry Morton Stanley are described in Stoker, *Personal Reminiscences*.

Stoker's writing vacations are described in Belford, *Bram Stoker*, and Murray, *From the Shadow of Dracula*. Stoker's sources are discussed in Stoker, *Bram Stoker's Notes for Dracula*; Miller, *Bram Stoker's Dracula*; and Clive Leatherdale, *The Origins of Dracula* (London: William Kimber, 1987).

Material on the original Count Dracula is from Raymond T. McNally and Radu R. Florescu, *In Search of Dracula* (Greenwich, CT: New York Graphic Society, 1972), and, from the same authors, *The Essential Dracula* (New York: Mayflower Books, 1979); Miller, *Bram Stoker's Dracula*; *Dracula: A Translation of the 1488 Nurnberg Edition*, with an essay by Beverly D. Eddy (Philadelphia: Rosenbach Museum and Library, 1985); *Bram Stoker's Dracula: A Centennial*

Exhibition at the Rosenbach and Library (Philadelphia: Rosenbach Museum and Library, 1997); and Elizabeth Miller, *A Dracula Handbook* (Bloomington, IN: Xlibris, 2005).

CHAPTER SEVEN. THE NOVELIST, "DREADFUL"

Leonard Wolf's careful account of Dracula's appearances is noted in Stoker, *The Annotated Dracula* (with notes by Wolf).

The account of Stoker's dramatization is from Ludlam, *A Biography of Dracula*; Belford, *Bram Stoker*; Stuart, *Stage Blood*; and David Skal's article "His Hour Upon the Stage, Theatrical Adaptations of Dracula," published in Stoker, *Dracula* (Norton Critical Edition). Additional material on the actors, and Stoker's original script, is from Bram Stoker, *Dracula: or The Un-Dead: A Play in Prologue and Five Acts*, ed. and annot. Sylvia Starshine (Nottingham, England: Pumpkin Books, 1997).

Reviews are reproduced from Miller, *Bram Stoker's Dracula*, and Senf, *The Critical Response to Bram Stoker*.

Lovecraft's letter to Donald Wandrei is quoted in H. P. Lovecraft, *Mysteries of Time and Spirit: The Letters of H. P. Lovecraft and Donald Wandrei*, ed. S. T. Joshi and David E. Schultz (San Francisco: Night Shade Books, 2002).

Conan Doyle is quoted in Miller, *Bram Stoker's Dracula*, and Charlotte Stoker's remarks are quoted in Ludlam, *A Biography of Dracula*.

CHAPTER EIGHT. THE MURDERER, "MORBIDLY FASCINATING"

Stoker's introduction to the Icelandic edition and the quoted reviews of the novel appear in Miller, *Bram Stoker's Dracula*.

Mansfield's characterization is taken from Richard Mansfield, *Jekyll and Hyde Dramatized: The 1887 Richard Mansfield Script and the Evolution of the Story on Stage*, ed. Martin A. Dahanay and Alexander Chisolm (Jefferson, NC: McFarland, 2005); John Ranken Towse, *Sixty Years of the Theater* (New York: Funk & Wagnalls, 1916); and William Winter, *Life and Art of Richard Mansfield* (New York: Moffat, Yard, 1910). I've also used a review of the play from the May 10, 1887, *New York Times*.

The Jack the Ripper murders are recounted from Melvin Harris, *Jack the Ripper: The Bloody Truth* (London: Columbus Books, 1987), and Maxim

Jakubowski and Nathan Braund, eds., *The Mammoth Book of Jack the Ripper* (Philadelphia: Running Press, 2008).

Stoker records Mansfield's dinner in Stoker, *Personal Reminiscences*.

CHAPTER NINE. THE SUSPECT, "DISTINGUISHED PEOPLE"

The Jack the Ripper murders are recounted from Harris, *Jack the Ripper: The Bloody Truth*, and Jakubowski and Braund, *The Mammoth Book of Jack the Ripper*.

Information on Hall Caine, and his early friendship with Tumblety, is from Allen, *Hall Caine*. Tumblety's story is recounted in Stewart P. Evans and Paul Gainey, *The Lodger: The Arrest and Escape of Jack the Ripper* (London: Century, 1995). Additional material on Tumblety and his interview in New York is from "My Life and Jack the Ripper," by Stewart Evans, a chapter in *The Mammoth Book of Jack the Ripper*.

Material on the Beefsteak Club and the Beefsteak Room appears in Belford, *Bram Stoker*.

CHAPTER TEN. THE ACTOR, "ABJECT TERROR, GRIM HUMOR"

I've quoted from David J. Skal's article "His Hour Upon the Stage," in *Dracula* (Norton Critical Edition), and Belford, *Bram Stoker*. Welles's anecdote is from Farson, *The Man Who Wrote Dracula*. Farson accused Welles of exaggerating, as the actor claimed to have heard the story from Stoker himself. This was impossible: Welles was born three years after Stoker died.

I actually believe that Welles read the *Chicago Tribune* review when he was fourteen years old; he was a precocious theater fan, living in Chicago at the time. This would account perfectly for his theory about Irving and Stoker. His exaggeration was to retell the tale in the first person—this was typical of his storytelling.

Terry is quoted from Terry, *Ellen Terry's Memoirs*.

Irving's story is told from Irving, *Henry Irving*, and Brereton, *The Life of Henry Irving*. His peculiar gait and pronunciation is from Rowell, *Theatre in the Age of Irving*, and Mayer, *Henry Irving and The Bells*.

Archer's observations are from Booth, *Victorian Spectacular Theatre*. Ellen Terry's remarks are from Terry, *Ellen Terry's Memoirs*. Terry and Shaw are discussed in Belford, *Bram Stoker*, and Shaw's critique of Irving is from Richard Foulkes, *Henry Irving: A Re-evaluation of the Pre-eminent Victorian Actor-Manager* (Aldershot, England: Ashgate, 2008).

The account of Irving's knighthood is from Stoker, *Personal Reminiscences*. In this book, he also discussed Shaw's criticism without naming Shaw. Shaw's quote is from Belford, *Bram Stoker*. Beerbohm's observation of Irving in his carriage is from Irving, *Henry Irving*.

Irving's travails are discussed in Stoker, *Personal Reminiscences*, and Irving, *Henry Irving*. Fussie's fate and Shaw's accusatory review are from Belford, *Bram Stoker*, and Farson, *The Man Who Wrote Dracula*.

The burning of the Lyceum scenery is recounted in Stoker, *Personal Reminiscences*. The story of *Sherlock Holmes* and *The Medicine Man* is from W. D. King, *Henry Irving's Waterloo* (Berkeley: University of California Press, 1993).

Donaghey's *Chicago Tribune* newspaper article is quoted in Skal, "His Hour Upon the Stage," in *Dracula* (Norton Critical Edition). Comments about Stoker's construction of the novel are based on his notes in Stoker, *Bram Stoker's Notes for Dracula*.

CHAPTER ELEVEN. THE POET, "PERENNIAL SWEET DEATH"

Stoker's letters are from Traubel, *With Walt Whitman in Camden*. Stoker tells the other side of the correspondence in Stoker, *Personal Reminiscences*.

Dennis Perry's article "Whitman's Influence on Stoker's Dracula," appeared in *The Walt Whitman Quarterly Review* 3, no. 3 (December 1986), pp. 29–35. Besides Whitman's poetry, I've used material from his biography, Jerome Loving, *Walt Whitman: The Song of Himself* (Berkeley: University of California Press, 1999).

Stoker's note to Gladstone and his essay on censorship are reproduced in Miller, *Bram Stoker's Dracula*.

CHAPTER TWELVE. THE PLAYWRIGHT,
"THE MYSTERY OF HIS SIN"

The discussion of Stoker's omissions is from Stoker, *Personal Reminiscences*. Shaw's obituary, and the controversy that surrounded it, is from King, *Henry Irving's Waterloo*, and Foulkes, *Henry Irving*.

The analogy of Jonathan Harker and Oscar Wilde is mentioned in Farson, *The Man Who Wrote Dracula*; Talia Schaffer's "'A Wilde Desire Took Me': The Homoerotic History of *Dracula*," *ELH* 61 (Summer 1994), pp. 381–425; and Diana Kindron's "Stoker's Use of Homoerotic Behavior in Dracula to Relieve Feelings of Guilt over Oscar Wilde" (published online, 2007).

Wilde's story is from Ellmann, *Oscar Wilde*; McKenna, *The Secret Life of Oscar Wilde*; Moyle, *Constance*; and Belford, *Bram Stoker*.

Labouchère and his amendment are discussed in F. B. Smith, "Labouchère's Amendment to the Criminal Law Amendment Bill," *Historical Studies* 17 (1976), pp. 165–175.

Clyde Fitch's letters are reproduced in Melissa Knox, *Oscar Wilde: A Long and Lovely Suicide* (New Haven, CT: Yale University Press, 1994), and additional material on Fitch is from Montrose J. Moses and Virginia Gerson, *Clyde Fitch and His Letters* (Boston: Little, Brown, 1924), and Winter, *Life and Art of Richard Mansfield*.

CHAPTER THIRTEEN. THE ACCUSED, "MONSTROUS AND UNLAWFUL"

The story of *The Picture of Dorian Gray*, the critical reaction, and the green carnation are from Ellmann, *Oscar Wilde*, and McKenna, *The Secret Life of Oscar Wilde*.

Stoker's notes are quoted from Stoker, *Bram Stoker's Notes for Dracula*. Florence's appearance at *Lady Windermere's Fan* is from Belford, *Bram Stoker*, and Irving's appearances are from Brereton, *The Life of Henry Irving*.

Wilde's association with Douglas and the problems with the Marquess of Queensberry are from Ellmann, *Oscar Wilde*, and McKenna, *The Secret Life of Oscar Wilde*. Fred Terry's story is from Marguerite Steen's *A Pride of Terrys* (London: Longmans, 1962). The story of Ellen Terry and the violets was reported by Irving, *Henry Irving*. Her correspondence to Constance was reproduced in Moyle, *Constance*.

Stoker reported the story of the knighthood in *Personal Reminiscences*.

Talia Schaffer's observations appeared in Schaffer, "'A Wilde Desire Took Me.'" Stoker's notes about the rosary and crucifix are taken from Stoker, *Bram Stoker's Notes for Dracula*.

CHAPTER FOURTEEN. THE STRANGER,
"HERE I AM NOBLE"

Reactions to Wilde, and his history in jail, are from Ellmann, *Oscar Wilde*, and McKenna, *The Secret Life of Oscar Wilde*. Fred Terry's joke is from Steen, *A Pride of Terrys*.

Hall Caine's reaction is from Allen, *Hall Caine*. Terry's remarks are from Terry, *Ellen Terry's Memoirs*. The story about seeing Wilde in Paris is from Steen, *A Pride of Terrys*. The story of Stoker taking money to Wilde is from Farson, *The Man Who Wrote Dracula*, and Florence Stoker's remarks are reported by David J. Skal, *Hollywood Gothic* (New York: W. W. Norton, 1990).

The inspirations behind *Dracula*'s characters are discussed in Miller, *Bram Stoker's Dracula*; Belford, *Bram Stoker*; and Murray, *From the Shadow of Dracula*. Stoker's later books were reviewed in Senf, *The Critical Response to Bram Stoker*.

The fate of the Lyceum was discussed in Stoker, *Personal Reminiscences*; Irving, *Henry Irving*; and Miller, *Bram Stoker's Dracula*. Ellen Terry's recollection is from Terry, *Ellen Terry's Memoirs*.

CHAPTER FIFTEEN. THE FRIENDS,
"INTO THY HANDS, O LORD"

Terry's description of *The Bells* is from Terry, *Ellen Terry's Memoirs*. The account of Irving's last performances is from Stoker, *Personal Reminiscences*, and Irving, *Henry Irving*. Shaw's remarks and Terry's response are from Rowell, *Theatre in the Age of Irving*.

The reviews of *Personal Reminiscences*, as well as Stoker's later fiction, are from Senf, *The Critical Response to Bram Stoker*, and Miller, *Bram Stoker's Dracula*. The last years of Stoker's life are taken from Belford, *Bram Stoker*, and Murray, *From the Shadow of Dracula*.

The Lair of the White Worm received fascinating discussions by Ludlam, *A Biography of Dracula*, and Farson, *The Man Who Wrote Dracula*. Obituaries of Stoker have been reproduced in Miller, *Bram Stoker's Dracula*. Farson discussed his syphilis theory in *The Man Who Wrote Dracula*; this has been debated in later books, particularly Murray, *From the Shadow of Dracula*, and Miller, *Bram Stoker's Dracula*.

Dracula's Guest is discussed in Miller, *Bram Stoker's Dracula*, and Stoker, *Bram Stoker's Notes for Dracula*.

CHAPTER SIXTEEN. THE LEGEND, "SPREAD OVER CENTURIES"

The story of Florence Stoker's battle with *Nosferatu* and the construction of the play for the West End and Broadway are taken from David J. Skal's masterly book *Hollywood Gothic*, as well as Hamilton Deane and John L. Balderston, *Dracula*, ed. and annot. David J. Skal (New York: St. Martin's Press, 1993); Ludlam, *A Biography of Dracula*; and Farson, *The Man Who Wrote Dracula*. Hamilton Deane's story is told in Ludlam's book.

I wrote about the English Grand Guignol productions, and its influence on other entertainments (like Sawing a Woman in Half), in Steinmeyer, *Hiding the Elephant* (New York: Carroll and Graf, 2003). I discussed *Dracula* onstage, and the mystery dramas that surrounded it on Broadway, in "The Spider in the Flies," *Gibercière* 6, no. 1 (Winter 2011), pp. 11–35. Reviews of *Dracula* are from Deane and Balderston, *Dracula*, and Samuel L. Leiter, ed., *The Encyclopedia of the New York Stage, 1920–1930* (Westport, CT: Greenwood Press, 1985).

Deane's appearance at the Lyceum with Lugosi is from Ludlam, *A Biography of Dracula*.

Elizabeth Miller has comprehensively, and entertainingly, discussed the various psychological and sexual theories that surround *Dracula* in her paper "Coitus Interruptus: Sex, Bram Stoker, and *Dracula*," *Romanticism on the Net*, no. 44 (November 2006). Skal's remarks are from David J. Skal, *The Monster Show: A Cultural History of Horror* (New York: W. W. Norton, 1993). Stephenie Meyer's remarks are quoted from her interviews with Gregory Kirschling (*Entertainment Weekly*, July 5, 2008) and with Rick Margolis (*School Library Journal*, October 1, 2005).

INDEX

ILLUSTRATION CREDITS